Sophia Parnell-Evans

Feminism, Farming and Politics in 19th century Portrane

GERARD RONAN

Comhairle Contae Fhine Gall
Fingal County Council

libraries.
fingal.ie

Title Spread: Toil and Pleasure, by John Robertson Reid (1851-1926), Courtesy of Tate Images, Image ID: N01600.

ISBN: 9781999973872

Also by Gerard Ronan

The Irish Zorro
William Kelly of Portrane
The Round Towers of Fingal
Margaret Evans – Poet of Portrane

FOR KAREN AND LAUREN

'Sophia Parnell (sister of the first Lord Congleton) was a woman of great ability and learning – a *maitresse femme* with a strong and resolute character and a face singularly like that of a lioness'

Boston Post, 26 December 1885.

CONTENTS

ACKNOWLEDGEMENTS

I owe particular debts of thanks to Nicholas Dunne-Lynch who very kindly shared me with copies of the Evans letters from the French Military Archives; to Mary Cockerill at the Hartley Library for providing me with copies of the Congleton Manuscripts, and to Patricia Phillips in Gloucester, whose assistance was invaluable in assessing the Evans family papers in the Edgeworth Collection.

I would also like to thank Peadar Bates for permission to use the photograph of Portrane House, John van Wyhe for the image of Erasmus Alvey Darwin, and Alec Silke for the photos of Rathleague Lodge. I am most grateful also to John, Sheila and Ambrose Evans-Pritchard, and to Bruce Ross-Smith, for all of the Evans family lore, editorial advice and the photographs of the plinth and bust of George Evans.

Finally, especial gratitude is due to Helen O'Donnell, Senior Executive Librarian with Fingal County Council, without whose assistance and support this book would not have been published. Last but not least, I owe the usual debt of gratitude to my wife, Cliona, and my daughter, Eleanor, for their continued support and indulgence.

PREFACE

A VERY MUCH abridged version of this biography was included in a previous book I authored in 2019 under the title *The Round Towers of Fingal – Their Hidden History*. At the time my interest in Sophia Evans was purely in relation to the construction of the round tower at Portrane. I had not intended to produce a biography, nor did I believe at the time that there was sufficient material available to warrant one.

However, the interest sparked by that book has generated more questions from readers about Sophia than any of the towers or the forgotten personalities associated with them. In fact on several occasions subsequent to publication, I have been stopped in the street or on the Portrane Cliff Walk and told by readers that they had just visited the round tower at Portrane for the first time *because* of the chapter on Sophia Evans.

As a result of this renewed interest I elected to continue with the research and to attempt to uncover more about Sophia's life than was perhaps necessary to illuminate and explain her motivation in building that tower. In diving deeper, the succeeding years have revealed a number of new sources that allow us to better know Sophia and her family. Unfortunately, as is often the case with research, newly discovered sources have all too often a habit of contradicting those already relied upon. While these new sources do not in any way alter the facts of Sophia's story, as told in *The Round Towers of Fingal*, they do slightly affect the chronology of her early life, giving rise to a need to revise some of her siblings' ages.

So little has been written about this family, and so few printed resources have come to light, that it is entirely possible that further documents lie waiting to be discovered and that this volume, too, may need yet again to be revised, or at the very least enhanced. It has, for example, been a source of constant frustration to be able to read George's reassuring letters to Sophia, but not to be able to read the letters that necessitated such reassurance. One can, of course, deduce much from the context, but there is the constant risk of erroneous assumption.

Sophia Evans was the protofeminist, deist and politically astute wife of a liberal-minded member of parliament. She funded and established two primary schools in Donabate for the poor children of the peninsula and, along with her land steward, William Kelly, helped to preserve the lives of her poorer neighbours when people were dying in their hundreds in the surrounding districts. She erected a replica round tower at Portrane in honour of her devoted husband, George, a man who for nine consecutive years had served as M.P. for the county of Dublin in the British House of Commons. Today, that tower stands equally as a monument to Sophia, and for a time it even carried the epithet of 'The Widow's Tower', before the widow, too, faded to obscurity.

Though my interest in Sophia Evans was sparked primarily by the existence of this abandoned round tower on the Portrane peninsula, in researching its history, I came to know a little of the life of Sophia but found myself having to postpone further investigation as I became engrossed in the story of her land steward, the incomparable William Kelly, who had similarly been written out of the history of the area, and indeed of the country, but about whom it was surprisingly easier to access information.

The primary problem in researching the life of Sophia and her brothers was not just the paucity of material, but the very understandable need of her family for privacy given that four out of her five brothers would suffer from mental health issues of one kind or another. Henry Parnell's depression never really became a matter of public knowledge until his suicide, Thomas Parnell's religious mania only really became a problem as he reached middle-age, and Arthur's 'madness' was a family secret that would have pretty much remained a secret had it not been for the actions of a little-known whistle-blower, who would identify Arthur in a narrative of the abuses he had witnessed at the infamous Whitmore House asylum in London.

Indeed, Arthur Parnell's name did not even appear in the many genealogies of the family that I had earlier relied upon when writing the history of the Portrane Round Tower. In its essence, then, this book is as much about Sophia's family as it is about her, for Sophia did not live in a vacuum. It will, for many, come as a surprise, as those details that were hardest to uncover had remained hidden for a reason, and are all the more interesting for that.

Over recent decades there has been a renewed interest in the roles of women in Irish History: roles that were very much curtailed by the gender politics of the nineteenth century. But that does not mean that they did not exert influence, or that it cannot be traced. The extraordinarily low death rate in Portrane, for example, during the Great Famine, can be traced in large part to Sophia Evans' partnership with, and support, of William Kelly. The higher than average levels of female education amongst the poor of the peninsula, can also be traced to the two privately funded primary schools that she established on her land.

That Sophia Evans has never been the subject of serious study before is hardly a surprise, given the attitude of earlier historians and family members to the role of prominent women in the community. In consequence, researchers have often had to rely on secondary and tertiary sources to compile what little *was* known about them.

Having said all that, it came as something of a surprise to discover a syndicated newspaper article, written just thirty-two years after Sophia's death, in which Sophia's auto-didactic education and subtle political influence were lionized. What made such an article extraordinary was that it was in all likelihood written by a man, and very much within the lifetime of those who would have known her personally.

Given the paucity of the material, one can never really hope to complete a full and proper biography, as those resources that are most easily found are inevitably positive in nature, and no man or woman is ever the sum of their good works alone. A further complication is the cultural risk of interpreting nineteenth century female personalities through the prism of the rich literary heritage of stereotypical characters with which we are all too readily familiar.

One of the most potent of those stereotypes is that of 'The Ingénue', the sexually innocent young girl schooled by her mother in all the feminine virtues until she passively passes from the protective care of her father to that of her husband. Such literary and dramatic characters are generally portrayed as having very little power over their own destiny and as little more than an empty vessel for their husband, or lover's, imagination. But the truth was often more complex than that, and women, like Sophia Evans, frequently played a greater role in the determination of their destiny than tradition would have us believe.

But for all the difficulties, Sophia Evans, like William Kelly, played a major role in the history of the Portrane peninsula, and for that reason alone, deserves to be remembered. Her story is part of the landscape, if not the memory of the area. It is my hope that this initial effort will raise awareness of her, and of her extraordinary family, and help to uncover such resources as yet lie undiscovered. Perhaps somewhere, in some great house or other, there might still hang a portrait of this lady that will enable us to put a face to her words and deeds. One can but hope.

1

FAMILY HISTORY

IT WAS A time of change and a time of challenge: a time when everything seemed up for grabs. A time of experimentation and invention; when industry raced ahead of science and great new machines were born of the imagination of young men who were far from university educated engineers. It was, it seemed, a time when science itself seemed to have changed direction, becoming less of a vehicle for increasing our understanding of the world, as a vehicle for changing it. It was a time when the very nature of existence began to be seriously challenged and the presence of a god, or gods, in an increasingly mechanical universe began to seem more and more unlikely. It was the best of times and the worst of times, a time of war and peace, of revolution and rebellion, of famine and disease, of profit and loss. It was both an exciting and challenging time to be alive, and to be a part of ... if, you happened to have been born male.

The children of Sir John Parnell would spend their childhood in one century and their adulthood in another. Half of them would know their mother, and

Sir John Parnell

half of them would not, becoming, as a result, a family of stark contrasts and fatal flaws. They would vary in their personal philosophies from political conservatism to naïve liberal idealism, and in their characters from unshakeable optimism to the type of extreme melancholia that seemed to go hand in glove with the then fashionable cult of Sensibility. The Parnells would follow their personal passions with a uniquely focused intensity and their great wealth would allow them an almost unfettered opportunity to do so. All of them, that is, bar one.

At a time when women were starting to openly publish literature in their own name, to engage in the study of science and medicine and indulge themselves in the first tentative expressions of feminism, the one arena from which young women with the appropriate talents remained effectively barred, was that of politics. And, in many respects, Sophia Parnell had been born to it.

At the time of his marriage, in July 1774, Sophia's father, John Parnell, a thirty-year-old graduate of Trinity College Dublin was a sitting member of the Irish Parliament. His bride, Laetitia Brooke, was the second daughter and co-heiress of Sir Arthur Brooke. Of the two John was considered the more fortunate, having bagged a renowned beauty a good decade his junior. John, in contrast, was considered a mild mannered and highly moral man, but hardly the most striking or masculine in appearance.

Following the marriage, John and Laetitia Parnell would split their time between their townhouse on Dublin's Dawson Street and their country estate in Rathleague, County Laois. As he was required to spend a great deal of time in Dublin during the parliamentary season, he would later lease a seaside retreat in Newtown Avenue in Blackrock for the pleasure of his wife and children (a lease he would surrender upon his wife's demise).

The couple's primary residence, however, would always be Rathleague House, described at the time as one of the finest mansions in the country. It was an idyllic place to live, and to raise children, but a long way from medical help. Whenever Laetitia became pregnant, therefore, her 'lying-in' would take place in Dublin, where a higher standard of medical care was to be found. Parturition, after all, was a dangerous business in the eighteenth century and newspaper announcements of successful childbirths invariably contained some version of the word 'safe'.

Laetitia Brooke Parnell

The couple's first son, John Augustus, was born at the Parnell's townhouse on Dublin's Dawson Street on 14 May 1775, just ten months after their wedding. A tragic accident prior to the birth resulted in the child entering the world as a 'deaf and dumb imbecile' (some sources also refer to him as a 'cripple'). Details of the nature of the 'accident' are scarce. The solitary mention of it that survives comes from a newspaper obituary.[1]

Laetitia's second son, Henry Brooke Parnell, arrived in July 1776 and was followed their only daughter, Sophia, who arrived late in the summer of 1779. Sophia was followed by William, born in August 1780; Thomas, born January 1782; and Arthur, who arrived late in 1783.

Some months after the birth of Arthur, Laetitia Parnell fell seriously ill. The nature of this illness has never been recorded, but it was short-lived, and fatal. She died at the family's Dublin residence on Dawson Street, on 11 Nov 1783. At the time of her death, her daughter, Sophia, was three years old. The dominant female figure in her life now became her seventy-year-old paternal grandmother, Anne.

The dearth of youthful female company meant that Sophia spent far more time in male company than was usual for a young girl at the time. She learned quickly not to be intimidated by masculine self-confidence, and how to fight her corner. What she never learnt, was the 'feminine' habit of considering herself intellectually inferior to her brothers, or indeed any man. She became an 'oddity', in a family of oddities, and gained a profile that was not always to the advantage of a young woman in a society that suffered from a congenital fear of idiosyncrasy.

The Parnells had 'form'. They were an old family, long established in Congleton in Cheshire, where one

---

[1] National Register, London. 'Death of John Augustus Parnell', p16. 16 Aug 1812.

of their number had been mayor during the reign of James I. They first came to Ireland following the restoration of the monarchy in England in 1660 and the return of Charles II as king. Cromwell's commonwealth having failed, and the bishops having been restored to parliament, many former supporters of Cromwell fled in fear of reprisals.

Sophia's great-granduncle, Thomas Parnell, had been Archdeacon of Clogher and a famous poet championed and befriended by such literary luminaries as Swift and Pope. He was also an acknowledged influence on the work of Goldsmith. Following the death of his wife, in 1711, he fell prey to bi-polar disorder, a susceptibility that would recur in subsequent generations together with a natural empathy for the underdog.

Thomas Parnell died suddenly in 1718, at the age of thirty-eight and was buried in the family vault in Chester. Samuel Johnson and Oliver Goldsmith would write epitaphs for him, though neither would ever be inscribed on his grave. They would both also publish biographies of him and Alexander Pope would publish a collection of his poetry. The sculptor, Edward Smyth, would later be engaged to sculpt his bust. It sits to this day in the old library of Trinity College Dublin.

Sophia's great-grandfather, John Parnell, was Thomas Parnell's brother. His son, John, Sophia's grandfather, would sit in the Irish House of commons as MP for Maryborough. Created a baronet in 1766, he died in 1782, when Sophia was two years of age. As John Parnell's only son, Sophia's father, also called John, inherited the family estates.

How much Sophia saw of her father during her early childhood is difficult to say, but his political career was on an upward trajectory and he would have been spending more and more of his time in Dublin where he held the post of Commissioner of Customs and Excise. Opposed to corruption and nepotism, he was

widely lauded for his fairness and his refusal to use his position for the advancement of his own family.

In September 1785, when Sophia was just five years of age, her father became Chancellor of the Exchequer of Ireland, a position he would hold for the next fourteen years. The following year, on the 27 October 1786, at the Court at St James, he would be appointed by King George III to his privy council. Such weighty responsibilities would have left little time for family life and Sophia, in consequence, would have had only her elder brothers and her grandmother to turn to for guidance and affection in his absence. That said, she was close to her father, and as soon as she was old enough she would come to live with him in London.

In 1791, during the construction of Dublin's Grand Canal, the bridge joining Clogher Road to the South Circular Road, was named after John Parnell in recognition of his efforts in promoting the building of Dublin's Canal systems, a transport route so quickly overtaken by the invention of railways that it led to the financial ruin of a great many investors. Despite all that he had achieved in politics the bridge, known locally as Sally's Bridge[2], remains the only memorial in Ireland dedicated to his memory.

---

[2] The road to the left/south of this bridge is named Parnell Road, but this was named in honour of Charles Stewart Parnell.

2

THE WALLED GARDEN

NEW EXPLANATIONS WERE beginning to emerge, but the idea that disability and mental illness had some sort of God-given or astrological cause had not entirely disappeared. An element of stigma still attached to physical and mental handicap that attracted as much shame as sympathy. Growing up with a profoundly intellectually disabled brother, would not have been easy for Sophia, or for her brothers.

Support for people with disabilities was not seen as the duty of the state, but as the charitable responsibility of the individual. Hospitals and homes were poorly run and underfunded, with some even allowing paying visitors to view their 'curiosities'. There was little real understanding or accumulated experience in dealing with mental illness or intellectual disability, and what little there was had resulted in widespread public disquiet regarding treatments and standards.

In 1763 *The Gentleman's Magazine* condemned the

'many unlawful arbitrary and cruel acts' which went on in madhouses, the proprietors of which were often not medically qualified.[3] In the year prior to John Augustus's birth, furthermore, the government had been forced to introduce a licensing system[4], following public concern that some non-lunatics, including children with purely intellectual disabilities, were being unlawfully detained at the whim of their families. Little surprise, then, that Laetitia and John elected to care for John Augustus at home.

His younger siblings grew up, therefore, in an environment where their elder brother's needs frequently and necessarily usurped their own. On a daily basis they would witness the difficulties inherent in caring for him and, privy to the worries and concerns of their parents, most likely sought age-appropriate explanations for his condition.

Even today, when the stigma is less acute than it was then, responses to the stress of having a profoundly disabled sibling vary enormously and individually at different stages of development. During the very early years of childhood, comparison and embarrassment is quite common, as is the worry of non-disabled children that they, too, might somehow catch whatever they imagine their disabled sibling to be affected with. They may even feel guilty that they themselves have been spared, or wonder what could possibly be wrong with *them* that their parents gave them less attention than their disabled sibling.

As they become older the non-disabled siblings may begin to suffer from anxiety or stress, being quite rational in their explanation of the disabled sibling's condition to outsiders, but angry and resentful at home of the double standards and unequal attention that the disabled sibling enjoys. They may also

---

[3] Sayce, Liz. *From Psychiatric Patient to Citizen Revisited* Macmillan International Higher Education, Palgrave, London, 2015.
[4] Regulation of madhouses act (1815).

experience guilt on those occasions when they opt to leave their disabled sibling to play alone, or express resentment at the expectation that he or she be integrated into childhood games or peer groups.

The non-disabled siblings may also feel obligated to compensate for the disabled sibling by acting as a surrogate parent or by being so impossibly good that they feel unable to express their natural resentments or anxieties. The ways in which a profoundly disabled child affects his or her siblings can be both positive and negative, but it *never* leaves them unaffected, and there are myriad different ways in which it can influence the course of their own development.

We have no way of knowing how Sophia and her siblings were individually affected, but as three of her four non-disabled brother's would suffer psychiatric issues in adulthood, we cannot entirely ignore the unusual nature of their childhood and their largely parentless, upbringing. Given the beliefs of the day, however, we can be certain that Sophia, as the sole female, would have been affected very differently to her brothers. As a girl, a greater degree of empathy and consideration would have been expected of her. She was, after all, being prepared for marriage and motherhood; the boys for education and careers. It was in her interest to develop her maternal skills and instincts.

The boys, in contrast, would have known from an early age that they would escape their fraternal responsibilities when sent abroad to boarding school and university. For a girl, such things were impossible. She would remain at home, and part of her disabled brother's care team, until such time as she married. It wasn't fair, but it was the way of the world. It is unlikely she would have questioned it, or if she did, that she would have dared to give a voice to such questions. To do so would have been seen as un-Christian, and unfeminine.

Rathleague Lodge today - photo © Alec Silke

This house was renovated c.1810, incorporating the fabric of
Sophia's childhood home, built c.1740. The stables to the rear of the
house are from the original lodge.

As John Augustus grew up, the ability of the family and their servants to keep a constant eye on him became ever more challenging and so Sophia's father arranged to have a large garden behind the house enclosed by a ten foot high wall. Within the confines of this garden, John Augustus could play, safe from the possibility of wandering off, which suggests that, the description of 'cripple' notwithstanding, John Augustus was actually quite mobile.

But a ten foot high wall? What was that all about? The height is far in excess of anything that might have been required to confine an intellectually disabled cripple to the garden. It suggests, rather, a need for privacy; a desire to keep John Augustus out of sight of prying eyes.

The garden wall at Rathleague Lodge.

With little opportunity to mix with other children, the importance of John Augustus' relationship with his siblings would have intensified as he matured. As Henry and William reached their early teens and were sent away to Eton, he would have become increasingly dependent upon his nurse, and his remaining siblings, Sophia, Thomas and Arthur, for company. That in itself was an unfair burden, and most likely intensified the great age of their grandmother, who would have lacked the energy or strength to cope.

With the passing years an even greater source of anxiety began to occupy their collective thoughts. What would become of John Augustus as he got older? What would happen to him, and them, should their father die prematurely, as their mother had done?

The same thoughts had obviously crossed their father's mind and in 1789 he made an application for a private act of parliament to disinherit his eldest son in favour of his second. Should the act be granted, Henry, and not John Augustus, would become his legal heir. The application would be made on the grounds of John Augustus's mental and physical handicaps. It would be a very public affair.

But this was not as simple as making an application to the King. John Augustus had first to be declared legally incompetent, and that meant an independent examination. In April 1789, John Augustus was taken to be examined by a commission of the Lord High Chancellor of Ireland and they declared him to have been 'an idiot from his nativity'. News of the granting of the act was carried in *Saunders' Newsletter* of 27 May 1789:

> *An act for vesting the settled estate, in the Queen's Co. of the Right Hon. Sir John Parnell, Bart. In his second, third, fourth and fifth sons, in the same manner as if his eldest son John Parnell had been dead without issue male, and for providing a maintenance for the said John Parnell during his life.*

The newspapers were perhaps kinder than the act itself, which was actually worded:

> *... as if the said John Parnell, the Idiot, had been dead, without issue male ...*

The act, all ten pages of it, made Henry the de-facto heir to Sir John's estate and, in the event of his father's death, head of the family and responsible for Sophia until such time as she married. An annual annuity of £200 sterling was also provided to pay for the care of John Augustus during his lifetime. To protect John Augustus from exploitation, the act finally declared that, should John Augustus marry before he was re-examined by a commission of the Lord High Chancellor and found to be of sound mind and body, his marriage would be declared null and void. The condition effectively made John Augustus 'the idiot'[5] the legal responsibility of his family for life.

---

[5] In 1789 the terms 'imbecile' and 'idiot' had legal status. An 'idiot' was one whose mental development never exceeds that of a normal two-year-old, whereas an 'imbecile' was one whose development was higher than an idiot, but not greater than a normal seven-year-old.

3

EDUCATION

Children of wealthy parents saw little of their parents for long periods of the year and were generally raised by nurses and governesses until such time as they came of age or were sent away to boarding schools. As very young children, they would spend most of their time in the nursery and only see their father when he was in residence, and even then only at mealtimes or for a few hours before bedtime.

With John Parnell working in Dublin during the parliamentary season and cities generally seen as moral obstacle courses unfit for young children, they would have been left at Rathleague for months on end without seeing their father. The only exception would be the summer months when they would repair to their seaside house at Blackrock, in south County Dublin.

Sophia's recreational activities at this young age would initially have revolved around doll's houses and dolls, the dressing of which had become so popular a pastime during the eighteenth century that French dressmakers would send doll-sized versions of their work to London and Dublin to meet the demand for the latest fashions. She would also have been prohibited from going anywhere unaccompanied. The daughters of the wealthy were always gossiped about. This was a truth – and a social control – that young girls learnt early. A girl, or a woman, who was prone to leaving the house unchaperoned ran the risk of being considered morally suspect. The same did not apply to boys.

As for Sophia's education, that, too, would have been gender specific. Throughout the eighteenth and well into the nineteenth century, gender roles were well established in Ireland and Britain. Men were seen as the breadwinners and women the housekeepers and homemakers. Women were not thought to require much in the way of education to fulfil their roles in society and, amongst the upper classes at least, what learning was available to them was generally restricted to the 'three R's' of reading, writing and religion.

Under the ideology of the 'separate spheres', gender roles for women were consigned to the private sphere of the home and family, and those for men to the public sphere of economics, politics and industry. Wealthy families, as a result, rarely educated their daughters alongside their sons, and daughters were raised to be wives and mothers, to manage servants and make prim and 'delicate' conversation. They were not expected to have political opinions, or display knowledge of science and philosophy, let alone opinions that might contradict or embarrass their husbands. An 'intelligent woman' was still, to many men, a contradiction in terms.

Women, as a result, had little say in society beyond the influence they could exert over their husbands. They were denied the right to vote, to own property or to work in their own right while married. They were seen as fragile beings, more emotional than rational, and prone to poor judgement. For those reasons, and others, they were excluded from public life and political debate.

For young girls of Sophia's class, the little education they did receive, from largely untrained governesses, was aimed at making them attractive marriage partners. Apart from reading, writing and scripture, Sophia would have learned French, some English literature and rudimentary arithmetic. She might also have received tuition in pianoforte or harpsichord, and in drawing.

Alongside these, she would have been schooled by professional 'masters' in the social graces of decorum, fashion and dancing. She would have been taught to reflect deeply upon her moral character and the Christian duties of a daughter and a wife. Anything further, was considered a risk. A woman with a passion for learning was looked down upon as a 'blue-stocking' and considered unfeminine. It simply wasn't acceptable for a woman to attempt to challenge a man's 'natural' intellectual superiority'. The entirety of her education, therefore, was concentrated about a single goal – the making of a good marriage.

Young girls of high intelligence, like Sophia, were not particularly wanted by society, nor were they trained to make use of their exceptional abilities. But, having learnt to read, they often quickly outstripped their governesses and educated themselves by means of the family library and daily newspapers. Watching their brothers being sent away to school might grate on their sense of fairness, but it was the way of the world, and generally accepted, until such time as they might be exposed to a world where other possibilities existed, as happened to many when they visited continental Europe for the first time, and in particular the salons of post-revolutionary France.

All of that lay ahead of young Sophia, but for now the matter of educational inequality was felt primarily in loneliness, as one by one her elder brothers were sent away to boarding school. By 1792 Henry had already left for Eton, one of the most elite and prestigious public schools in Britain, and a break with family tradition. Henry's father, Sir John Parnell, had himself attended Harrow, where he had formed a lasting friendship with the classical poet Sir William Jones (who would dedicate poems to him).

The curriculum Henry faced at Eton included

classical studies, writing, arithmetic, geometry, literature and antiquities. This would have been very different from the rather rudimentary education that Sophia would have been receiving at Rathleague, though even this would have been far more than most young women of her class would have received.

At Eton Henry would be expected to form friendships and comradely relationships with other aristocratic children who might be of use to him in his adult life. The same would have been expected of him in 1794, when he progressed to Trinity College, Cambridge. But Henry ultimately chose to leave Cambridge without completing his degree in order to pursue a career in politics.

In 1796, when William became the next brother to depart Rathleague for Eton, Sophia was left at home with John Augustus, Thomas and Arthur. At sixteen years of age, she was approaching marriageable age and would have been expected to take a more maternal role in the care of her younger brothers in preparation for her future role as a wife. In the process, she became the closest either Thomas or Arthur would ever have to a mother. That onerous sense of responsibility would remain with her for the rest of her life.

To add to Sophia's woes, on the 20 April 1795, her paternal grandmother, Anne Parnell, died at Rathleague. She was eighty-two. Following a funeral service in Maryborough, her remains were sent to Dublin and transported by ship to Parkgate, on the Wirral peninsula, from where they were taken to Chester, and interred, on 25 April, in the family vault in Trinity Church. The Chester Chronicle of 1 May 1795 declared that 'a better character perhaps never adorned society than this venerable lady.'

At just sixteen years of age, Sophia was now effectively mistress of Rathleague. With her mother and grandmother gone, and her father spending long periods away from home, the role that Sophia played in the household had to change. There were two younger brothers in their early teens who needed all manner of control and education; two young boys who would later fall victim to mental health issues. Sophia would now be expected to become an example to them, a moral authority who would guide them into adulthood, or at least until such time as they, too, could be sent away to school. The only escape from such expectation and responsibility lay in marriage, but that particular possibility must have seemed a distant and unwelcome lifetime away to a sixteen-year-old girl.

That same year, the family's property portfolio increased substantially when a distant cousin, Samuel Hayes died, leaving the bulk of the estate that would later become known as *Avondale* to his cousin, Sir John Parnell, on the understanding that it should be left to one of the younger children upon his demise, and not to his heir apparent. The family would add considerably to this estate over the years and by 1840 it would be even larger than their holdings in Queen's County (Laois). It would eventually become the property of William, through whom it would later pass to his grandson, Charles Stewart Parnell.

By the time Sophia reached her nineteenth birthday, her brother Henry had entered parliament as the Member for Maryborough and William was fast acquiring a reputation as an intelligent and original thinker. Indeed, such was William's reputation and influence that, at the age of eighteen, he was already was counting amongst his closest friends, the controversial economist, Thomas Robert Malthus, who, in 1798, produced his ground-breaking *Essay on the Principle of Population.*

In this work Malthus, whom William most likely first met at Cambridge, observed that an increase in a nation's food production would only temporarily improve the well-being of the people as it would inevitably lead to a growth in population, growth which would undo the benefits of increased production. In other words, humans would always utilize abundance to increase their numbers rather than maintain a high standard of living. This view of economics has come to be known as the 'Malthusian trap' and is still widely debated.

In the Malthusian view of the world, populations would always to grow until such time as the lower classes fall prey to famine and disease. In a letter to his brother Henry, written from Hampstead sometime in 1798, William claimed to have not just challenged Malthus personally on some of his reasoning, but to have actually changed his mind:

'I have talked to Malthus about his book, and I think I have convinced him that he [is] wrong in supposing that population can only be checked by vice and misery and that no country can be without a class of poor. The fact is that the great check to population is prudence and the spirit among all ranks of preserving their respective situations in society; and Holland is a proof that industry and economy joined with a spirit of comfort can raise the lowest ranks to a sufficient competency.

But these can never exist under an oppressive government, and hence we learn the great merit of liberty in raising a pride and self-importance in the people which will make poverty a disgrace and restrain them from imprudent marriages. If you examine different nations you will find that the people breed in exact proportion to the tyranny of the Government.

I have scarcely seen King as he has been forced to be at Ockham and I could not leave Sophia. I saw him in town yesterday and he returns tomorrow. He has turned out what I have long foretold, quite a moral principle particularly with regard to talents.

You shall hear from me soon. My knee is much better. The change of weather has had some effect on Sophia, but I hope it will not continue.

Your affectionate brother
W. Parnell'

The 'King' referred to above is Lord Peter King of Ockham, who in years to come would travel with William and Sophia in France. But the importance of this letter, as far as Sophia is concerned, that it is the first indication we have of the fact that Sophia is ill, and so seriously ill that her brother is reluctant to leave her on her own.

4

THE ROMANTIC DISEASE

TUBERCULOSIS, OR 'CONSUMPTION' was a killer disease caused by bacteria spread from one person to another through coughs and sneezes. The AIDS of its time, once contracted it was considered a death sentence. Few survived.

The symptoms of the disease were many. They included flushed cheeks, pale skin, bright eyes, coughing up blood, pain with breathing, fatigue, fever, night sweats, chills and weight loss from loss of appetite. The debilitated patient would need constant care and attention, not to mention good nutrition. It was not an inexpensive process.

In later life Sophia's husband would often refer to her as 'delicate', a word often used as a euphemism for TB sufferers. In a novel her brother William would write while travelling with her in France, the heroine would be an intelligent girl with a hunchback who struggled to find love and acceptance in a family obsessed with good looks. There is no evidence that

Sophia was even mildly hunchbacked, but the condition was a common symptom of the disease and a handy visual metaphor. Pelvic TB was also a common cause of female infertility, with which Sophia would later be cursed.

Sophia's survival can be attributed largely to wealth. Only the wealthy could afford appropriate nutrition, and only the wealthy could flee to Lisbon, the retreat of choice for wealthy English sufferers. It can also be attributed to the fact that her father didn't hang around.

In his *Essay on the nature and cure of the Phthisis Pulmonalis*, published in 1782, Dr. Thomas Reid, lamented that all too often sufferers left it too late to travel to warmer climes:

> *'Of late years it has been the custom to send consumptive persons to Lisbon, and other parts abroad; but this, like every attempt to cure, being generally used when in the last period, we are not to wonder that it seldom succeeds …*
>
> *When a distant voyage is eligible, the southern climates should be chosen. Lisbon is near, and accessible by the packets going every month. Madeira is still better, being at a greater distance, and the air more to the southward, from its insular situation. But the Mediterranean is what I would prefer to all other sea voyages.'*

On 29 October 1798, in a letter to Lord Castlereagh, a certain Richard Marshall wrote that:

> *'I understand that Sir John Parnell is here, or, rather, at Hampstead, with his daughter … Mr. Pelham understands that Sir John talks of going to Lisbon with Miss Parnell.'*

Treatment for TB was non-existent. The wealthy often travelled to warm countries in the belief that Mediterranean sunshine was curative. Chopin went to Majorca and Robert Louis Stevenson to the South Seas. Both died there.

The most peculiar aspect of this largely incurable and fatal disease, was the degree to which nineteenth century Europeans romanticized the image of its victim as 'slowly and gracefully fading away, transcending their corporeal body, their immortal soul

Lisbon 19th Century

shining through'.[6] The high mortality rate among young and middle-aged adults and the persistent surge of Romanticism, led to the idealization of the sufferer as a romantic exile, a dropout wandering in endless search of a healthy place. The disease was even thought to bestow a heightened sensitivity upon the sufferer and its slow progress to allow for a 'good death' in which sufferers had time to arrange their affairs.

As the disease came to represent spiritual purity and temporal wealth, many young, upper-class women began to purposefully whiten their skin in order to achieve a consumptive appearance. Lord Byron even wrote that he 'should like to die from consumption', helping to popularize consumption as the disease of artists.

One can only too readily imagine the effect of such romantic notions on the mind of an impressionistic, self-conscious and frightened adolescent acutely aware of the nature of her disease and unable to find much in the way of recreation or entertainment apart from that found in the pages of her books. For if there was one experience that all tuberculosis sufferers quickly came to share, it was the sense of time passing unimaginably slowly, measured not in days or weeks, but in the distance between moments of change and novelty or, as Sophia might have put it, between visitors, chapters and books.

In her books Sophia could retreat into a world of adventure, education and refuge, a fantasy world in which life was lived vicariously and *everything* was possible. And if all of this did not fail to leave her gauche and pliant personality untouched, then there was always the death-bed indulgence of her carers and visitors. George Sand once called her consumptive lover, Frédéric Chopin, her 'poor melancholy angel'.

---

[6] Manoli-Skocay, Constance. *A gentle Death in 19th Century Concord*, William Munroe Special Collections, 2005.

Sophia had become the Parnell equivalent, a dying teenage girl, being slowly habituated to silence and tranquillity.

It was, of course, in the nature of TB to be a lingering illness and over the course of the following year, Sophia's condition gradually deteriorated. In October of 1799, Sir John was once again compelled to take her to Falmouth and board the packet ship the *King George*, bound for Lisbon. Her health had deteriorated so much by this time that their departure made the Irish papers. But at least the packet was fast. With a crew of just twenty-six men and a complement of just six guns, the ship was designed to outrun pirates and corsairs rather than engage them.[7]

Sir John Parnell, with his daughter, who is in a bad state of health, sailed last Tuesday from Falmouth on board the King George packet for Lisbon.

This morning at 4 o'clock, Mr. Justice Ford, with Townsend and Saver, the Bow-street officers.

Limerick Chronicle, 09 Oct 1799.

Lisbon would do the trick and Sophia's health would gradually improve, but her overriding impression of Lisbon would always be that of endless boredom and 'enervating heat'. She was no doubt happy, therefore, to return to London much improved a year later but it would be some considerable time before she saw Rathleague again. The Act of Union (1800) had changed everything.

Following the passing of this act, Sophia and her father settled more or less permanently in London, where Sir John, now sat in the British House of

---

[7] Norway, Arthur H. *History of the Post-office Packet Service Between the Years 1793-1815*, Macmillan and Company, 1895.

Commons. Their London townhouse, at 22 Eaton Square, would become Sophia's home for the next five years. John Augustus appears to have been left behind in Ireland, to be cared for at Rathleague. It is not known what arrangements were made for Thomas and Arthur.

As she approached her twentieth birthday, Sophia found herself obliged to enter society and be made available as a potential wife. But she was far from the average debutante. She had contrived to survive a disease that for many was a death sentence, and it had left its mark. She had become accustomed to her own company and a voracious consumer of books.

By the standards of the time, women of marriageable were not expected to remain in the family home and become an unreasonable burden on their siblings. Sophia's 'delicacy' notwithstanding, it would have been expected that she at least make an effort to find a life for herself with someone else. But her attractions were far from commonplace, or conventional. She had grown up in a predominantly male environment with little in the way of female company or role-models, and in a family of intelligent, plain-spoken and introverted individuals. Male society was so much bread and wine to her that she intimidated young men. Even her future husband would have to be encouraged by her brother to declare his feelings, so intimidated would he be by his 'better genius'.

The dominant female in her life at this time was Lady Anna Maria Jones, wife of the poet Sir William Jones, a distant relation of her father. Indeed, Lady Jones had become so close a family friend of late that Sophia had come to look upon her as an aunt, and Lady Jones in turn to treat her like a favourite niece. Sophia could not have had a more inspiring mentor.

Anna Maria Jones had no children of her own and had been about as unconventional a woman as it was possible to be in her heyday. Possessed of a dry sense

Lady Anna Maria Jones

of humour and a daring and adventurous spirit she had, during her time in India, once undertaken a perilous expedition up the Ganges and through the jungle to Benares. The Indian climate, alas, eventually got the better of her. In 1793, as a result of frequent bouts of fevers and digestive disorders, her husband was forced to send her home, promising to follow after as soon as he was able.

Before she left Calcutta, Anna Maria published a volume of poetry titled *The Poems of Anna Maria.* Heavily influenced by the cult of Sensibility, many of the poems had previously been published in the *Asiatic Mirror* and the *Calcutta Morning Post.* Many women of her class wrote poetry, but few would have dared to risk publication. It simply wasn't done. And yet, the list of subscribers represented a virtual roll call of upper-class English society in Calcutta at that time.

The authorship of the poems was recently called into question[8] on the basis that Lord and Lady Jones were both listed amongst the subscribers. But this would surely have been an expected subterfuge from the wife of a famous poet endeavouring to find fame in her own right at a time when it was considered socially unacceptable for women. William Jones never re-joined his wife. Shortly after her departure he fell ill with an 'inflammation of the liver' and died.

Lady Jones would often correspond with Sophia and her letters are rich with materteral familiarity and wry humour. She would also be an early example to Sophia of an intellectual and independent woman daring to indulge her passions for science and literature. During her time in India, quite apart from poetry, Anna Maria developed a keen interest in botany – an interest that may well have rubbed off on Sophia – and her botanical sketchbooks are to this day preserved in the

---

[8] Gibson, Mary Ellis. Angles: English Verse in Colonial India from Jones to Tagore, Ohio University Press, 2011.

archives of the Royal Asiatic Society.

Lady Jones also spoke several European languages, including Latin and Greek, which she had been taught by her father as a child, and had only recently edited her husband's literary, linguistic and scientific works for publication. She was a formidable and talented woman whose Mayfair townhouse on South Audley Street was just a short walk from the Parnells'.

Sir William Jones

Lady Jones and her four sisters also moved in the highest intellectual circles. One sister, Georgiana, was a close friend and correspondent of Benjamin Franklin[9] and another, Penelope (later Mrs Pelham Warren), the wife of a member of The Royal Society. They were cousins, furthermore, to the controversial Georgiana, Duchess of Devonshire, an eminent member of the peerage then infamous for her unusual marital arrangement, love affairs, political influence and gambling.

A measure of the closeness of the Jones and Parnell families can be gleaned from a gift, made by Sir John Parnell to Lady Jones in November 1801. This gift was one of Sir John's most treasured possessions: a collection of poems written by Anna Maria's husband, Sir William Jones, a man Thomas Mortimer had dubbed *The British Plutarch*. This collection, written while both Jones and Parnell were children at Harrow, had been gifted to Sir John by his closest friend, Sir William, in 1763, and included an early version of the poem that Jones would later famously publish as *Arcadia*.

What elevated this act of friendship beyond that of a simple gift was the fact that amongst the handwritten manuscripts was a poem, addressed to Sir John in imitation of a well-known Ode of Horace[10] that had been composed when both he and William had been in their early teens. It represented a very personal testament to their friendship. The third verse of the ode reads:

> *In vain, my Parnell, wrapt in ease,*
> *We shun the merchant-marring seas;*
> *In vain we fly from wars;*
> *In vain we shun th' autumnal blast;*
> *(The slow Cocytus must be pass'd;)*
> *How needless are our cares!*

---

[9] Her correspondence with Franklin is preserved in his papers housed at the American Philosophical Society.
[10] Ode 14. lib. Ii.

This was the most enduring friendship of Sophia's father's life, and one that had since been shared by Sir William's wife, Anna Maria. That she should take such an interest in Sophia following the death of her mother, and especially as she herself had been widowed young and left childless, was perhaps only natural and over the years Sophia would develop an equally close relationship with Anna Maria's sister, Penelope, of whom more anon.

5

HENRY & CAROLINE

IF THERE WAS pressure on Sophia, at nineteen years of age, to enter into society and find herself an eligible husband, it paled in comparison to the pressure being heaped upon her academically minded older brother, Henry, who was now in his twenty-second year and finding life as a Member of Parliament somewhat lonelier than anticipated.

Following the Act of Union, in 1800, Henry, like his father, found himself transported to London with all of the other Irish MPs, where, outside of his parliamentary duties, he found he had far too much time on his hands and little imagination regarding what he was meant to do with it. Henry Parnell was not a party animal. Nor was he, by all accounts, much of a conversationalist. He was once described as a man 'prepossessing in his general aspect and appearance, but possessing a voice that was unclear and indistinct, and whose speeches abounded with facts and calculations'.

Henry was not equipped for flirtatious behaviour or

41

the demands of a prolonged courtship, and his prospects of a love match appeared slim. In the autumn of 1800, however, while on a visit to his uncle Thomas, the first Viscount de Vesci, he happened to meet with Lady Portarlington and her daughters, Caroline, Louisa and Harriet.

Lady Portarlington, better known as the famous painter, Caroline Dawson, 'a genius in painting and musick'. was not wealthy, at least on a par with the Parnells. It came as a shock to her to learn that Henry was even remotely interested in one of her daughters. He had played with them while they were children, but had never shown any interest in them as women, let alone as eligible young women.

Being painfully shy, mild-mannered and not a little intimidated by the artistic and accomplished Dawson females, Henry had not spoken much with Lady Caroline, or her daughters, at the time of his visit. He found himself, nonetheless, so charmed by the good looks of the second daughter, Louisa that not long afterwards he decided to write to Lady Portarlington and propose marriage.

But Henry was as inarticulate in love as he was in politics and so clumsily did he word his proposal that Lady Portarlington took it to be for the hand of her eldest daughter, Lady Caroline Elizabeth Dawson, then aged eighteen. It was a reasonable assumption, the daughter that Henry had actually admired, Louisa, being still underage. The proposal was discussed in a letter from Lady Portarlington to her sister, Louisa, on the 28 November 1800. There was simply no holding her:

'My dear Louisa,

You will be surprised when I tell you I do not know how long Caroline may keep the name of Dawson, as she has had a very agreeable proposal which she is inclined to accept. It is now time to tell you his name is Parnell, Sir John's eldest son, and if I were sure he would like her and make her a good husband, it is the match of all others I would have wished, as I have known him from a child, have a great regard for all his family and connections, and their house just half way between us and Lord de Vesci. He is remarkably handsome, very sensible and well-informed, and of a very active mind; he was at Abbeyleix when we were there about a fortnight before we left Ireland. He did not seem to observe my girls, and has always been more reserved to them than was natural, considering they used to play together as children.

We thought all the admiration he had met with in Dublin had made him conceited, and that he was too fine to take notice of my shy timid girls. I have not yet written him an answer, as I hardly know what to say. Car. has no objection to make but the very natural one of not feeling sufficiently acquainted with him. By his letter (which is to me) it would appear that his father was not acquainted with his intentions, as he says, with our joint permission to acquaint his father, he has every reason to think he will act by him in the most liberal manner.

He says that he has but a very small income independent of his father, but you know I cannot expect any great things for my daughters, who have so little to bring to a family. I can't tell you how happy this event would make me if I could think he had taken a fancy to her. If this event should take place, I suppose it will bring me to town sooner than I intended, for I conclude he will come over, and I could not make him stay in this place, where he would not have another man to speak to.

Poor Caroline does not know what to think of it, she is so surprised, and indeed so are we all, for they have never been asked to think of husbands. Louisa and Harriet are as much children in their way as they were five years ago, and poor Car was only in the world for the small space of two months, half of which time being Easter, people went to the country and there was hardly anything going on, and she, not being forward or used to the ways of town misses, made very few acquaintances.

If I dispose of her I believe I shall be tempted to bring out Harriet and Louisa together, as Harriet is more grown up in her person than Louisa, but she is very awkward, and it may take that off. The Duchess of Gordon admired Louisa, but I think Harriet will be thought the best looking. Caroline is certainly the least, so therefore it shows it is mere luck and not beauty that attracts husbands.

I think I shall be very vain of my son-in-law if Henry Parnell becomes so, and I shall long to introduce him to you. Adieu, my dear sister. My mind is so occupied with this unexpected event I can think of nothing else.'

When Henry discovered that he had been accepted by the wrong sister, he had not sufficient courage to explain matters and the marriage to Caroline proceeded. They were married on 17 February 1801. He had acquired his father's permission by then, but it had been given grudgingly. Less than two months prior to the wedding Henry had even written to Sophia to see how the land lay with his father regarding where he and Caroline should live after the wedding, he being too afraid to approach him directly.

Sir John's reservations were to prove well-founded. The couple were totally unsuited. In after years Caroline would confess to her daughter, Emma, that she had been 'chilled' by Henry's coldness towards her after the wedding. Though never entirely happy with each other, the couple nevertheless strived to make the best of it and Caroline gave birth to a daughter, Mary Laetitia, the following year, giving her a fresh vessel into which to she could now pour her love.

6

THE FRENCH CONNECTION

HER PATH TO marriage started not with a ball, but with a funeral.

On 6 December 1801, Sir John Parnell, having just returned from a debate in the British House of Commons, died suddenly of a stroke while returning to his town house in London's Belgravia. He was by that time a former Lord of the Treasury, a Chancellor of the Irish Exchequer and one of the wealthiest men in Ireland. He left his children more than adequately provided for, and heirs to a political legacy that each in their own way would struggle to come to terms with.

Anxious to escape the tide of condolences that represented the first real awareness of their own mortality, William and Sophia decided to run away for a while and live a little on the fruits their inheritance. Following in the wake of friends who had departed the previous November, they set sail for post-revolutionary Paris.

They were not the only Parnells to go. The signing of peace preliminaries between Britain and France had seen hordes of curious nobility to race to the continent to experience the aftermath of revolution. Their older brother, Henry, recently married to Caroline Dawson, also travelled to Paris, but separately. He was never recorded in his younger siblings' company, or even within the same social circles.

The younger Parnells, as liberal as their elder brother was conservative, held unconventional political and divergent religious beliefs. Not having a political career to protect, they could indulge their intellectual curiosity. Sophia even contrived to underscore her newly acquired independence by infiltrating a circle of radical society women who would forever influence her view of the world.

The war of 1793-1801 had effectively closed France to tourists. During that time the French monarchy had been swept away by revolutionary forces that in their turn had been brushed aside by Napoleon. With newspaper reports proving an unreliable witness to events, those educated and wealthy enough to do so took advantage of the peace to witness the new republic for themselves. Their morbid curiosity satisfied, they reverted to type. Their 'grand tours' became more about pleasure than education, and vast sums were spent on entertaining themselves and their guests.

The Parnells were sufficiently wealthy and well-connected to travel and dine with the best of them. William, in particular, was a close friend of the extraordinarily wealthy Lord Peter King, 7th Baron of Ockham. The pair had been at Eton and Cambridge together. They would also socialise with Lord Stephen and Lady Margaret Mount Cashell.

The only female in her family since the age of four, Sophia Parnell was a tall, slender and intelligent young woman. Denied the educational opportunities of her brothers, who had been educated at Eton and

Cambridge, she had slaked her thirst for knowledge in the family library and in her private reading had developed a love of Voltaire, Hume and Gibbon: reactionary agnostic thinkers that few governesses of the day would have dared to introduce to an impressionable young lady. Forceful in her liberal convictions, she represented something of a social risk to prospective suitors and, despite several London 'seasons' and a sizable marriage portion, she had, at the age of twenty-three, still to attract the attention of a suitable marriage partner.

Margaret King Mount Cashell (1801)

Lady Margaret Mount Cashell was also an intelligent and self-educated woman. Having chosen to marry for position she now found herself trapped and trammelled in unhappy wedlock with a man whose political views were the polar opposite of her own. The Irish diarist, Katherine Wilmot, a travel companion of the Mount Cashells described Margaret as 'socially charming and attractive, highly cultivated, upright and refined'. She would also describe her as 'harsh to her children, a freethinker in religion, and imbued with what were then the most extravagant political notions'. In the young and impressionable Sophia Parnell, Margaret Mount Cashell found what she could never find with her husband – an intelligent and sympathetic audience.

Margaret Mount Cashell's 'extravagant political notions' had largely been sown and watered by her childhood governess, the proto-feminist writer, Mary Wollstonecraft. An early campaigner for women's rights, and the author of *The Rights of Women*, Wollstonecraft had tutored Margaret for just a single year, but her influence had been so profound that Margaret would forever look upon her as the surrogate mother who had 'freed her mind from all superstitions'.

A writer in her own right, Margaret had also, much to the annoyance of her husband, written pamphlets for the Society of United Irishmen during the 1798 rebellion and befriended the infamous Lord Edward Fitzgerald. During her stay in Paris she had also become acquainted with Robert Emmet who, less than a year later, would be executed for leading an armed rebellion in Ireland.

Sophia's future father-in-law, Hampden Evans, was also friend of Fitzgerald, and was similarly visited by Emmet in Paris during this time. It is more than probable, then, that the Evans family were also friendly with Margaret Mount Cashell – a woman whose political leanings had once been considered so extreme that she had no sooner settled into married life in Ireland than she had incurred the suspicion of the Government.

Throughout their time in France, Sophia and William Parnell would travel widely with the Mount Cashells, the siblings charming English and Parisian society alike with their wit and intellect. Wilmot, was particularly taken with them. On Sunday, 25 April 1802, from her room at the Hotel de Rome, she wrote:

> *'A son and daughter of Sir John Parnell's have been at Paris, and often at Lord Mount Cashell's. William Parnell is the son I allude to. I speak of him with a sort of pride as being an Irishman, and such a character take it for all in all, as any country wou'd look upon as doing it the highest honor.*
>
> *'Tis pleasant to have an idea of the person, to whose character your attention is drawn, and therefore you may scatter every improvement you please over a countenance, which at first sight is only distinguished by good temper, and intelligence. He is tall and slight, with small face and features, colouring cheeks, and smiling eyes.*
>
> *The circumstances of this young man's life have I believe, been peculiar, from his cast of thought running in direct opposition to his natural disposition. His experience of mankind makes him talk of self-interest being to be reverenc'd above everything else, at the very moment that involuntary benevolence looks out from his countenance to mellow down the rigour of such a principle.*
>
> *Nature and education are at such cross-purposes in him, that he reminds me of the shot silk tissues of various colours, which, sometimes run green in one direction and rosy in another, and tho' he has thoroughly convinc'd himself he is proof against all the visitings of human nature,*

> *yet I declare I hardly know the person I cou'd sooner ask to relieve me from every species of affliction than himself.*
>
> *His sister resembles him a good deal. But they are gone to Bordeaux and when they return I will tell you more about them, for they strike me as being a very extraordinary pair of Beings.'*

Ten years before the publication of *Child Harold's Pilgrimage*, it would appear that the youthful William was trying to affect a Byronic pose. It was juvenile and unconvincing, but at the same time an alluring paradox. Margaret Mount Cashell, a decade older and heavily pregnant, was equally intrigued. In June 1802, when she gave birth to her second son, Richard, she asked William to stand as godfather.

Sophia was younger than William by three years but so closely were they said to resemble each other they might as well have been twins. They were also said to be intellectual equals. Since the influential liberal politician, Charles James Fox, once described William as 'one of the best as well as one of the cleverest men I ever knew' one must assume that Sophia was possessed of an equally formidable intellect.

Physically, the pair were unremarkable, despite their mother's renowned beauty. Sophia's appearance was never commented upon and Wilmot described William as a young man with a 'small face and features, colouring cheeks, and smiling eyes.' Portraits of the time show him balding prematurely in his early twenties.

Resentful of a society that placed greater value on looks than intelligence, William, at the time of his visit to France, was in the process of putting the finishing touches to his first novel: *Julietta: On the Triumph of Mental Acquirements over Personal Defects*. It told the Cinderella-like story of a humpbacked[11] child and her

---

[11] A deformation often caused by tuberculosis.

struggles to find respect and affection in a family obsessed with feminine beauty.

At the crux of this novel, the aged and ailing Lord Marsham advises eighteen-year-old Julietta on how an intelligent woman might make herself the mistress of politics, economics and all the sciences, without becoming insolent, contemptible or untrue to herself. Julietta, under his tutelage, eventually finds happiness courtesy of her persistence, guile and intelligence.

Published later that year by Joseph Johnston, William's book reads, in retrospect, like an instructional fable for his sister. But William need not have worried, for Sophia's unconventional attractions were not without their admirers. One man in particular had begun to take close notice of her.

William Jones Burdett was the thirty-year-old brother of the radical English politician and friend of Thomas Paine, Sir Francis Burdett[12]. A frequent companion of the Mount Cashells in France, his family were also close friends of the O'Connors, who in turn were frequent visitors to the Condorcets, at whose home Sophia had become a regular guest.

Katherine Wilmot describes William Burdett as 'a young man exceedingly fond of improvement and highly amiable'. All other accounts describe him as a pale shadow of his brother, Francis. Nothing would come of the attraction in France, but Burdett's interest in Sophia would become much more intense following his return to London the following year.

Their liberal philosophy notwithstanding, the Parnells were not beyond a bit of celebrity gazing. They may even have managed to wrangle an invitation to the Tuileries, Napoleon's official residence in Paris, where guests were presented each month to Madame Bonaparte (later the Empress Josephine). Katherine

---

[12] It would be Sir Francis Burdett who gifted Thomas Paine the money that enabled him to discharge his debts and return to the United States.

Wilmot also attended, William and Lord King having travelled to Versailles on 16 May 1802 specifically to collect her for the occasion:

'When I was here a fortnight, Lord and Lady Mount Cashell, Mr. Parnell and Lord King came to Versailles, to take me back to Paris for a few days. The object was our presentation to Madame Bonaparte. They spent the day here, and we all dined together at the Inn. This Mr. Parnell is the one I spoke to you of before; he and Lord King are the greatest friends upon earth and, tho' very different, it speaks volumes for both parties.

Lord King is very handsome, and as a painter said of him "looks like a fine Spartan Youth". He is very boyish in his manners and totally unaffected. His sense everyone knows about, and tho' eloquence does not strike one as particularly his gift, yet I have heard he is one of the best orators in the House, whenever he speaks, which is very seldom. This was the only day I ever knew to turn out pleasantly when the parties were forewarn'd they were to like one another. But it really was delightful and we all set off for Paris as gay as larks.

And the next day, at three o'clock, Lady Mount Cashell and I drove off in State to the Thuilleries to be presented to Madame Bonaparte. The Room was crowded and Madame Bonaparte was seated on a sofa, when M. Merry, our Minister, brought up to make our obeisance before her. She is that sort of looking woman, that if chance had not placed her on such a pinnacle, would escape minute observation. Her manners are gentlewomanlike, amiable and pleasing, and her caption of us was easy and excessively polite. After staying a quarter of an hour, she rose, made a regal courtesy and withdrew.

Everybody then drove about Paris, making

visits to the House of Bonaparte, Lucien, Louis &c., and the Prefect of the Palace. This ended the business and this incense to Royalty is administered every month. The next day Lord and Lady Mount Cashell, Parnell, Lord King and myself, spent the most entertaining and pleasant day possible, at "Bagatelle", beyond the "Bois de Boulogne", and built in six weeks by the Prince of Condé. It was an entertainment given by Mr. Rowley and, as it is a Publick garden, multitudes of people were parading about and amusing themselves in a thousand different ways. This "Bagatelle" is so beautiful! Such a wilderness of Flowers, and so gay, that I delight in it!

The next day Lady Mount Cashell, Miss Parnell and her Brother came with me back to Versailles, and left me at Monsieur de Pescheloche's. They return'd back to Paris. Two days ago Monsieur de Pescheloche, Monsieur Mongein and I, rode to Vanciesson to dine with an English family of the name of Hervey. It is half way to Paris, and we met Lord and Lady Mount Cashell, and Mr. Parnell there.'

The Parnells may also have dined with Napoléon at one of his monthly dinners, as they regularly attended such functions in the company of the Mount Cashells. On the face of it that would have seemed unlikely, but for the fact that in December of that same year, Sophia's older brother, Henry, would receive a letter from a certain Madame de Brissac regarding a parcel that he had delivered to her. Madame de Brissac was Napoléon's mother.

During her stay in Paris, Sophia would frequently share the company of many of the city's independent-minded and influential *salonnières*; intelligent women who appeared lived a life of intellectual freedom and pervasive influence. Most notable amongst her acquaintances was Sophie de Condorcet, widow of the late French philosopher and mathematician, Nicolas de Condorcet. Courtesy of his opposition to the Jacobin administration, Nicolas had lost his life during the Reign of Terror.

Parc de Bagatelle, Paris.

More than twenty years younger than her famous husband, and renowned as an early feminist, Sophie de Condorcet was fluent in English and Italian, and already an accomplished translator of the works of Thomas Paine and Adam Smith. Her salon regularly attracted the leading figures of the enlightenment. Unlike many of her fellow *salonnières*, Sophie's salons always included other women, especially the infamous Madame de Staël, an opponent of Napoleon and a friend of the United Irishman, Arthur O'Connor. An occasional house guest of both de Staël and the Condorcets, O'Connor was also a frequent guest of the exiled Evans family of Portrane, the eldest son of which, George, was a close friend of Sophia's brother, William, and secretly in love with her.

De Staël would make a particularly deep impression

Sophie de Condorcet, née de Grouchy (1764-1822)

upon young Sophia, but they would never become more than casual acquaintances. Her relationship with the Condorcets, on the other hand, became quickly intimate, most especially with Sophie's daughter, eleven-year-old Eliza, a delightful, intelligent and animated child who had lost her father at the age of five (and who would later marry the aforementioned Arthur O'Connor).

Eliza's mother, Sophie de Condorcet, was, like Margaret Mount Cashell, similarly possessed of extravagant political notions. A century before women would be given the vote, and a full twenty-eight years before slavery would be outlawed in the British Empire, she and her husband, Nicolas, had championed such radical ideas as a liberal economy, free and equal public education and equal rights for women and people of all races.

The salons of Paris presented a novel and educational experience to a young lady accustomed only to the morning parties and languid luncheons of English polite society, where the primary preoccupations were gossip, fads and fripperies. The French salons, in contrast, were all about ideas. They offered intelligent and imaginative young women a safe place in which they could openly debate with men. London was about the body, Paris about the mind. It left a lasting impression.

There had, of course, been 'bluestocking' salons in London since the 1750s, where intellectual men and women had mixed freely and on an equal footing, but these had been largely revolved around the gatherings of single or widowed middle-to-upper class women such as Frances Boscawen, Elizabeth Vesey and the so-called 'Queen of the Blues', Elizabeth Montagu. Of these women only Boscawen was still alive. But she was now eighty-three and neither Sophia nor William were ever recorded as moving in such circles in London.

Courtesy of her informal French education, when

Sophia finally returned to London, she took with her more than a journal full of memories. She took with her a newfound self-confidence and a head full of 'extravagant' notions, such as the idea of purchasing, as a single woman, a home of her own. With her brothers' help, she settled into an emancipated and independent life at 45 Welbeck Street in Marylebone.

7

GEORGE HAMPDEN EVANS

FOLLOWING HER RETURN to London, Sophia moved into her new townhouse on Welbeck Street, where she proceeded to live alone on the fortune of £600 a year that her father had provided for her in his will. Into that house she brought much of her father's library, including a priceless portfolio of proof copy prints by William Hogarth that the artist had once gifted to her grandfather, and also some quarto volumes of the works of Alexander Pope that had belonged to her father.[13]

In her new house she entertained her friends and enjoyed the attachment of romantic admirers, though admittedly *these* were few and far between. She had been 'out' in London society for some seven seasons now, but had little to show for it. A decorous and

---

[13] She would later gift these to her nephew, Henry William Parnell, son of Sir Henry Parnell, when he let the house for her following Sir Henry's death.

59

45 Welbeck Street.
Photo courtesy of Mark Philips, Edward Charles & Partners LLP.

personable young lady, Sophia was no shrinking violet. Firm in her unorthodox opinions, she was as willing to debate them as any man and *with* any man. Her intelligence, though worn lightly, was no less intimidating than that of her brothers, and of late only one young gentleman appeared to have found the staying power to last the course.

William Jones Burdett, whom she had previously met in Paris, had hopes of taking the relationship further and it was widely expected that he would eventually propose, and that she would accept him. There were even some who believed that he had already done so, and that the pair were secretly engaged.

One such person was George Evans of Portrane, a close friend of Sophia's brother, William. George had met Sophia on several occasions and was absolutely besotted with her. His heart had been so badly pierced by Cupid's dart that he feared to return fire lest his trembling hands cause him to miss, Sophia had become his 'all-in-all', the unsated hunger of his life.

But what hopes could an inarticulate and diffident oaf like him realistically entertain, when his every rational instinct denied them? It was simply an impossible infatuation, a thing to be escaped or managed, not horribly, embarrassingly, acted upon. He was, he believed, quite plainly and simply unworthy of her and his infatuation remained a secret, even from his closest friends.

But then one day the mask slipped and he unburdened his heart's load on his dear friend, William, who convinced him that he had misjudged his sister and that he had, at the very least, an honest chance, *if* he moved quickly. With the risk of embarrassment still uppermost in his mind, George decided to write to Sophia and have William forward the letter to her with a heartfelt plea for discretion. William, however, did more than simply pass on George's note. He intervened on his behalf and actively encouraged his sister to consider him.

Sophia, received the letter, but temporised in answering. For days George fretted and fidgeted, nervously alert for the answer that would injure or elevate his feelings. In the end he could withstand the torment no longer. On 11 May 1805, emboldened by the absence of an outright and peremptory refusal, and contrary to the societal rules that generally governed such delicate transactions, he took up his pen:

'I am not going to ask a question, or to extort a confession which I can not as yet hope for, but to which I fondly look at some further day; I am a novitiate in the art of paying my court and as such am entitled to some excuse if I have not succeeded – I have had no opportunity of expressing the esteem I set on your high accomplishments, and with that mind I have had no opportunity of claiming a large share of indulgence when I have appeared deficient in little attentions and should hope it was not set down to the want of a feeling that has long been paramount with me.

In your company I am happy, your voice is music to my ears and pleasing to my heart; I could dwell with pleasure on many topicks relating to you, and account with delight, the hours I have passed in such contemplation. I have but little to say of myself, I am but too well aware of my true deficiencies, particularly an impracticality of manner which may at first raise a prejudice against me, and the want of a polish which is sometimes overrated – if I may offer an equivalent, it is in the proffer of a warm heart, and a pledge that from the day we shall be united, my chief object shall be the furthering your happiness; a blush for my honour or conduct as a man shall never suffuse your cheek.

I consider I have gained a prize rich indeed and must repay somewhat in a generous affection. I am confident it will be durable, it is fixed in the firmest foundation, it was not alone the charms of your person, your family, or fortune that made so deep an impression (the latter I could have obtained in a triple ratio) but a simplicity and elevation of character that to me was irresistible – do not ask why I have written, I may have erred against the dictates of good judgement in writing, yet my heart tells me I am justified, and the heart devoted to you can not be wrong,

Etc etc etc,
G.E.

On the face of it they made for an unlikely couple: George was a keen sportsman with an insatiable appetite for riding and shooting and possessed of considerable skill at both. Sophia, for her part, appears to have hated sport and to have treasured her peace and quiet. George was a cautious and unassuming young man; Sophia, an opinionated 'blue' from a family known for oddities. Both were educated and erudite, George having graduated with a law degree from Trinity College Dublin, and Sophia, a largely self-educated woman, naturally drawn to politics and philosophy and exuding an intimidating veneer of self-assurance that he would in time discover to be paper thin.

As George waited anxiously for her reply, William, too, became impatient. Sometime in May 1805, Sophia wrote to him, questioning his motives for interfering in so delicate a matter. From his home in Avondale, on 31 May 1805, he wrote to reassure her, and to press the practical benefits of her choosing George in preference to Burdett:

My Dear Sophia,

I was aware that Evans was attached to you; but like all people of great worth was too diffident to declare it. A report I heard from Henry that Mr. Burdett was paying his address to you determined me to write to him and I enclose his answer which I trust if you really are otherwise engaged you will mention to no earthly person.

You have seen Evans and therefore can pretty well decide and Mr. B. as far as personal accomplishments go; Evans' fortune will be every way respectable, I make no doubt his father would immediately settle £1500 a year on him and in case of his father's death he would have a property of at least £4000 a year. If he accepted him, I know he would purchase a seat in parliament which would secure your residency a certain portion of the year in London.

Pray hesitate at least if you do not decide in his favour and at least see more of him,

Your most affectionate,

W. Parnell.

Sophia was not about to be rushed. She had been seeing Burdett for some time now and not without some expectation on his part. She had *his* feelings to consider. But William would not let up. On 10 June 1805, fearful that his sister was about to make a grievous error of judgement, he wrote again:

My Dear Sophia,

I hope you received a letter of mine enclosing one of Evans to me; I send you another of his that I may do justice to his suit. He takes it for granted that you are engaged to Mr. Burdett which I hope sincerely is not the case, as I suppose his fortune is not great and I never heard anything of his accomplishments etc.

Evans is a man that a sensible woman must feel a preference for, and he is the only person I know I should wish you married to. I am certain his fortune will not be less than 6000 per annum before he dies.

Your most affectionate,

W. Parnell.

Sophia finally relented and agreed to see George. Beneath the inevitable decorum and guarded compliments that beset such meetings, a certain naturalness quickly developed between them that spelt the end of her interest in William Jones Burdett. They found themselves, in the parlance of the day, exceptionally 'well met'.

When she finally accepted him, George's joy was not without a certain apprehension. Had he simply wooed and won her, things would have been simple and uncomplicated, but he had not. He had deprived another man of her, and she of him. His greatest fear, as he prepared himself for the task of bringing home the new Mrs Evans and parading her amongst his relatives, was that he would yet prove unworthy of her.

At the beginning of his relationship with Sophia, George appears to have had little interest in politics beyond its effect on his legal work, his family's estates, and the hospitality he was obliged to offer the more dangerous acquaintances of his father. Not even the visit of Robert Emmet, who dined with him in October 1802, could persuade him to offer support to another rebellion.

With his entire family dependent upon the income from the estates he now managed on behalf of his exiled father, George refused to involve himself in anything that could jeopardise their collective futures. In 1798, his father, Hampden Evans, had escaped the hangman's noose by the skin of his teeth. George was not about to make the same mistake.

Less than a year later, on 20 September 1803, Robert Emmet would be hung and beheaded on Dublin's Thomas Street for his part in a failed rebellion. Such would be the fear of being tainted by association, that not a single person would come forward to claim his remains. George had been prudent in his caution.

George was not, however, without political opinions of his own, or beyond giving aid or support to non-violent campaigns. In the year following Emmet's execution, and before his marriage to Sophia, Lord King had approached William Parnell to discuss his intention of moving a bill to abolish what remained of the penal laws. Advised by the prominent Whig statesman Charles Fox that the necessary majority would be difficult to achieve unless a petition for relief was first received from the Catholics, the pair had undertaken to ensure that such a petition would be forthcoming.

On his return to Dublin, William Parnell went straight to Portrane to call on George, who took him to meet his friend, James Ryan, a wealthy Catholic merchant. Together the pair attempted to persuade Ryan to get up the petition. Ryan had agreed to canvas other influential Catholics, but neither George nor William were prepared to go any further at that stage.

The *Martial Law* and *Suspension of Habeus Corpus* acts were still in force, and under the provisions of these acts anyone who was merely *suspected* of being a member of the United Irishmen could be imprisoned without trial. For George Evans they posed a real and present danger to his liberty. His father, after all, had participated in the United Irish rebellion of 1798, and Robert Emmet himself had been a guest at his home.

George had every reason to be cautious, and William appears to have respected that.

That brief foray into the world of politics with William Parnell may have been but a small step for the liberal-leaning George, but it was to prove significant. The political arena was the realm of the Parnells and the world in which the woman he loved had been born and raised. It was never going to be his last foray, especially when his good friend, William, in his *An inquiry into the Causes of Popular Discontents in Ireland,* had just described an entire class of absentee landlords as a 'horde of tyrants':

> *'A horde of tyrants exist in Ireland, in a class of men that are unknown in England, in the multitude of agents of absentees, small proprietors, who are the pure Irish squires, middle men who take large farms, and squeeze out a forced kind of profit by letting them in small parcels; lastly, the little farmers themselves, who exercise then same insolence they receive from their superiors, on those unfortunate beings who are placed at the extremity of the scale of degradation – the Irish Peasantry! ...*
>
> *Are these men supposed to have no sense of justice, that, in addition to the burthen of supporting their own establishment exclusively, they should be called on to pay ours; that, where they pay sixpence to their own priest, they should pay a pound to our clergyman; that, while they can scarce afford their own horse, they should place ours in his carriage; and that when they cannot build a mass-house to cover their multitudes, they should be forced to pray under a shed!'*

George himself may have been reluctant to get actively involved in politics, it being a chapter that could not easily be written while he lived in the dominating shadow of his radical and patriotic father, but such was his family's reputation that, on hearing of his engagement, Lady Anna Maria Jones couldn't help teasing Sophia about it. On 16 July 1805, from her home in Ravensbourne near Bromley, she wrote:

'*My Dear Sophia,*

You used me most shabbily last year and I have been meditating a scold; upon hearing you were gone to Daensfield for the summer, fearing you intended to behave no better to me this year: but my wrath on that head is assuaged, tho' I think I have fresh ground for a quarrel by hearing that you are on the brink of committing matrimony without having asked my consent. I however give it most freely as I understand it is quite a choice of your own.

I always advise all my young friends to marry & to choose for themselves. I assure you that the little I saw of your future does not diminish the high opinion I always had of your good sense and discernment. And that he has proved his I fancy none who know you will doubt. In short you will both be very happy if you escape being hanged (you know your Bro. W. introduced him to me as a great rebel) ...

If Mr Evans finds it expedient to live much in Ireland: or even with his Brother Rebels on the continent, I so far from object, to you doing the same. It will always be my earnest advice to young married women to accompany their husbands wherever they are called by choice or business to reside, and that is the only piece of advice I shall leave you with; but my wishes and prayers for your happiness are more unbounded, they are guided by the sincere affection I ever felt for your dear parents and which I always felt a melancholy pleasure in transferring to you.

*ZP My Dear Sophia
affectionately
AMJ.'*

On Wednesday 31 August 1805, the marriage settlements having been signed by Sophia's eldest brother, Henry Parnell (but, significantly, not by George's father, Hampden, who was still exiled in Paris), thirty-three-year-old George Evans stood at the altar rails of Marylebone Church to wait for twenty-five-year-old Sophia Parnell. The church was just a short walk from Sophia's townhouse on Welbeck street. Shortly after the wedding they departed for Portrane, where Sophia settled into a substantial south-facing Georgian house that looked out over expansive lawns to Howth Head and the Wicklow Mountains. It was somewhat isolated compared to her house in Belgravia, but it was quiet and peaceful and very much to her taste.

In becoming mistress of Mount Evans, Sophia entered a coterie of idealistic artists (even her mother-in-law wrote poetry) and the company that gathered at her table was a far cry from the political strategists and pragmatists that had once congregated at her father's. Having experienced the intellectual freedom of the French salons where wealthy educated women steered a course of their own charting, scorned 'delicate' conversation and debated freely with men on matters of science, politics, economics and the arts, the new Mrs. Evans chaffed at societal restrictions in Ireland and rarely accompanied her husband on shooting expeditions outside of her immediate family circle.

She missed the cut and thrust of London life and the ease by which political and philosophical books could be bought. Of her brothers, only Henry was now actively involved in politics, but he lived in London, too distant for regular contact, and he was father now to two further children, Emma, born in 1804, and John, born in 1805.

Over the succeeding years Henry's wife, Caroline, would give birth to another daughter, Fanny, and then to two further sons, Henry and George. Sophia, therefore, had no shortage of nieces and nephews to dote upon during her visits to London, where she continued to keep a townhouse, but as of yet no children of her own.

Following the marriage, some issues arose regarding the marriage settlement and her house on Welbeck Street. The primary cause lay in George's inability to get his exiled father to sign the marriage articles. The lack of this signature appears to have caused some financial difficulties for the couple and for a time Sophia battled with a decision as to whether or not she might have to sell her house on Welbeck Street. While visiting her friends and family in London, she wrote to George, who had returned to Portrane alone. His reply was gracious to a fault for a man of that era:

'I am quite at a loss to explain to you in the way I could wish, my opinion about the house in Welbeck Street. Need I assert, my dear Sophia, the pre-dominant and ever present sustenance of my heart is to render you happy …

I have been entrusted with my father's property; and have I been faithful to my heart. If our marriage articles were signed by him the case would be altered, then I should have money at command, and your jointure would be secured; now your jointure rests on the security of your own fortune which I can not bear to diminish by any act of mine.

I will not confine myself to the selfish gratification of making you comfortable during my life, however, to come to the point, and to avoid any embarrassment, cross purposes, or guesses, I must insist on leaving the decision of selling or not selling entirely to you. My advice to you is to keep the house. I was confident you have a kind of attachment to it, and I think it very natural you should, you felt more an exclusive property in it before your marriage, than in any thing else ...

If a thing should fix us again in London we should then have no trouble in providing a house, because it looks so very comfortable that I am quite in conceit with it myself. I propose therefore that you should take it to yourself. I will make over all claim to it, if you can prevail on Arthur or any other person to pay to our joint assessment 25% which is something about the money we have lost by it. This will be securing about £13.15 a year the surplus that will accrue to you. By taking it, when in Ireland, may be a considerable addition to your pin money[14], and when in London, will be most pleasant to go to.

This is my advice, and a further inducement to my giving it is to prevent your regret at a further day for parting with the house. From hence forward I will take no part in your decision...'

In the end, Sophia decided not to sell. Her childhood home in Rathleague, on the other hand, was already in the process of being sold off, the implication being that John Augustus was now being cared for somewhere else. The process of selling the estate, however, was proving far from simple on account of her brother, Thomas, who had recently become something of a religious zealot with little understanding of the value of money or how the property market worked.

By insisting on selling his inherited portion of the estate at below market value to get a quick sale, Thomas was driving down the price that his other siblings could get for their own portions and insisting that if they were that concerned they should buy the land from him themselves. On 4 December 1808,

---

[14] At that time this meant a lady's clothing allowance.

George, who had estate business of his own in the area, wrote to Sophia:

> *'Tom's excuse is that he does not care for money and that he can live on little, that if Henry did not take it he would have sold it to any one. I hinted what you desired, it made no impression'*

This incident was to prove the beginning of Tom's downward spiral into extreme eccentricity. His inability to handle money would become a source of much contention and bad feeling in the years ahead.

8

PORTRANE HOUSE

PORTRANE HOUSE SAT on a shelf of rising ground in the centre of a seaside peninsula surrounded by trees and lawns and visible from neither road nor sea, except for the chimney tops that craned their necks above the evergreens. It was a quiet sequestered spot, perfect for study and peaceful contemplation, except at dusk when the ravens wheeled and homed in cacophonous clamour above the treetops and the horses whinnied in the stable yard.

The trees protected the house from the worst of the easterly and westerly winds and from the corrosive salt air that swept in from the Irish Sea. Clearings to the north and south allowed expansive views towards Rush and Howth, but planting to east and west shielded the house from the joys of dawn and dusk. Wrapping the house in their collective embrace the trees stole the softest colours of the sun. If you wanted to enjoy the best of what the demesne had to offer, you had to wrap up well and venture outside.

In 1837, in his *A Topographical Dictionary of Ireland,* Samuel Lewis described the demesne thus:

'The coast is remarkably grand and bold, and the sea has worked its way into the rocks, so as to form several excavations of large extent, in one of which is a curious well of fresh water called Clink. Portrane House, the property and residence of George Evans, Esq. M.P. is a spacious brick building nearly in the centre of a demesne of 420 acres, well stocked with deer and commanding extensive and splendid views'

Portrane House. Photo courtesy of Peadar Bates.

The house itself was a standard T-plan three-storey over basement country house with a five-bay limestone façade. A central breakfront featured tripartite windows on the first and second floors, with square-headed windows, tooled limestone sills and timber sash windows to either side of the breakfront. A pedimented entrance consisted of timber and glazed double doors and decorative fanlight. It was accessed up four limestone steps flanked by a plinth wall.

Built around the middle of the 18th century the building had three stories to the front and four to the rear, enabling the downstairs servants to enjoy the light of day as they went about their work. This basement story, sunk below ground, was exceptionally large and spacious, and a back staircase led to the servant's apartments that were situated in a separate wing attached to the main house.

The ground floor contained a large entrance hall which led directly to an even larger dining room. A double staircase led to the upper floors. To the right and left of the entrance hall were four drawing rooms, a library, and a billiard room that led to a large conservatory. The upper floors consisted of sixteen bed and dressing rooms with toilets and bathrooms attached. No matter how many guests Sophia and George would entertain, there was always somewhere within the house where one could find solitude.

Apart from the main house there were also offices, and stabling for nine horses, as well as several coach houses and apartments for visiting coachmen and grooms such as can be seen still at Rathleague. Beyond the stables again, there was a pump house and a large rainwater tank in an enclosed yard connected to the main house by means of an underground passage. The house was centrally heated in winter by hot water pipes.

The form of the house would have appeared conservative when it was built and represented the aspirational middle ground between farmhouse and mansion, embellished and extended as and when funds permitted. In its form it bears striking similarities to Milltown Park House in Shinrone, Co. Offaly. It may even have been built by the same architect. An idea of what the interior looked like can probably be gauged from the heavily stuccoed interiors and marble hallways of this building, which still stands today.

Portrane House was a place of stillness and shadow, a place of hospitality and convalescence that functioned like a small hotel or spa. And it had to, in order to draw visitors from the city to such an isolated and windswept location. Each year it would attract a host of early autumn guests, invited to 'take the sea-air' or indulge in the latest health fad of 'sea bathing'. The poet Mary Tighe would visit for four weeks during her recuperation from tuberculosis in 1807, and in 1835 Lady Morgan would record the following in her diary:

> *'We are going to-day to Portrane (the Evans' thank God!) ... Whilst here, Morgan, who is ill and weak, would take no exercise, so my sole object in coming here was disappointed.'*

That same year, following the marriage of Sophia's favourite nephew, Henry William Parnell, to Sophy Bligh, the seaside location of Mount Evans would also begin to draw Henry's wife and children for September holidays.

The health attractions of the mansion would further be enhanced, in the years following the famine, by the addition of a Turkish bath. This strange and short-lived therapeutic fad swept so thoroughly through Ireland in the mid-nineteenth century, that by 1860 a public bathhouse would open on Dublin's Lincoln Place. It would cater for as many as ninety bathers a day.

The attractions of Portrane, however, lay not just in the comfortable rooms and scenic surroundings, but in the munificent hospitality of the hosts and, most especially, the delights of their dining table. The Evanses understood only too well the value of a skilled chef and fine wines. Lady Morgan, who was a frequent guest at Portrane House, records in her diary of 5 January 1834, that:

> *'They are both excellent, and I always enjoy my sea-girt dwelling; in spite of the wind howling without, all within is peace, comfort, and good cheer; by-the-bye, à propos to the latter, they possess the first cook in Europe.'*

The final attraction of Portrane lay in its abundance of game, for George was a keen and talented horseman who loved to shoot and ride. Visitors during the shooting and hunting seasons, therefore, were also quite common, except when George was shooting at someone else's estate. The house would generally fall quiet between March and July of each year as George and Sophia decamped to London for 'the season'.

First and foremost, however, Mount Evans was a working farm, the workings of which were immediately of interest to Sophia. Just two months after their marriage George would write to Sophia, a great admirer of the agriculturist Arthur Young:

> *'I hope you will not fatigue yourself. I shall be home as soon as possible ... I hope you will superintend the planting in all directions and generally the business of the farm.'*

From the very start, it seems, this was a very modern marriage and George was happy to delegate to Sophia the day to day running of the farm, while he took care of his law practice and those financial transactions that were dependent upon his signature such as the buying of stock etc. It says much for Sophia's self-confidence and abilities, and indeed George's recognition of them, that he would consent to this, as much of the work that Sophia would take on was normally the preserve of the land steward. A few paragraphs from the *Boston Post*, of 26 December 1885, give us a flavour of how Sophia may have been seen at the time by those who would later remember her:

'Sophia Parnell (sister of the first Lord Congleton) was a woman of great ability and learning – a maitresse femme *with a strong and resolute character and a face singularly like that of a lioness. She was a Deist of the old school and her greatest delight in old age was in reading her magnificent editions of Hume, Gibbon and Voltaire and the encyclopaedists.*

Before her marriage she lived alone in her house in London on her fortune of £600 a year, which in those happy times sufficed to enable the possessor to keep a good establishment and a carriage. She went to France also, and became very intimate with Condorcet and his family, for whom she had great admiration, and likewise knew Arthur Young, Madam de Stäel and most of the other notabilities of the time.

Rather late in life she married her countryman, Mr. George Hampden Evans of Portrane, a beautifully situated estate on the Irish Coast about 10 miles north of Dublin. There, her energy and ability soon worked wonders.'

Boston Post, 26 December 1885.

With estates all over the country, and numerous invitations to join hunting parties, George was frequently away from home, leaving Sophia with a surplus of free time and solitude. Feeling vulnerable alone in the house at night, she would often take to sleeping in one of the guest rooms closer to the servants' quarters.

At such times, whenever it was possible, William

would come to stay with her, or she would visit with him at Avondale, but such visits never entirely filled the gap and, at every waking, the pattern of her solitary days at Portrane seemed to be set in stone. Her retreat of choice, into the world of books, had been severely curtailed since she left London, the reading tastes of the Evans clan having for a long time been so very different to her own.

The one part of her new domain, therefore, that Sophia was keen to set about improving from the start, was the library. She had grown up surrounded by books, and had inherited many valuable volumes and rare prints from her father, most of which were still in London. One of her firmest and most long standing business relationships would now be with her London bookseller.

George was not unaware of his wife's frustrations; indeed her intelligence and learning were part of what attracted him to her in the first place. In June 1807, having firstly enquired as to how she was getting on with the sheep shearing, he added:

'I just sent you by Mr. Ryan on Sunday a large packet of letters and papers, which considering your long privation of literary and philosophical correspondence must have been a great treat.'

The constant flow of guests to Portrane, were not just a reflection of George and Sophia's popularity and hospitality, they were essential to the mental health of a childless couple living in a remote countryside mansion with only their servants for company. Guests were spoiled, and a top class chef employed, for a reason. The library was enhanced, primarily for Sophia's pleasure, but also that of their guests.

If the result of all that was that their home became something of favoured retreat for recuperating invalids, then so much the better. Silence was golden, but solitude could be poison. Her brother Arthur, currently resident and working in London, was about to learn that very lesson in the most awful way.

9

ARTHUR AND THE ASYLUM

UNLIKE HIS ELDER brothers John and Henry, Arthur Parnell was never sent to Eton. The reason for this is not known; all we know is that Arthur was resident in London from at least 1799 and that by 1809 he was noted as being resident at the Royal College of Physicians, at Warwick Lane, in London. Here he laboured as part owner and shareholder in the firm 'Puget[15], Bainbridge & Parnell, merchant bankers. Since 1801, this firm had been handling receipts and payments on behalf of the Irish Treasury and certain members of the French Aristocracy[16]. A lot of money was passing through their hands on a daily basis.

On the 6 August 1809, Arthur presented himself at the offices of Paget and Co., Solicitors, in London and

---

[15] Possibly a relative. Henry's daughter, Emma, would spend a lot of time in the company of a certain Mrs. Puget, whom she would refer to as her father's 'cousin'.

[16] MS 49,491/2/1146, National Library of Ireland.

proceeded to draft his will. He was twenty-six at the time. The will was witnessed by Thomas Bainbridge. As Bainbridge was a business partner of Arthur, one must assume that Arthur was in reasonably good health at the time.

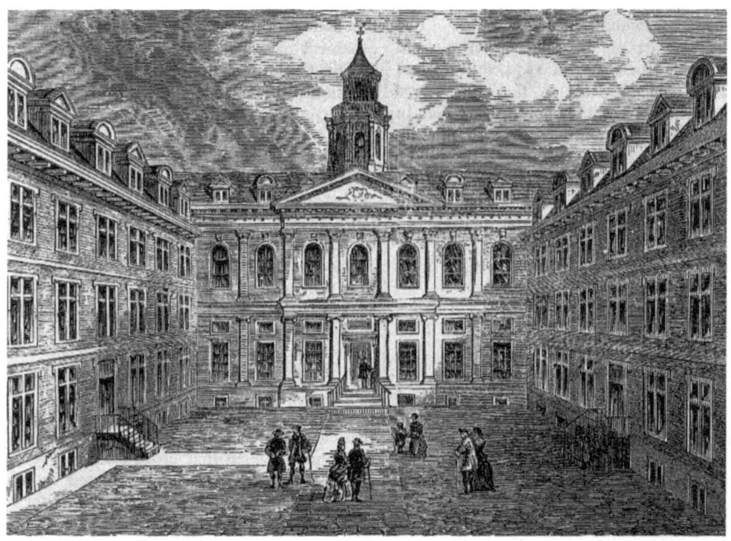

Royal College of Physicians, Warwick Lane. Interior Quadrangle.

In this curious document, Arthur left all his property to his brothers Henry, William and Thomas, subject to certain legacies being paid out within a year of his death to one Elizabeth Dobson, daughter of James Dobson and mother of three children, Arthur, Mary-Anne and Elizabeth. The mother of these children was to receive the enormous sum of £4000, and the children, £1000 each. To put these sums in context, they would in total exceed the entire annual income of George Evans vast estates in Ireland.

A further legacy was to be granted to John Parnell, eldest son of Arthur's brother, Henry. Three weeks after the will had been signed a codicil was added regarding the age at which the Dobson children could inherit. That Elizabeth Dobson was identified by her maiden name – and her children likewise – suggests that she was unmarried. The bequest itself, furthermore, suggests a personal relationship of some seriousness with Arthur Parnell. The name of her eldest child may even suggest the nature of that relationship but there is little other evidence to support what would appear, on the face of it, to be a natural conclusion.

Everything surrounding the Dobsons is shrouded in secrecy, and it is impossible at this remove to know for certain the exact nature of Arthur's relationship with them. Relationships between a 'gentleman' and his 'miss' were not uncommon at the time, and usually took place on the understanding that the woman and her offspring would be taken care of. If, or when, the relationship had to end, the 'gentleman' would be expected to compensate the woman for her loss of virtue with sufficient property or income as to not just make her economically comfortable, but an attractive prospect for another man. But Arthur was not doing *that*. This was a will. The money would only be paid out after he died. It would seem likely, therefore, that the relationship was current, and thriving.

A degree of moral leniency was frequently attached to a gentleman's 'miss' and the surrender of her virtue assumed to be an act of financial desperation. Nevertheless, with the drafting and witnessing of that will, the relationship was now out in the open and publicly acknowledged, at least within Arthur's inner circle, and concern began to be expressed for his wellbeing.

Early the following year, Arthur suffered some form of mental breakdown. The severity of his illness was such that the Parnells believed that he needed a holiday in a bracing, temperate climate. Arthur suggested Lisbon, a climate that had worked wonders for his sister. Sophia, however, believed that heat and lethargy was the last thing he needed in his current mental state and instead offered to care for him at Portrane.

Sophia would receive regular updates on Arthur's condition from Henry, but Arthur himself refused to write, or to answer her letters. Sophia was hurt by the snub (she had after all, been the dominant female personality in Arthur's life since the death of their mother). On 6 February 1810 she wrote to Henry:

'I do not wish to write to him myself for I cannot help feeling very much hurt by his silence and reserve to me ... I never regretted more my absence from London as it would give me great pleasure to see Arthur before he went abroad. I think Lisbon is the worst place he could have chosen, if he was determined not to come here he should have gone to Madeira, the climate of this place would, however, have been more likely to restore his health ... he would have derived all the benefit of extreme mildness of weather without being enervated by the heat of the sun which he will find in Lisbon and Madeira. He will not get to Lisbon during the rainy season and he will not perhaps be able to quit the house for some weeks after he gets there ...'

At this stage, it would appear that nobody believed Arthur to be a danger to himself, but that slowly began to change. Arthur began to procrastinate about seeking help and divesting himself of his interest in Puget, Bainbridge and Parnell. In consequence, Sophia's husband, George, had to be prevailed upon to come to London and use his connections to procure a consultation for Arthur with Robert Waring Darwin[17], the famous physician and fellow of the Royal Society.

A consultation was duly arranged at Darwin's clinic

---

[17] Father of the naturalist Charles Darwin.

in Shrewsbury, but Arthur refused to go, or to visit the offices at Warwick Lane to sort out his affairs. As his condition worsened, an increasingly frustrated George wrote to Sophia at Portrane:

Robert Waring Darwin

'Arthur has deferred his departure till Monday, on which day I ardently hope we may leave town for Shrewsbury, as I begin to fear he is not a little capricious. Ill health and seclusion can not fail to

have an effect on any tempers. I have had a good deal of conversation with Francis which I think will be of essential use to Darwin in forming an opinion on his case. As Will is in town, and as he proposes to go to Ireland in a fortnight, if he unhinges Arthur in his resolution of coming on Monday next or some early day in the week, I do not see any great use in my staying much longer in London when no object is gained by the delay.'

Three days later, George was beginning to despair of Arthur's temporizing. On 19 March he wrote again to Sophia:

'Arthur has taken not one step to prepare for his departure though he must have very essential business at Warwick Lane to sign powers of atorney and the transfer of stock. He however promises to go there on Monday; and Wednesday is the day fixed for leaving town. He feels as much reluctance to go to the Country House as he ever did formerly to leave it.

I believe finding his health would not permit him to continue the struggle with Bainbridge, he dislikes visiting the scene of (his) actions from shame or vexation. I never liked Bainbridge yet I can't help saying that he must have had a very hard card to play with Arthur, who instead of conciliating was in a constant state of warfare with him. From every appearance, when Arthur once leaves Warick Lane after settling his business, it will be a long time before he returns to it. This will be so much the better if we can quite restore him in Ireland.

The only way I can account for not hearing from you since I came to London is the state of the weather ... I firmly hope this is the only reason why I get no letter. We have had much cold weather since I came to London. It every moment

*threatens to snow. If it is as sharp at Portrane as
here I hope you did not begin your planting. April
for your evergreens will be time enough.'*

Two days later, George wrote again:

*'Arthur having got a slight cold, the physicians
think it better he should not leave London till the
middle of May. I therefore set off in a few minutes
for Shrewsbury, where Darwin will have much to
do if he detains me above 2 days. I hope to see
you in a shorter time than I imagined. Yesterday I
got your letters, they came as great consolation to
me. I have volumes to say to you.'*

At this point George appears to have given up and
returned to Portrane, leaving responsibility for Arthur's
welfare firmly in the hands of his eldest brother,
Henry. By 1811, Arthur's condition had deteriorated so
much, that Henry was forced to have him committed
to Whitmore House, a private lunatic asylum in
Hoxton. To spare Arthur, and the family, further
embarrassment, Arthur was admitted under the alias
of 'Mr. Palmer'.

The inmates at Whitmore House included family
members of many of titled and prominent families,
including the son of British Prime Minister, Henry
Addington. Fees were not cheap, varying from £500 -
£1200 per year depending on the type of
accommodation and care that was sought, but the
treatment of patients was no better, and no more
effective, than anywhere else.

Seeing no improvement in his brother, Henry went
to the Court of Chancery and, on 4 December 1811,
applied to have a Commission of Lunacy convened to
examine his brother's situation. These commissions,
established to decide whether or not the subject of the
inquisition was of sound mind, had as their priority
the proper administration of the lunatic's estate.

Indeed, the primary objective of getting a person declared of unsound mind by a Chancery inquisition was not to get them the medical help they needed, but to take away his or her power of independent legal action in the disposition of property. Committal to an asylum was an entirely separate, and medical, procedure.

The Chancery inquisition convened on 4 December 1811 and five days later the Master declared Arthur Parnell to be a lunatic 'not enjoying lucid intervals' and to have been 'in that state since 25 March 1810'. Critically, this date did not precede the drafting of Arthur's will.

Whitmore House (also called Balmes House).

While all this was going on, Arthur continued to be confined at Whitmore House, whose number of inmates totalled approximately thirty of each sex. But despite the lack of overcrowding, and the fact that it was a private institution, the full horrors of what went on inside would be not be exposed until 1825, when a former employee, John Mitford, decided to tell all.

The owner and keeper of Whitmore House was the infamous Thomas Warburton, owner of several asylums in London. Originally a butcher's boy in the country, he fled to London before he had served the full term of his apprenticeship on account of having a bastard-child sworn to him. According to Mitford, Warburton was:

> *'... first employed under the porter at the gate of Whitmore House, to beat coats, clean shoes, and carry messages, for which he was rewarded with his meat. Being expert at conveying liquor into the house for the keepers to dispose of amongst their patients, (a practice still pursued) he obtained a footing as a servant, and in that situation, by a little help, and much industry, he learned to read and write.*
>
> *His strength of body (a necessary qualification for a demon in one of those hells,) and his zeal, raised him to the dignity of a keeper, and he assumed the control of the lash under happy auspices. He is more than six feet high, broad shoulders, heavy built, with knock-knees, and a visage on which is a proboscis three inches long, quite sufficient to frighten a person of weak mind and delicate nerves into a fit of insanity.*
>
> *I have heard one of the myrmidons who attended at Windsor say, that the old King could not bear to look upon him, and used to exclaim: "Take away that fellow with the long nose — take him away — away — away." In time, he attained the confidential office of first keeper (lately held by Tom Harris,) and by his treatment of the lunatics under his care, gained the good graces of his mistress, who, upon the death of her husband, married him, and he became ruler over the mansion of affliction.*

Tom possessed a great deal of low cunning, and insinuating manners, which worked him into the good graces of many not awake to his duplicity. When he was raised to his mistress' bed, there were not many patients in the house, and no regular medical attendant. Tom having scraped together two hundred pounds, presented it to the late Doctor Willis, and engaged him for that sum annually, to recommend his house.

He soon had every ward in it filled, and managed to get a lease of the extensive premises at Hoxton for a mere trifle. I have heard how this was done. The keeper of St. Luke's had a son, an apothecary — one of Tom's daughters is that son's wife, and he physics the patients to some purpose.

The visiting physicians are not to blame if they make good reports of Hoxton mad-house, as they are deceived. A week or two before their visitation, the patients are better fed, and more kindly used, Tommy himself sometimes dines with them in the parlour, in order that he may say — " Oh, the patients live so well I frequently dine at their table from choice!"

The house is moreover cleaned, and new clothes distributed to those in rags; so that, to outward appearances, the physicians are satisfied. If any poor wretch (confined and in his senses) dare complain, a score of keeper and keeperesses, that is, rogues and prostitutes, are ready to testify that it is only a " lucid interval." If the poor fellow becomes enraged at these falsehoods, as it is natural he should be, it immediately is set down as a proof of the truth of the keeper's assertion!'

Henry Parnell truly felt that he was securing for his brother the best care available and for a substantial period of time remained oblivious to the truth of what was happening behind closed doors. The whistleblower, John Mitford, however, had been there at the time and remembered Arthur Parnell, or 'Mr. Palmer':

'Mr. Palmer, (Whose real name is Parnell,) occupied a front room, and had a keeper entirely to attend upon him. His brother, Sir Henry Parnell, Member of Parliament, paid for this servant, and also for a separate table, when in truth, he, Palmer, received his scanty meal from what was left at the parlour table, and which, when it happened to be anything eatable for a sane person, his keeper appropriated to himself, and gave him bread and cheese.

The same keeper had a certain quantity of tea and sugar from the housekeeper every Monday morning, for his use during the week, which he sold to a person in Hoxton, and gave Mr. Palmer small beer for his breakfast. The keeper carried a small dog-whip, and I have seen him beat his patient till the blood flowed from his legs, merely because he refused to go to bed before the regular time. His clothes were furnished from his brother, of the best kind, and the keeper always managed to take them away before they were worn a month, frequently demanding a new suit, alledging that he had torn the other to pieces, or burnt them.

A greater robber of the poor patients did not exist than Jemmy Davis, who had charge of the Hall, and accumulated a little fortune by his atrocious peculations. Mr. Palmer was, at length, sent over to Waterford, with a keeper, by his brother's desire, who had found out the infamous treatment he received ; it would have been as well if he had punished the authors, but gentlemen hesitate before they attempt a general good when it costs them a painful family exposure.'

When Henry Parnell finally discovered the truth about Arthur's care, he had him promptly removed from the establishment and brought back to Ireland. But such institutional mental health care as was available in Ireland at the time was no less barbaric than that available in England and the majority were heavily overcrowded and run primarily for profit.

Bethlem Hospital, London: the incurables being inspected by medical staff, with patients represented by political figures. Drawing by Thomas Rowlandson, 1789. Courtesy of Wellcome Collection.

Following a change in the law in 1800, it had become a lot easier to have someone committed as a criminal lunatic, even if they had not committed a crime. This allowed families with ill, disabled or otherwise burdensome relatives, to place of them in an asylum. The inevitable happened. The asylums were soon bursting at the seams.

There was only one option left open to Henry, and that was to provide private individual care for his brother. But there was still the awful stigma attached to mental illness, fueled in no small part by the widespread belief that such things were inherited. Privacy, therefore, remained an important consideration for a member of parliament known to suffer from bouts of 'melancholia'.

Taking Arthur home to Ireland via Dublin, where he might easily be recognized, was probably never going to be an option, and so he was taken home to Wicklow via Waterford, and privately cared for at Mount Avon, near Rathdrum in County Wicklow, where Henry owned vast tracts of lands. To have even considered this course of action would seem to suggest that Arthur still did not pose a threat to anyone's health but his own.

Henry thus passed responsibility for Arthur on to William, and to a lesser extent, Sophia. As a serving member of parliament, and a member of the government, he was ill-suited to caring for Arthur. He also had his own demons to deal with. That being said, things didn't quite end there for Henry. Arthur had left quite a mess behind him and, in March 1813, the *London Gazette* carried the following notice from the High Court of Chancery:

> *'Pursuant to an Order of the Lord High Chancellor of Great Britain, made in the matter of Arthur Parnell, Esq. a lunatic, the creditors of the said Arthur Parnell, the lunatic, late of the College of Physicians, Warwick Lane, London, are, on or before the 30th day of April next, to come in and prove their debts before Charles Thomson, Esq. one of the Masters of the High Court of Chancery, at his Chambers, in Southampton Buildings, Chancery Lane, London, or in default thereof they will be peremptorily excluded the benefit of the said Order.'*

The closest we can get at this remove to

understanding the nature of Arthur's illness is the use of the word 'lunatic', a legal term that was understood at the time as a person who was 'sometimes of good and sound memory and understanding and sometimes not'. It would appear, on the face of that definition, Arthur's refusal to leave his house, and the attempts by his family to get him out of the city to a place with a bracing climate, that Arthur was suffering from some form of psychotic depression. He was not the first, and would not be the last, of his family to do so.

10

THE EMPTY CRADLE

ONE CANNOT OVERESTIMATE the effect of infertility on a nineteenth century marriage, when childbirth was still seen as a woman's primary function in life. It was an attitude that had a long history. The entire Judaeo-Christian tradition began with the story of Sarah and Abraham's desperate desire for a child, and classical literature was littered with stories of childlessness, miraculous births and adoptions. Five years into a childless marriage it would have been unusual had she *not* been struggling to come to terms with the fact.

As late as the eighteenth century, childless women were encouraged to 'take the waters' in spa towns to ease their nerves and prevent spasms of the womb, and French doctors were currently linking childlessness to abortion, venereal disease, and promiscuity. The stigmas attached to infertility were many and varied. There were even some who persisted in the belief that it was a punishment sent from God.

The birth of children was not just expected, and

expected quickly, of a newly married woman; the successful production of a child, and particularly her first male child, brought with it a certain elevated status amongst her peers. The unfulfilled desire for that status, on the other hand, often resulted in all manner of worries and insecurities, for it was generally to the female partner that blame was attributed.

Nor was there much to be found in the way of medical help. As early as 1797 an American physician, a certain Dr J. Walker, felt compelled to admonish his colleagues for their disinterest in infertility; a disinterest they attributed to the fact that the inability to conceive rarely placed a life in danger. Walker, recognising the social stigma and negative psychological effects, urged his colleagues to reconsider. They needed to take a greater interest, he asserted, because of the 'anxiety of mind' that an unfruitful marriage often engendered.[18]

For most couples childlessness was regarded as a great personal tragedy, involving much emotional pain and grief, especially when resulting from miscarriage. Often perceived as a loss of feminine identity, it frequently led to a sense of powerlessness and despair. In many respects little has changed in the intervening centuries. Mothers have always sought other mothers to share their experiences, and childless women have always felt marginalised.

We do not know the exact nature of Sophia's problem and whether it was down to a failure to conceive or a failure to carry to term, but if, as seems likely, it was as the result of a previous bout of tuberculosis, both were certainly possible. Tuberculosis bacterium primarily affected the lungs, but it could also cause secondary infections to the uterus and fallopian tubes. Pelvic TB infections,

---

[18] Walker, J. *An inquiry into the Causes of Sterility in Both Sexes with Its Method of Cure.* (Ph.d. diss., University of Pennsylvania, 1797), esp. 7-8, American Collection, New York Academy of Medicine, New York.

furthermore, could cause the uterine lining to become so thin that it would be unable to bear an implantation, resulting in miscarriage.[19]

What we do know, or can at least deduce from her husband's letters, is that it affected Sophia deeply and became the source of much doubt and soul searching during her marriage. Her letters to her husband on such matters have not survived, but his replies to *her*, over several years, speak of a man deeply in love with his wife and having to battle constantly to reassure her of his continuing affection:

> *'I never can avert to our union, my dear Sophia, without feeling the most sensible pleasure. I assure you my affection has much increased.'*

George Evans
19 April 1806.

---

[19] Sharma JB, Dharmendra S, Agarwal S, Sharma E. Genital tuberculosis and infertility. Fertil Sci Res 2016;3:6-18.

'I never feel so happy as with you, we have lived long enough together for you to judge of my feelings. You will credit me when I say I do not think there is another person in the world I would have united myself to.'

George Evans
20 June 1808.

'I do often regret my absence from you yet this country and this season of the year has a strange effect, by contrast, of producing a pleasurable sensation, for it was this time 3 years ago I was greatly agitated between hopes and fears of winning your hand, the object dearest to my heart ... my heart expands as fully at your presence as ever it did."

George Evans
13 December 1808.

The announcement of a pregnancy was, and often still is, taken as evidence of male virility, and Sophia would have expected herself to be a high achiever in whatever she attempted. Both she and George had come from large families. Neither would have ever considered the possibility of infertility. The burden of disappointment, however, was not equally shared.

Even today most women experiencing or sharing that burden regard it as a discreditable attribute.[20] Sophia would have felt, in a way her husband could not, the stab of injustice that every woman who has ever struggled to conceive feels in their encounters with women who seem to get pregnant at the drop of a hat. She would have struggled to affect a passable impersonation of joy at every announcement of a

---

[20] Miall, Charlene E. "The Stigma of Involuntary Childlessness." Social Problems, vol. 33, no. 4, 1986, pp. 268–282. JSTOR, www.jstor.org/stable/800719.

pregnancy in the family, while at the same time concealing the very natural, and very personal, sadness it would have rekindled. To do less would be to risk being seen as selfishly unhappy, or resentful of the happy couple.

Despite the continuing monthly cycles of hope and disappointment, George and Sophia's affection for each other never diminished. They had, despite everything, a strong marriage, and could always lean on each other for support. George, in all of his letters to Sophia, is empathetic and supportive; their infertility only ever alluded to obliquely, and with a well-practised reserve:

> *'I might have wished for your sake that our lot had been more splendid.'*

As the stigma of childlessness begins to weigh ever more heavily upon them, one can perhaps read in George's letters to Sophia the sense that his wife is blaming herself for their misfortune; that she believes she has somehow 'cheated' her husband in marriage. Left frequently alone to ponder her misfortune, it is perhaps understandable that she feels the need to let off some steam.

George's letters indicate frequent absence. Sophia never accompanied him on his shooting expeditions by choice, and George rarely asked her to, though he did once, in 1816, write to her from Mountrath, where he had been shooting with the Coote family, expressing the hope that she might join him on his next trip there because the house was so quiet that she would feel quite at home there. In the same letter he confessed to feeling 'most sensibly the loss of my better genius.' There was pleasure in solitude, but also in being missed.

It would, of course, have been their joint assumption in marrying, that they would have children. But with each passing month it began to look increasingly unlikely and each slowly, but surely, had to adjust to the difficult transition from anticipated parenthood to anticipated childlessness. Each had also to adjust their perspective of self and their relationship with the other; to grieve for the future they desperately desired, but which was looking increasingly unattainable.

In the midst of all of this uncertainty and change, Sophia began to indulge a new interest. To complement her already extensive agricultural interests she began to study botany. She had a fine conservatory, heated by hot water pipes, and plenty of space to indulge her studies. In no time at all she had garnered a reputation for being exceptionally green-fingered. When the Percival family came to stay in August 1816, instead of bottles of fine wines or brandies, they brought her gifts of 'so many handsome plants'.

Sophia's Conservatory

11

LITERARY CONNECTIONS

SOME YEARS PRIOR to George Evans' wedding, the poet, Mary Blachford Tighe, composed a poem that gently poked fun at him and eulogised the intellectually competitive nature of the artistic gatherings into which Sophia now found herself thrust. In her *Letter from Mrs Acton to her Nephew Mr. Evans*, Tighe assumed the voice of George's maternal aunt, Sidney Acton, as she warned him to be prepared to deliver an entertaining and cultured performance if he planned to spend Christmas with the Tighes:

> *I am happy, dear George, to hear you intend,*
> *Some time at Rossana this Christmas to spend;*
> *I am pleased in my nephew to see such a spirit*
> *To enterprise boldly I know you inherit*
> *Yet before in so arduous task you engage,*
> *Tho' I know you superior to most of your age,*
> *I think it but friendly to caution you thus*
> *Lest, your memory failing, you come to nonplus.*

Whatever you learned at school or at College
Brush up for your use at this seat of all knowledge.
For my nephew's appearance I own I must quake
When I think what a moderate figure you'll make;
When with Latin of Greek not a marvel too much,
With Italian and French and a little high Dutch
In the midst of such scholars you find yourself placed
And with questions in Hebrew and Syriac disgrac'd,
Lest staring around you, you fancy it Babel
When you hear fifteen languages spoken at table,
Or venture in English to ask for some beer
At the poor ignoramus the butler will sneer.
Not a groom but his "aes in presenti" can say
And the son of the cook in pure Latin can pray;
To the housekeeper to should you happen to speak
'Tis fifty to one she will answer in Greek;
The ladies think these are but vulgar attainments
Thrown by to their maids with their old fashion'd raiments
On their toilets no books but Arabic you'll see,
And with native Chinese they present you their tea;
On the carpets are charts of biography spread,
And quilts geographical cover the bed;
In alembics by blowpipes with chemic perfection,
The meat is oxided by Harry's direction;
While in sallads they search for the stamens and pistils
The rice pudding cools in rhomboidal crystals,
And the carver takes care, tho' the venison he mangles
To part every portion in proper triangles.
Bread and butter is cut in forms mathematic,
And the tea urn distils with art hydrostatic;
Nay their dances are measured by just trigonometry
And they move in the radii as ordered by geometry;
Nor language nor science enough can adorn
For each poetical genius is born;
While infants they couplets could form in a trice
And lisp in soft numbers of geese and of mice,
Not to speak of that wonderful genius from England
Who Priestly and Blair has surpassed by his single hand,
Whose talent for rhyming so copiously flows

His labour is only to speak in plain prose,
When the family, call'd by the bells' silver tine
Assembles to supper, each offers his own,
Whether epic or comic or tragic they choose
Each worships his favorite appropriate muse.
Not a person appears in the family circle
But has verses deserving bays, laurel or myrtle.
Not with pencil alone is it Caroline's care
The vices to task, but the persons to spare;
For tho' on her labours the muses all smile
Yet the high polish'd satire's her favorite style
Miss Butticuz modest and timid declares
That nothing beyond a poor sonnet she dares;
But it has been whisper'd and I think that the fact is
She prepares for the press a new system of tactics;
Of the georgics an elegant version I hear
From the chymical farmer will shortly appear
Concentrated essence of gypsum and dung;
Mr. Jones too, I hear, in a poem didactical
Gives hints of politeness both courteous and practical,
Tho' as yet he has only pastorals dealt,
And in smooth strains of sentiment sung what he felt,
Yet this fault I have heard has by critics been found
That in S's too frequent his verses abound;
Camilla, indeed, as a foreigner, says
From her lips are expected no vulgar tongued lays,
But in the Mandingo, or verses Arabic,
She now and then ventures lines enigrammatic;
Then Mary sings plaintive in notes elegiac,
While her brother I'm told prefers the alcaic.
To ensure your reception dear George I must hope
From your pen some little production may drop;
Some small epic poem or encyclopaedia,
(For fifty large jokes, at once they will read ye)
Some treatises critical or philological,
Or at least you may show a new chart Chronological.

The Sidney Acton mentioned in the poem was the
sister of another female poet, George's mother,

Margaret[21]. Unlike Mary Tighe, Margaret Evans had yet to publish. It would be quite some time before she found the courage to do so. Sophia was no artist; her interests lying more in science, politics and philosophy than in literature, but if George was going to spend time with the Tighes at Rosanna, then there was at least the prospect of news of mutual friends and relatives to look forward to, and of one scandalous pair in particular.

Shortly after Sophia and William left Paris, their close friend, Margaret Mount Cashell, began an illicit relationship with George Tighe, brother-in-law of Mary Tighe. Since then, Stephen Mount Cashell had taken possession of his sons, abandoned his wife in Germany and left her to flee with George Tighe to Italy. In love for the first time in her life, Margaret relinquished all trappings of social respectability, renamed herself Mrs. Mason (after the governess in Wollstonecraft's children's book *Original Stories from Real Life*) and plunged headlong into a life of poverty with the only man she would ever truly love. To some of her class she appeared heroic. To the remainder she cut a somewhat ridiculous figure.

Mary Tighe, meanwhile, had contracted tuberculosis and her health had begun to fail. While receiving medical treatment in England she was invited to publish a volume of poetry but decided against public authorship in favour of private publication. Just fifty copies of her *Psyche; or the legend of love*, were printed and distributed to family and friends. So widely were they copied, however, that she would be widely celebrated as the author of *Psyche* for the remainder of her life.

Mary Tighe was not just a close friend of Sophia's husband; she was equally close to Sophia's brother, William. Back in 1804, when William published his *An*

---

[21] See Ronan, Gerard. *Margaret Evans – Poet of Portrane*, Fingal County Council, 2020.

Mary Tighe: Frontispiece from *Psyche, with Other Poems*. 5th ed.
London: Longman, Hurst, Rees, Orme, and Brown, 1816.

Enquiry into the Causes of the Popular Discontent in Ireland, Tighe referred to it in her journal as 'A very spirited, lively gentlemanlike pamphlet containing truths, alas too just'. On the title page of the presentation copy of *Psyche* that she gifted to William, she inscribed the following dedication:

'To William Parnell from his obliged friend M.

Tighe July: 1805'.

The following year, when William Smyth published the fourth edition of his, *English Lyricks*, the preface contained a poem written by William in which he addressed Mary Tighe and spoke of 'the destruction of the business of printing' in Ireland. The following June, when William expanded his arguments in favour of Catholic Emancipation in his *An Historical Apology for the Irish Catholics*, Mary found it to be:

'Full of very curious ancient anecdotes & written with spirit & temper in favour of a cause which had truth and justice on its side vainly oppos'd to prejudice illiberality & power'.

Sophia's literary connections did not stop there. Her husband was also friendly with Sydney Ownenson (Lady Morgan), and at the same time as Mary Tighe was recording her thoughts on William Parnell's latest publication, her brother William was entertaining Thomas Moore at his estate in Avondale.

For a long time there was a dispute amongst the noblemen of Wicklow as to whose house Moore had been visiting when he wrote his famous song *The Meeting of the Waters*. William had always contended that it had been written at Avondale, a claim that Moore would later deny; but so keen was William to have his family associated with the song that he once wrote to Moore begging him to confirm it, a fact Moore would later record in his journal:

'Poor William Parnell, who now no longer looks upon these waters, wrote to me many years since on the subject of those doubts, and, mentioning a seat in the Abbey churchyard belonging to him where it was said I sat while writing the verses, begged me to give him two lines to that effect to

*be put on the seat. "If you can't tell a lie for me,"
said he, "in prose, you will perhaps, to oblige an
old friend, do it in verse"'.*

Alas for 'Poor William', Moore couldn't bring himself
to lie, even for an old friend.

Thomas Moore

Mary Tighe, meanwhile, having finally returned to
Ireland, found that her struggles with tuberculosis
continued to plague her and, in September 1807, she
was invited by George and Sophia to come and stay
with them at Portrane and take the sea air. Sophia
herself had suffered from the disease: there would be
no-one more knowledgeable or understanding of her
needs. Mary stayed for four weeks and according to

her mother, Theodosia Blachford, she was 'very hospitably entertained'.

Avondale House

The following summer Mary spent some time with Sophia's brother at Avondale. It was to be her last visit. She would die two years later, in March 1810. During this visit she composed the following sonnet for William:

To W.P. Esq. Avondale

We wish for thee, dear friend! For summer eve
Upon thy loveliest landscape never cast
Looks of more lingering sweetness than the last.
The slanting sun, reluctant to bereave
Thy woods of beauty, fondly seemed to leave
Smiles of the softest light, that slowly past
In bright succession o'er each charm thou hast
Thyself so oft admired. And we might grieve

Thine eye of taste should ever wander hence
O'er scenes less lovely than thine own; but here
Thou wilt return, and feel thy home more dear;
More dear the Muses' gentler influence,
When on the busy world, with wisdom's smile,
And heart uninjured, thou hast gazed awhile.

Over the course of such a long friendship, one could hardly expect the matter of Mary's brother-in-law not to be discussed, especially since the unconventional couple had now decamped to Jena, where tall and muscular Margaret had begun to cross-dress as a man to study medicine at the local university. Some years later, the infamous couple would move to Pisa, where Margaret would continue to attend University and give birth to two daughters, Laurette and Nerina. Sophia and George, meanwhile, had all but resigned themselves to a childless marriage and their undiluted affection was now spent entirely on the other.

12

OF WILLIAM AND GOD

JUST SEVEN MONTHS after the death of Mary Tighe, on 1 October 1810, William Parnell married Frances Howard, daughter of the Hon. Hugh Howard, son of Viscount Wicklow. Over the course of the next three years she would give birth to a son, John Henry and a daughter, Catherine. Sophia had now a niece and a nephew to dote on who did not live on the far side of the Irish Sea, news that was almost as welcome as the elevation of her brother Henry to the peerage.

> *'This last* (Henry) *made up for his brother's* (John Augustus) *defects by talking incessantly in public and running up and down perpetually between London and Dublin, being the principal originator of the great highroad from Shrewsbury to Holyhead, which opened up Wales for the first time to ordinary travellers. The Menai Bridge, which constitutes the crowning glory of the achievement, was looked upon in its day as one of the wonders of the world. In recognition of this,*

*and other public services, Sir Henry Parnell was
created first Baron Congleton in 1811.'*

Boston Post, 26 December 1885.

1812 saw the death of John Augustus. He died on
30 July at the age of thirty-seven. The location of his
death is unknown, but his passing brought a close to
many of the complicated emotions, fears and
responsibilities that his disability had engendered in
his siblings.

Two years later again William's wife, Frances,
passed away and he began to develop a close
friendship with the evangelical preacher, the Rev.
Robert Daly. Daly had recently landed himself the
prestigious parish of Powerscourt, giving him access to
some of the most influential aristocratic families in
Ireland, including William's in-laws, the Howards of
County Wicklow. By the following April he had become
so regular a face at William's social gatherings that
William would feel comfortable encouraging him to get
married.

William had form in this endeavour, having all but
arranged his sister's betrothal. Daly, however, was a
realist. 'For your comfort I will tell you,' he replied, 'I
am not in the least against it, if Providence (in whom I
believe) should put it in my way.'

William never embraced Daly's brand of evangelism
to quite the same extent as his late wife and his
brother Tom, but following the death of Frances it was
to be Daly, and not Sophia, to whom he most regularly
turned for consolation. The result was that William
began to read the Bible.

Shortly after he had buried Frances, Daly wrote to
William:

*'I am very happy in thinking that you are reading
the New Testament, and with interest, for I cannot
conceive any one to read it without prejudice and*

111

not be made a real Christian by it.'

Unfortunately for Daly, William's reading of the New Testament had the effect, not of guiding him into the communion of evangelists, but of driving him to a more ecumenist view of Christianity, and to an even more pro-Catholic position. And he was not alone amongst the Parnells.

William Parnell, by John Comerford.
Image courtesy of National Gallery of Ireland.

By April 1815, Sophia's brother, Henry, had begun to converse with Daniel O'Connell and others about presenting a Catholic petition to parliament. By

December of the following year he was receiving letters from the Roman Catholic Bishop of Kildare and Leighlin, promising to support him in the forthcoming election. Henry was being besieged by letters urging his support for emancipation. They came from politicians, bishops, and from William, who wrote to him in June 1817. By July, Henry was even publishing a pamphlet of his own on the matter.

With both of her brothers now actively involved in the cause of Catholic emancipation, it would be nigh on inconceivable to believe that Sophia was not similarly engaged in the debate, at the very least with her husband, who at this time was beginning to undergo something of a political awakening of his own (of which more anon). Inspired, perhaps, by William's decision, in 1817, to finally follow in the family tradition and enter parliament as the member for Wicklow, George began to consider a similar course of action.

At this time William was widely seen as a naïve and impractical theorist rather than a serious politician, an impression that wasn't exactly helped by a letter he sent that year to the Irish secretary Robert Peel who, not for the first time, had disappointed William with his approach to the economic and social problems of Ireland:

> *'I have been rather unfortunate in my applications to you, so much so that I think some explanation is due to myself for having made them. I have always been miserable at the state of Ireland and have felt something of a personal gratitude to those who seem to wish her well, however they may have mistaken the means.*
>
> *I was a friend to Lord Hardwicke though his government was detestable and to the Duke of Bedford though his was not much better, but both intended well. But in your good intentions there appeared more warmth and vigour, and though I*

could not approve of your administration, which seemed to have the vice common to all of receiving the Irish in a state of pupillage and keeping them so, yet I was so far captivated as to attempt to urge you to the adoption of those measures which can alone confer lasting honour on an Irish administration, those which tend to raise the lower orders in this country from the degradation into which they have been driven down.

What was intended kindly ought not to be charged to interference or indiscretion. But though sanguine I am not quite absurd, and in future my good wishes shall be equally warm without being quite so troublesome.'

Two years later, in the introduction to his polemical novel of Irish rural life, *Maurice and Berghetta; or the Priest of Rahery*, William declared that the author:

'... scarcely remembers the time, when a passion for his native country, and a painful commiseration of the deplorable state of the peasantry in Ireland, were not the strongest feelings in his breast'.

This book, which he dedicated to 'the Catholic priesthood of Ireland', whose 'merits have always appeared to me equal to their privations', was savaged by a Tory journal as 'mischievous and absurd' and William portrayed as 'a child playing with fire-arms; an innocent who, by way of giving light to his neighbours, sticks his farthing candle into a barrel of gunpowder'. The subsequent failure of William's 'Irish Paupers Bill (1820)', together with that of an earlier attempt to protect impoverished children employed in Irish cotton factories, was seized upon by the *Quarterly Review* in 1820. In their retaliatory attack on his response to the ridicule of his novel, his political theories were described as wild, idle and impracticable and he himself as an amiable, weak, well-intentioned and extravagant 'purveyor of follies'.

In the years that followed his election, William spent a good deal of his energy trying to negotiate and promulgate an agreed set of Christian Gospels for use of both Catholic and Protestant schoolchildren. He presented a set of extracts to the Rev. Father Doyle, the Catholic priest of Bray, with a request that he be introduced to Dr John Thomas Troy, the Roman Catholic archbishop of Dublin.

As a result of William's meeting with Troy, Doyle was given the job of vetting William's gospels with a view to using them in schools for 'the lower class of society.' Doyle suggested a few changes, all of which were accepted, and following Troy's approval, William ordered, at his own expense, the printing of one thousand copies by Blenkinsop & Co., printer to the Catholic Seminary at Maynooth. His ecumenist agenda promised a long career in parliament, even if he no longer shared his sister's views on religion.

Ever since her time in Paris, and possibly even before that, Sophia's philosophical views had veered sharply towards deism – a position that rejected revelation as a source of religious knowledge and asserted that reason and observation of the natural world were sufficient to establish the existence of a Supreme Being or creator of the universe.

During the Age of Enlightenment, British and French philosophers began to reject revelation as a source of knowledge and to appeal only to truths that they felt could be established by reason alone. Such philosophers were called 'deists'. Sophia was known in later life to be an avid reader of David Hume, a philosopher, whose views on religion have led to many a heated debate as to whether he was a deist, atheist, or something else entirely. In his *Natural History of Religion* (1757), furthermore, Hume had contended that polytheism, not monotheism, was 'the first and most ancient religion of mankind' and that the psychological basis of religion was not reason, but fear of the unknown. The deists of the enlightenment, in denying revelation as a valid source of religious knowledge had similarly rejected all books, including the Bible, that claimed to contain divine revelation, and also the 'incomprehensible notion' of the Trinity and other religious 'mysteries', along with all reports of 'miracles and prophecies'.

Although hardly mainstream, Sophia's views were not uncommon in Dublin at the time. Indeed the Rev. William Hamilton Drummond had been preaching something similar at the meeting house on Strand Street since 1819. By the 1840's that particular congregation would have fully embraced the doctrine of Unitarianism, the religion of choice at the time for the scientifically or industrially minded, or, as Erasmus Darwin, grandfather of Charles, had put it, a 'featherbed to catch a falling Christian'.

It is impossible to know exactly what Sophia's privately held beliefs were with any real degree of certainty, but from the little we do know it is obvious that Sophia was on a different philosophical path to both Thomas and William, and ever so slowly they became more distant.

But if she was not entirely in step with William in matters of religion, then William's passion for the education of the poor was at least something on which they could find common ground. In time that passion, and her brother's inspiration, would lead her to take a personal hand in the education of the poor on her own doorstep.

13

THE O'CONNORS

SOPHIA ALMOST RETURNED to Paris in August 1809. George's younger sister, Mary Lawless, was still living with her parents on the Boulevard des Invalides, and had taken so seriously ill that the family feared for her life. Mary had fallen in love with a frequent visitor to the family home, a former surgeon by the name of William Lawless. Exiled with Hampden Evans on account of the part he played in the 1798 rebellion, Lawless was currently serving in the Irish regiment of the French army.

So well did Mary Evans conceal her infatuation, that neither Lawless, nor the Evans family, suspected a thing: until, that is, rumours of Lawless' death at the Siege of Flushing trickled into Paris. Poor Mary all but died of grief. Not even the ministering of Wolfe Tone's widow, Matilda, could console her. Her health only recovered when Lawless was discovered to have survived.

Hampden Evans quickly acquainted Lawless with

117

his daughter's feelings and a speedy marriage was arranged. Two funerals were averted and Sophia remained in Portrane. She continued to maintain her own connections to the French capital, however, through her friendship with Sophie de Condorcet and her daughter Eliza.

Little Eliza! How the years had flown! She was twenty-years-of-age now, and married, with two baby boys, Arthur and Daniel. She had even followed in her mother's footsteps, by marrying, at the tender age of seventeen, a certain Arthur O'Connor, a United Irish veteran who was twenty-seven years her senior and a serving general in the French Army.

Eliza's new husband had been a fellow prisoner of Hampden Evans in 1798. Like Hampden, Arthur had been spared execution with a last-minute reprieve and forced into voluntary exile on the continent. Arthur had also been a house guest of both Madame de Staël and Sophie de Condorcet during Sophia's time in Paris. Sophia would have known him at least as well as her husband. More importantly, her husband remained to this day a close friend of Arthur's famously prodigal brother, Roger.

Roger O'Connor was a legendary wastrel who was content to live a life of dissipation on his brother's inheritance. A fellow member of the United Irishmen with Hampden Evans, he had served a term of imprisonment in Fort George, in Scotland, and following his release had never been far from controversy. His home at Dangan Castle, heavily insured, had burned down in suspicious circumstances; he had eloped with a married woman, and he had been arrested and tried for the robbery of the Galway mail train only to be released for lack of evidence.

As for Eliza, she and Sophia would not have been short of things to write about since Sophia's last visit to Paris. Ever since that unusual wedding, in which the groom was almost exactly the same age as the

Arthur O'Connor

mother of the bride, the newlyweds had been increasingly in contact with George on account of Arthur's desire to liquidate his assets in Ireland and purchase the Chateau de Bignon – a 100-acre estate about seventy miles outside Paris.

Arthur needed help. His landed property in Ireland had been put under the management of his brother, Roger, who had treated it as his own and was reluctant to see it sold. Arthur's own solicitor, Sir Francis Burdett, brother of the man that George had stolen Sophia from, had been unsuccessful in persuading Roger to part with it and uncommonly lenient in his dealings with Roger. It was

Roger O'Connor

time for fresh minds and a fresh approach. Desperate for funds, Arthur asked George Evans, whom he regarded not just as a friend, but as an intimate of Roger's, to intervene and secure his £10,000 inheritance by pleading with Roger to:

> 'submit the account of his agency, and all accounts between him and me, to the arbitration of some common friend or friends'.

George was initially so hopeful of an amicable solution that, in early 1807, he wrote to Arthur assuring him that Roger's account with him was 'likely to be settled by arbitration'. Arthur immediately wrote to his friend William Putnam McCabe:

'Since I saw you, I have also received a letter from Evans, by which I learn that Roger's account with me is likely to be settled by arbitration, and, though most inconvenient, I have agreed to take the payment in five years. If you go to Dublin, I beg of you to see Evans, and bring me a letter from him about all my affairs; tell him how entirely I rely on his friendship to draw me out of the cruel situation I am in. If this estate that offers slips through my hands for want of £4,000, it will be a constant source of regret to me all my life, for it is the place, of all others, where I could be happy. There is a rapid stream that tumbles down through the whole property, with every other advantage we could wish, do not let me lose it if you can.'

McCabe didn't reply and by 17 March, Arthur's desperation was becoming ever more apparent. In a letter to his eldest brother Daniel, he wrote:

I have just received a letter from my good friend Evans, by which I find he has written to you, acquainting you with the state of affairs with that wretched being, Roger. I hope the arbitration may be agreed on; but, in case he is mad enough to expose the matchless depravity of his conduct, I request you will inform Evans of the attorney you wish to have employed, should he force me into a lawsuit. In order to leave all to arbitration, I have pointed out an easy way for him, to discharge the debt he owes me.'

But George was being overly optimistic and trusting. Constantly frustrated by Roger's stalling tactics, he was forced, in May of 1807 to write again to Arthur:

'The six weeks asked for by Roger, and granted by me, have been nearly spun out to three months, with assurances from time to time that this delay would not be much longer. One day he must be in England; another day must be in Dublin, on what he would call his own business; the beginning of this week, I understand, he sets out for Cork ... The fact is I much doubt if any thing can be done with him, but through the hard and cruel path of law.'

Arthur was forced, somewhat reluctantly, to agree with George and to file a legal suit against his own brother. At the beginning of 1808 he declared:

'I was necessitated, as my only resource, to have recourse to the laws, and file a bill against him, and to force him to account.'

The legal proceedings dragged on, and in an attempt to speed things up, Arthur decided to send twenty-five-year-old Eliza to Dublin to plead with Roger. But this was no easy matter. England and France were still at war. Permission had to be granted at the highest level.

On February 1, 1815, Eliza's application to visit London and to proceed to Ireland on matters pertaining to the affairs of her husband was finally granted by the British prime minister, Robert Peel. In another letter, addressed to the Lord Lieutenant, Lord Sidmouth ordered that she be carefully watched for as long as she remained in Ireland.

And so it was, in 1815, that Eliza and Sophia were finally reunited. The visit, alas, was to prove short and unproductive. Roger knew that Eliza's visa was limited and found excuse after excuse to avoid meeting with her. By the time she left Ireland, Eliza had enjoyed no more success in her attempts at friendly arbitration than George Evans, who was now left with little option but to have Roger arrested and jailed.

It would take until 1834, but eventually Arthur would manage to recover what remained of his inheritance. He had lost a brother in the process; but in George Evans he had gained a loyal and trusted friend.

14

A FAMILY SCANDAL

FOLLOWING THE DEATH of his youngest daughter, Fanny, at just five years of age, Henry Parnell's marriage began to fall apart. The subsequent death of his mother-in-law, so soon after the death of his daughter, sent his wife, Caroline, into a downward spiral of grief. Caroline fell into ill-health and, unable to endure her 'uncongenial home' any longer, she decided to flee.

In 1813 her sisters, fearful of her deteriorating mental health, contrived to obtain permission from the Emperor Napoleon, then at war with Britain, for her to travel through France to Switzerland. Passports were granted on condition that the party should contain no boy or man above the age of twelve – a significant concession by the Emperor at a time when the only English people in France were diplomats or prisoners of war. But that was no hardship for Caroline. It meant she could not be followed.

A runaway wife was exactly the sort of salacious

tittle-tattle upon which the gossips of London and Dublin society were wont to feast. It was simply unheard of; a sinful, shameful and scandalous thing. A husband might desert a wife – such things were far from inconceivable – but this? This was something else again.

Lady Caroline Parnell hadn't just left her husband, she had fled to a place where he could not possibly follow. She had travelled, moreover, through a war zone to get there. There was a statement in that – a very *public* statement – and it did not just hurt Henry's reputation, it hurt the entire family, on both sides of the Irish Sea. News like that could neither be concealed nor explained away. It did not reflect well on either party.

Leaving London, Caroline took her children firstly to Calais and then overland to Switzerland, where she spent some time recuperating. Her intention at this point in time had always been to return. On the return journey, however, she made a stopover in Paris, where she made such firm friends with local families that she suddenly felt happier than she had in years. Life, all of a sudden, seemed to be offering her new possibilities that did not include a cold and unfeeling husband.

No longer able to face the prospect of returning to an unhappy marriage she elected to make her life in Paris and made arrangements to settle there permanently. Henry ordered Caroline to return, but on each and every occasion he was ignored and Caroline's return continuously postponed.

Their time in Paris would have a marked effect upon Sophia's nieces, and in after years Emma, who would have been nine at the time, would often regale the family with stories of the fine house they lived in, the charming French officers who would visit them, and the day she saw Napoleon reviewing his troops. On the darker side, she would never forget the hatred visiting French officers would express for the allies whenever they received news of the death of a comrade, or when any of their friends or relatives returned maimed or wounded.

We know that Caroline and the children were still in Paris in 1814, during the entry of the allied sovereigns, because Emma would never forget the sound of the guns at Montmartre before the city surrendered. By 1815, however, they were living in Passy, a village outside of Paris. Following the Battle of Waterloo she would recall how pretty the tents of the victorious English army looked as they camped on the Bois de Boulogne.

Henry junior, although five years younger than Emma, would remember a beloved French nurse who used to sing to him *Malbrook s'en va t'en guerre*. He would also 'remember' that Napoleon had requisitioned his mother's English travelling carriage for his own use. To anyone who would listen, he would claim that Napoleon's carriage at Madame Tussaud's, captured after the battle of Waterloo, was the same one that had been taken from his mother.

Caroline's son, John, on the other hand, would remember Paris as an unhappy period of his life, a time when he was so miserable in his French school that he would repeat the few prayers he knew two or three times over, hoping that God would hear his plea and remove him from the school.

There would have been all manner of speculative whispering in London society concerning Caroline's reasons for fleeing, and it is doubtful that Henry could have so insulated himself from them as to become immune to their sting. The only effective answer to the most salacious of the rumours was the return of Caroline Parnell. But Caroline was not for turning.

Henry wrote again, this time demanding that the children be returned. Paris was now under British control. Faced with the choice of losing her children or returning to a depressive husband and an unhappy marriage, Caroline chose the former, and the children returned to London without her.

Napoleon's Carriage at Madame Toussaud's.

Caroline has been portrayed by many commentators since then, not least by her granddaughter, Lady Elizabeth Cust, as 'preferring, it would seem, her liberty to either husband or children'. In truth, Caroline had little choice. Women had very few rights under the law at that time and her only other option was to return to a cold and unfeeling husband who was already prone to the dark bouts of depression that would eventually lead to his suicide. The truth of the matter was that Caroline was not an unfeeling mother and over the years that followed she would keep in constant touch with her children by letter.

Some years later, when Emma had children of her own, she would write to Caroline in Paris:

'I have often felt myself excited to attend to my dear children's health and welfare by recollecting your great attention to us when we were all little children. I remember very well your coming to see us undressed and settled in our little beds, and your visits at night to the nursery to see that the nurses were taking proper care of us.'

When the children arrived in London, however, they found themselves subjected to a very different, and less personal, sort of care. Their father, Henry, always more at home with facts and figures than people, quickly found that he had grown too accustomed to living alone and, unable to cope with the chaos of children about the house, he packed them off to live with a Dr. and Mrs. Crane at Brentford Rectory, until such time as they could be farmed out amongst their relatives. At this time the plan was that, when she reached her eighteenth birthday, Emma would be sent to her Aunt Sophia at Portrane, who would take care of her introduction to Irish society.

In the meantime, despairing of Caroline ever returning to London, Henry began legal proceedings, and, on 03 July 1816, he and Caroline were granted a deed of separation. It brought closure, of a sort, to the unfortunate affair, but the emotional repercussions would last for decades.

While all this was going on George and Sophia prepared to celebrate their tenth wedding anniversary. It was a time for mature reflection and the counting of blessings. Sophia, however, now thirty-six, was still childless and though all hope was not lost, both she and George had by now resigned themselves to a medical assessment of improbability and the expectation that that unexplored region of the heart would be forever closed to them.

While on yet another visit to Lord and Lady

Portarlington, on 4 June 1815, George wrote to Sophia:

'It is with a certain glow of heart I refer back in my mind to this time two years, when I was much agitated between hopes and fears over your assessment. It is with pride and satisfaction, after so long a period, I can say that in no instance have I been disappointed in my expectations of happiness as far as related to you, that in that lapse of years I have not seen one individual who I could for a moment prefer or estimate above you.

I might have wished for your sake that our lot had been more splendid, but perhaps we should not have the happiness for it. It is true I have moments of some internal despondency but upon the whole I am much contented ...'

The anniversary came and went that August, but the period of reflection continued. On 24 September 1815, while joining a grouse shooting party at Portarlington, he wrote to Sophia:

'Presently it is now upwards of 13 years that I walked up this road in a state of considerable anxiety of mind. I had proposed for you and my agitation was great until I had an answer that for these 13 years has made me, as far as relates to yourself, the happiest of men. It was a gratification to me to contrast the present state of my mind with what was past, in walking up this road, I know many would laugh at me for this ...
I do not of course know how long it may please Providence that we shall co-exist in this life, but if my existence is prolonged to another state my most arduous wish is that I may again rejoin you. I know that my temper is not too good and that I have often treated you in a way that I ought not,

but for that I have often had poignant regrets ... I am afraid I have tired you out, but you will excuse me when I tell you the chief pleasure I have in being absent from you is to say to you in this way how much I love you.'

15

POLITICAL AWAKENINGS

GEORGE EVANS HAD hitherto maintained a low political profile. But he was not without strong political opinions, particularly on the subject of nepotism and corruption. At Maryborough, in December 1808, he commented:

> *'I have read a speech of Sir F. Burdett's to the electors of Westminster that pleases me greatly and is so vulgarly un-Whiggish ... that I view in it the true state of the country. The fact simply is this, both Whigs and Tories wish to keep up the systems of corruption and to keep down the people and keep out the French; all incompatible with each other.'*

Having won Sophia's hand George could afford to be magnanimous with regard to the political speeches of his former love-rival's brother, but his regard for Sir

Francis Burdett, and his friendship with William Parnell, suggest that he was very much a liberal in his political views; views that were hardly congruent with those of his father. Thus far, however, he had avoided becoming actively engaged in the political arena.

All of that changed on the 16 August 1819, when cavalry charged a crowd of 60,000 protestors at St. Peter's Field in Manchester. The protestors had been demanding the reform of a system of parliamentary representation that gave only 2% of the population a vote. This gathering had been provoked by the famine and chronic unemployment that had followed the end of the Napoleonic Wars and, more latterly, by the introduction of the hated Corn Laws that had driven up the price of bread and caused it to become more of a luxury than a staple.

The meeting was to have been addressed by the 'brass-lunged' orator of the parliamentary reform movement, Henry Hunt. Banners bearing slogans such as 'Liberty and Fraternity' and 'Taxation without Representation is Unjust and Tyrannical' flew provocatively in the breeze, awaiting the arrival of 'Orator Hunt' with his trademark white top hat. The atmosphere was peaceful and cheerful. Contingents came from Bolton and Bury; 6,000 marched from Rochdale and Middleton, and more from Saddleworth and Stalybridge. Two hundred women dressed in white arrived from Oldham with their children and their picnics. Their dresses did not remain white for long.

Female reform societies had recently sprung up across the north-west of England, calling for votes for women. They were depicted by cartoonists such as George Cruickshank as sluts and whores, abandoning their families to meddle in things they had no business thinking about. They wore white on the day to symbolise purity of character and motive. It was why the cavalry singled them out for attack. If they wanted the same rights as men; they could face the same treatment.

Women in White, from *The Peterloo Massacre* by Richard Carlisle.

An estimated 18 people, including four women and a child, died from sabre cuts and trampling that day, and 650 men, women and children were seriously maimed and injured. News of the atrocity outraged George Evans. He immediately made a donation of fifty pounds to an appeal seeking funds to aid the victims and convene an inquiry into what was soon to become popularly known as the 'Peterloo Massacre'. The name was coined by a local journalist named James Wroe in a punning reference to the Battle of Waterloo four years earlier. Wroe paid for the pun by seeing his radical newspaper, the *Manchester Observer*, closed down. He himself was sentenced to a year's imprisonment for seditious libel. Fifty pounds was an enormous sum in those days, and news of George's donation was carried in both the Irish and the British

Detail from *The Peterloo Massacre* by Richard Carlisle.

press.

From that moment onwards the cause of electoral reform would be the political passion of George Evans' life. Like so many others who had been horrified by the massacre, he confirmed himself in favour that day of extending the right to vote. They owed it to the victims. The bloody atrocity of Peterloo must never happen again.

Having well and truly nailed his colours to mast of Reform, it appeared to all and sundry that George Evans was about to form an independent alliance with his brother-in-law, William Parnell, in the cause of universal suffrage and the secret ballot. But it was not to be. Peterloo and its aftermath may have shocked the nation, but it did not lead to parliamentary reform and, as the authorities closed ranks against change, the massacre deflected the movement for political reform into a crusade for justice for the victims.

'Beginning reform,' said the Duke of Wellington, 'is beginning revolution.' Well the Evans clan had never been afraid of a little revolution when appropriately motivated. But it was not so much a lack of motivation that prevented George joining the fight, as a lack of time.

On 22 April 1820, at his townhouse at 35 North Great George's Street, Hampden Evans, George's father, passed away. In an instant George became tied up with the difficult settlement of his father's estate. When the legal dust had finally settled, George found himself the sole and proud owner of both the Dublin townhouse on North Great George's Street, and the Mount Evans estate at Portrane that he had effectively been caretaking since his father's exile. He also found himself at liberty to express opinions that would have been anathema to his father.

Down in Avondale, meanwhile, William Parnell was still beavering away at his education projects when, on the 22 December 1820, he paid a visit to the Secretary for Ireland and managed to secure an annual grant of

£3,000 to be vested in the Catholic hierarchy for the education of the poor. The day was, by all accounts, unusually wet, and William caught a heavy cold, which terminated in a fever. He died, just eleven days later, on 2 January 1821, at his in-laws home at Castle Howard, where he had gone with his children to spend Christmas. Regarding his death, *The Times*, on 11 January observed that:

> *'No man was more amiable in private life ... and even his opponents admitted that, as an honest public man, he had no superior.'*

Another obituarist in the same newspaper declared:

> *'Had Mr. Parnell lived ... the attention which he was in the habit of giving in Parliament to Irish affairs would have been productive, ere long, of lasting benefits to his country. Time only was wanting to enable him to give effect to those plans, which had been his constant study from his earliest years, for relieving Ireland from her grievances, and for ameliorating the condition of all classes of her people, in wealth, in manners, and in morals.'*

Finally, on 15 February, an individual signing himself as 'C' wrote to the *Freeman's Journal* to eulogise William Parnell as a man who:

> *'... not content to linger out his days in inactive and unprofitable sympathy had set out to improve the standard of living and education of poor Catholics.'*

16

THOMAS 'TRACT' PARNELL

ARTHUR PARNELL NEVER attended Eton or Cambridge, but his brother Thomas did, and the experience was to change his life, only not in the way that his father had perhaps intended.

Sent away to Eton at the age of thirteen, Thomas entered Peterhouse College, Cambridge, at fifteen, and quickly discovered that he didn't much like the arts and sciences. He elected instead to study divinity, and migrated to Emmanuel College in November 1798, after just eleven months at Peterhouse.

At Emmanuel Thomas began to flirt with Methodism, a form of Protestantism that derived its practice and beliefs from the life and teachings of John Wesley, and on his return to Dublin he fell under the influence of William Russell, author of a famous book on 'pulpit elocution'. In no time at all Thomas began to achieve some fame in his own right as an evangelical, celibate and somewhat eccentric preacher.

Thomas also appears to have been in contact with

William Wilberforce, the famous British politician, philanthropist, and leader of the movement to abolish slavery. The connection was probably made through some evangelical network or other, Wilberforce himself having embraced evangelical Christianity in 1785, a conversion that resulted in major changes to his lifestyle and a lifelong concern for reform.

Exactly how well Thomas knew the anti-slavery campaigner is not known, but when the Irish evangelical preacher, the Reverend Thomas Kelly of Athy, visited London with his wife in 1810, they spent quite some time in the company of Wilberforce largely on the back of letters of introduction they had procured from Thomas Parnell.

Emmanuel College, Cambridge.

Thomas was, by this time, veering sharply and publicly away from mainstream Anglicanism. Just how publicly is perhaps evidenced by a diary entry of Sir Vere Hunt, in May 1813, during a visit to Dublin. He referred to Thomas as a 'swaddler,' a contemporary term of abuse usually reserved for Methodists, but sometimes applied to radical Anglican evangelists.

Thomas had become a familiar sight around Dublin

by this stage, his pockets filled with religious tracts that he was forever stuffing under doors. He still received invitations to visit friends and relations, but such was his reputation by now that whenever he arrived as a house guest 'the household knew that they were in for a discourse, at least an hour long, after evening prayers.'

Down in Portrane, Thomas's increasingly eccentric lifestyle was slowly becoming a cause for concern, but they had other, more pressing concerns for at the same time as Thomas was marching about the streets of Dublin thrusting his religious pamphlets into the hands of passers-by, the Irish Regiment of the French army, was marching into battle at Bautzen, in eastern Saxony.

Among the Irish of Napoléon's 'Foreign Regiment', there marched George Evans' younger brother, Hampden Evans junior, and his sister Mary's husband, William Lawless. On 16 August 1813 having assembled at Goldberg in Silesia and repelled a cavalry attack, they suddenly found themselves exposed to an artillery barrage so brutally sustained that it carried off upwards of three hundred men. Five days later, on 21 August, Lawless led his troops into battle at Löwenberg, where he was seriously wounded; his leg shattered by a cannon ball. Carried to the rear on a door, he was treated by the Emperor's personal surgeon, Baron Dominique Jean Larrey, but the leg could not be saved. Lawless would be subsequently retired from military service. George's younger brother was not so fortunate.

It was something of a tradition at this time to receive the newspapers and morning post with breakfast, and letters from France would normally have been received in the breakfast room at Mount Evans with excitement, especially if addressed in a familiar hand. It was also quite common, that news of military defeats would reach the newspapers before the casualty list had been posted. And so, when a letter finally did arrive from France, whether in William Lawless' hand, or some other, it would have been received with some trepidation.

It was sometime in September, before that letter reached Portrane and news of Hampden Junior's death became common knowledge. He had been killed in action, it read, on 19 August 1813 in a clash with Prussian Cavalry close to the town of Mojesz, in southern Silesia, then part of Germany but now a part of Poland.

Two months later, the post brought happier news. George' sister, Mary, had given birth to a son. He had been born on 20 October and named William Hampden Lawless. It was a shaft of light in a darkened cave, but not enough to dispel the general gloom. In the wider scheme of things, Sophia's concern for her brother Thomas' mental health seemed somewhat petty concerned to the birth and death of her in-laws.

Thomas, meanwhile, found his niche, and a shield behind which his eccentricity could assume a degree of respectability. In 1814 some evangelical Protestants, led by Lady Lifford, began to campaign among their fellow English evangelicals for the establishment of a Hibernian Auxiliary to the London Missionary Society. Lady Lifford had already founded a Dublin Ladies Association of the Missionary Society, but had encountered stiff opposition from the primate and his bishops on the one side, and the rival claims of the London Missionary Society on the other.

In June of that year the London evangelists sent three missionaries to Dublin. They were warmly welcomed but given little in the way of concrete support until, in the words of Ford Keeler Brown, 'in came Mr Thomas Parnell, a gentleman moving in the first Dublin society, a subscriber to the London Jew Society and a life member of the Hibernian Auxiliary.' Prospects were suddenly bright.

But it wasn't all about religious tracts for Thomas at this time, as a curious incident related to Sophia by

George in 1816 confirms. It concerned Thomas' involvement in the trail of an infamous highwayman, Jeremiah 'Captain' Grant, a man whose trial had been taking place in Maryborough while George was on a shooting expedition at nearby Mountrath and staying at the Coaching Inn at Boughlone.

Jeremiah Grant cut an imposing figure, standing 6' 1" tall, with bushy eyebrows and short thick black hair. He had married, when just nineteen, a girl that was both younger than he and from a far wealthier family. Following the death of an uncle he had used his inheritance to lease a farm at Loughmore, in County Tipperary, where he had lived so reasonably prosperous an existence that he could comfortably support a family of seven children.

Having spent most of his inheritance improving the land and buying stock, Grant suddenly fell foul of a grasping landlord, one Gilbert Maher, who sent his steward to seize some of Grant's possessions in lieu of unpaid rent. During the subsequent confrontation, in which Grant objected to the sale of his wife's beehives, Grant produced a pistol, levelled his aim and pulled the trigger. The pistol failed to discharge, but the attempt was enough for landlord to have Grant charged with attempted murder. Grant fled to Moyne where, hidden by friends, he became a partner in an illicit distillery.

In the meantime, the landlord's son, Nicholas, entered into a romantic relationship with Jeremiah's sister, Mary, leading Grant to suspect that Nicholas's intentions were far from honourable and aimed less at securing his sister's hand as securing his own arrest. Hearing that Jeremiah and his brother, John, were looking for them, Mary and her lover fabricated a story that John had similarly fired a loaded gun at Nicholas on 22 Mar 1810, and missed. The Grant brothers were arrested but during their transfer to Clonmel gaol, Jeremiah managed to escape by getting their escort drunk when they stopped at an inn for refreshments.

Jeremiah's brother John was unable to break free of his captors and Jeremiah himself would be later re-captured while attempting to visit his wife and transported to Clonmel gaol to join his brother.

With her brothers facing the death penalty, Mary had a sudden change of heart and attempted to remove the only witness against her brothers, her erstwhile boyfriend Nicholas Maher. Luring him to the lonely cabin where they had enjoyed their secret trysts, she beat his brains out with a stone while he slept. She, too, was now arrested and taken to join her brothers at Clonmel.

Grant and his Companions attacked by the military.

The landlord now attempted to implicate the entire Grant family in his son's murder, but Jeremiah's wife was able to intercede with some of the gentry, who investigated the charges and discovered the truth of the matter. The sister was hanged in the Spring

Assizes, and John was sentenced to transportation to Australia. Jeremiah got twelve months in prison.

Following his release, a penniless Jeremiah fell into the trade of stolen horses. He was arrested in 1811, but released for lack of evidence. The following year he was cornered by troops at a friend's house but escaped by jumping from an upstairs window, landing on a goose, and swimming a river to safety. Arrested again for horse stealing in August 1813, he escaped by overpowering the sentry and, in spite of being shot in the leg, managed to flee to Enniscorthy, Co Wexford, where he proceeded to live under an assumed name with his wife and family.

Jeremiah Grant, alas, was too imposing a physical specimen to be capable of blending into a crowd and he was soon recognised, forcing the family to flee to Bray, in County Wicklow. Here he was eventually caught stealing cattle, forcing him now to flee to Drogheda, where he lived safely for a while.

In May 1815, while collecting rent from a man living in his old house in Moyne, he stole an old gig, was arrested, and conveyed to Thurles prison. Here he picked the lock on his handcuffs and tried to rush out of the gaol, only to get lost in the corridors and be overpowered. Transferred to Clonmel gaol in leg irons as well as manacles, he somehow managed to have the implements for sawing through the bars smuggled in to him, by which means he also sawed through the prison bars. On 11 July 1815, he organised a mass gaol break. All of the escapees were subsequently re-arrested, except for Jeremiah, who escaped by swimming the River Suir.

On his return to Drogheda Jeremiah, whose reputation had by now spread countrywide, was once again recognised and re-arrested. On this occasion he was conveyed via Dublin's Kilmainham Gaol to Maryborough, where he was dubbed 'The Captain' by his gaoler, a nickname that was quickly taken up by the press.

In Maryborough Jeremiah had a skeleton key sent in to him concealed in a herring. Using it to open his cell, he overpowered his guards and escaped yet again. In March 1816 he made yet another journey back to his native county, where he robbed the house of one Thomas Cambie of money and sliver plate. Mrs Cambie was at home at the time and Grant behaved with such politeness towards her that she ordered him supper and wine. Impatient to be going, Grant applied his teeth to extract a cork from a bottle; upon which the mistress observed 'it was a pity to spoil his fine white teeth,' and immediately stood up and procured him a cork-screw.

For much of the following year Grant survived as a highwayman becoming at the same time a widely feared and widely admired figure. As his fame spread he was likened at times to Rob Roy, and became a thorn in the side of the authorities. He was finally captured on 24 June 1816, and returned, this time under heavy guard, to Maryborough.

Grant's trial took place at Maryborough Courthouse on 16 August 1816, where he was found guilty of the burglary of Mr. Cambie's house and sentenced to death. When asked what reason he might have why judgment and sentence of death should not be passed upon him he replied, in a firm and collected manner:

'My lord, I only beg of the court some short time to arrange things before my departure for another place; not in the idle hope of escape or pardon, but to make restitution to the persons who have suffered by my bad line of life. I have been visited in my cell by some blessed people, who have, thank God. given this turn to my mind, and to which I implore your lordship's attention.'

One of the attendees at Jeremiah Grant's trial, and one of the 'blessed people' who had visited him in his cell, turned out to have been Sophia's brother,

Thomas. Thomas had long admired the romantic exploits of Jeremiah Grant, and the gentlemanly manner in which he had prosecuted his trade. The fact that Jeremiah hadn't actually killed anyone, according to Thomas, should be enough to warrant the blessing of mercy, and so he began to plan a petition to spare Grant's life. He related as much, with no little pride, to George Evans, when he had tea with him at Frederick Bourne's coaching house at Boughlone, on Monday 19 Aug 2016. George found him full of admiration for Grant, and proud of the fact that he was one of the 'blessed' that Grant had alluded to in his address in court. He was especially pleased to have 'cheated the priest of him'. Thomas' petition notwithstanding, Jeremiah Grant was hanged in Maryborough on 29 Aug 1816.

By 1817 Thomas Parnell had become a founder member of the Religious Tract and Book Society of Ireland, an evangelical and interdenominational Protestant organization, whose aim was to produce and distribute religious tracts to attract converts to evangelical Christianity. In one fell swoop the path of the remainder of his life had been set.

Two years later, he would find himself being made an Honorary Member of the Liverpool Religious Tract Society, on account of his 'active exertions' to which 'the Sunday School Society of Ireland, and many other excellent institutions owe much of their prosperity'. The key word here is 'prosperity'. Thomas, it would appear, had already started to spend his inheritance on his passion. He soon became a familiar sight about the city, going from door to door selling penny pamphlets, and in no time at all he had become commonly known as 'Tract Parnell'.

In his religious zeal, at least, Thomas was not unusual amongst his class. Helping him shepherd the Society were such luminaries as the banker James Digges La Touche, the silk magnate Samuel Bewley, and the bibliophile, evangelist and Irish-language enthusiast, Henry Joseph J. Monck Mason. Thomas would later become the Society's secretary, and later still its treasurer, and would spend the remainder of his life working out of their offices at 32 Sackville Street, Dublin.[22]

As Thomas grew older, his passion slowly evolved into something approaching mania and he became ever more eccentric and unreliable. Within the Society he found himself slowly reduced to the role of a mere committee member. He became somewhat less than scrupulous in his personal habits and grooming, causing Sophia to become increasingly concerned for his well-being.

At one point Sophia went so far as to organise a housekeeper to look after him, but it did not work out. The housekeeper's husband, in a drunken fit, got it into his head that Thomas had designs on his wife and fell upon him in a furious rage until someone came to his rescue. Thomas was left shaken and badly bruised, but suffered no permanent damage.

Invited frequently to Portrane, Thomas also became a familiar sight around the peninsula, where his sister once again became something akin to a surrogate mother to him, treating him as one might a difficult child. He was especially well known to Frances Power Cobbe, whose father was the Protestant Archbishop of Dublin, and to whose house Thomas was prone to make impromptu visits. She dedicates several paragraphs to him in her autobiography:

'A brother of this lady, who walked over often to Newbridge House from Portrane to bring my mother some scented broom which she loved, was a very singular and pathetic character. He was the younger brother of that sufficiently astute man of the world, Sir Henry Parnell, but was his

---

22 Now 32 O'Connell Street.

antipodes in disposition.

Thomas Parnell, "Old Tom Parnell" as all Dublin knew him forty years, had a huge ungainly figure like Doctor Johnson's, and one of the sweetest, softest faces ever worn by mortal man. He had, at some emote and long forgotten period, been seized with a fervent and self-denying religious enthusiasm of the ultra-Protestant type; and this had somehow given birth in his brain to a scheme for arranging texts of the Bible in a mysterious order which, when completed, should afford infallible answers to every question of the human mind!

To construct the interminable tables required for this wonderful plan, poor Tom Parnell devoted his life and fortune. For years which must have amounted to many decades he laboured at the work in a bare, gloomy, dusty room in what was called a "Protestant Office" in Sackville Street. Money went speedily to clerks and printers; and no doubt the good man (who himself lived, as he used to say laughingly, on "a second-hand bone") gave money also freely in alms.

One way or another Mr. Parnell grew poorer and more poor, his coat looked shabbier, and his beautiful long white hair more obviously in need of a barber. Once or twice every summer he was prevailed on by his sister to tear himself from his work and pay her a few weeks' visit in the country at Portrane; and to her and all her visitors he preached incessantly his monotonous appeal: "Repent; and cease to eat good dinners, and devote yourselves to compiling texts!"'

Thomas was constantly looking for money, especially from his soft-hearted sister Sophia, and then spending it as soon as he had it. Over time, however, even his devoted sister became exhausted by her attempts to care for him, and the pair became slowly more distant.

17

EMMA

IN 1820, HAVING reached her eighteenth birthday, Henry's daughter, Emma, was sent to live with her aunt Sophia at Portrane.

It appears to have been a difficult transition for young Emma. She had spent most of her young life travelling between the two great cities of London and Paris, and was totally unsuited to country life. She was not overly fond of outdoor activities and was, by her own admission, a very poor horsewoman. Portrane was also a long way from Edinburgh, where her brother John, the person to whom she was closest in this world, had been sent for schooling.

Sophia had never raised children of her own and found herself struggling to deal with an impossibly pious teenager with whom she had little in common. Intellectually there was a chasm between them. Sophia must at times have appeared impossibly dismissive to her young charge, who would have found her a far more challenging conversationalist than her previous guardians for whom every moral question began and ended in the pages of a holy book. Her aunt's interests, furthermore, were by the standards of the age, well, somewhat masculine.

Prior to her arrival in Ireland, Emma had spent a great deal of time in the company of one of her father's evangelical cousins, a certain Mrs. Puget, with whom she was wont to talk much on the subject of religion. Before her departure for Portrane, Puget had gifted Emma a little Testament that Emma would treasure for the rest of her life. Her religiosity, on the face of it, represented a remarkable transformation. Her brother, John, would later confess that their mother had taught them to say their morning and evening prayers as children, but they had never received any formal religious education and had known nothing of the Gospels.

Emma was reasonably cultured. She was fond of reading, especially history, and could draw fairly well. There was a large library at Mount Evans, stocked largely by Sophia, but the type of reading material available would have dismayed the naïve, affected, and somewhat puritanical teenager and her evangelical circle. Her letters from Portrane reveal a devoutly religious and sincerely pious young woman constantly at odds with her guardian.

Despite their philosophical differences, however, Sophia was still happy to undertake the materteral task of introducing Emma into Irish society and, in making their rounds of the Dublin season, she allowed a proposal of marriage from a Captain George Probyn, of the East India Company, to be presented to Emma. Emma, alas, was having none of it. Probyn she protested, was simply far too stout and 'middle-aged' (in actual fact he was just six years her senior).

Emma was considered remarkably good looking, with 'laughing black eyes' and still darker hair dressed in ringlets. She had a small straight nose, full red lips and a lovely pink and white complexion. Despite her teenage affectations of piety, she was vain enough to know that she could do better, that there would, in time, be no shortage of suitable suitors closer to her own age; suitors who would not be away at sea for months on end.

It is not known if Emma ever met any of Sophia and George's more famous literary friends, but while staying at Portrane, she would have had plenty of opportunity to chat with Sophia's mother-in-law, Margaret Evans[23] about her real artistic passion, poetry. A poem that Emma composed while at Mount Evans, harked back to her time in Paris and the end of the Napoleonic wars, an experience that Margaret Evans could understand only too well:

ST HELENA

Grave of the mighty, melancholy isle,
Whose sea-girt rocks, a high and gloomy pile
In lovely grandeur, on the Atlantic's maze
Look down with cold and stem repelling gaze,
When passion's meteor reign shall have expired
And other men with no resentment fired
Shall read the tale of Europe's wayward strife,
Shall feel with hurried throb the pulse of life
Beating within them, while the glowing page
Unfolds the records of this warlike age,
Shall they not often turn with wondering eye
And gaze where low Napoleon's ashes lie,
Conqueror of Europe, when in youth's bright hour
Italia owned thy stern resistless power
When awestruck France before thee kneeling low,
Beheld thee place her diadem on thy brow,
When the proud eagle fluttered in thy sky
And waved his golden wings in triumph high,
O mighty Emperor did thine eye of pride
Ere seek to draw the veil of fate aside.

---

[23] See Ronan, Gerard. *Margaret Evans – Poet of Portrane, Fingal County Council,* 2020.

Emma, having effectively been raised for the last eight years of her life by a Protestant Rector, soon found she had far more in common with Sophia's brother, the evangelical preacher, Thomas Parnell, than she had with her aunt Sophia. When 'Uncle Tom' took a shine to her, therefore, she was only too happy to forsake Sophia's company, and supervision, for his.

Finding himself more flattered by the attention of his niece than that of his older sister (who had never stopped treating him like a child), Thomas undertook to relieve Sophia of her materteral duties and to take Emma on the usual round of familiar visitations. It began, in 1822, with a visit to his great friends, the Earl and Countess of Roden, at their home at Tollymore House, near Newcastle in Co. Down.

The Rodens were a famously religious family and Emma felt very much more at home in Tollymore than she ever had at Portrane. The letters she wrote to her brother John from there resemble miniature sermons, obsessively concerned with matters of death and the fate of her immortal soul. They are indicative, perhaps, of the extent to which she had fallen under the influence of her Uncle Tom, who had promised to introduce her to all of the influential evangelical families of the time.

If a match had to be made, then Thomas Parnell was determined that it should be a match that *he* approved of, and the suitor a man after his own tastes. In January 1823, Emma wrote to John from Carnew, in Co. Wexford:

'In my next letter I mean to write you a long account of Lord and Lady Roden and the delightful time I spent there. Uncle Tom came down to fetch me, and brought me up to Lady Westmeath last Monday week. Mr. and Mrs. Henry More, great (friends) of Uncle Tom's, asked me to come and see them, and as Lady Westmeath was coming down she brought me

with her, and so I am here at Carnew, in County Wexford, a very wild part of the country, but a very pleasant place to be in. I have got such a number of nice friends through Uncle Tom, who is very much beloved and respected.

Some years ago there was hardly one person in Ireland of good family, or either of the higher class who had any idea of religion. He was the first, but now great numbers of the higher class in Ireland are religious characters and many of them through Uncle Tom's means. When you come to Ireland you must be acquainted with them all. I am sure you will be delighted with the Rodens especially.

I have never been to a ball and never mean to go (by) my own consent, because I could not go without feeling so much vanity and emulation, and hearing so much flattery and nonsense as would make me, I fear, grow indifferent to my spiritual welfare, but perhaps for a young man the case is different, though I dare say you will not find much pleasure in them. If you should however get fond of them, I would advise you to beware, for we are commanded not to love the world, I John iii. *I long to see you all ...'*

Two years later, Emma had grown out of her puritanical aversion to balls and would learn to dance the quadrille for her wedding. The puritanical zeal she inspired in John, however, would remain with him for the rest of his life and he, too, would eventually fall under the charismatic influence of his evangelical 'Uncle Tom'.

One can readily see in Emma's letter the sort of frustrations that Sophia would have encountered and, most likely at Emma's insistence, Henry was left with little choice but to remove his daughter from Sophia's guardianship and place her in the care of his brother-in-law, Lionel Dawson, or 'Uncle Li' as Emma was

Emma Parnell

wont to call him. Lionel and his wife, Lady Elizabeth, in consequence, took Emma and her sister Mary to live with them at Emo Court, Abbeyleix, until the end of the 1823, when Dawson, finding life at Emo beyond his means, decided to remove his family, Emma included, to Brussels.

The Dawsons had barely started from Ireland when Thomas set off in pursuit. He caught up with them at Dover. A stormy confrontation ensued that only ended when Emma agreed to return with him to Ireland, where he undertook to provide for her. Thomas, alas, was no more suited to caring for a wilful teenager than his sister and responsibility for Emma was finally delegated to his cousins, Lord and Lady de Vesci, who took Emma to stay with them at Abbeyleix. Much to Sophia's chagrin, Emma would grow to consider Abbeyleix, and not Portrane, as her home, at least until her marriage in 1825.

George Tighe and Margaret Mount Cashell had by this time been joined in Pisa by the poet Percy Shelley and his wife Mary (daughter of William Godwin and Mary Wollstonecraft and the author of *Frankenstein*). At the same time, William Godwin was filing for bankruptcy. The man handling his affairs was none other than George Evan's brother, Joshua. Throughout 1824 Joshua was a regular visitor to Godwin's house in London.

Margaret Tighe would feel a maternal bond with the young Mary Shelley and would help her to set up her household, find lodgings and hire servants. She would also give the illness-prone and hypochondriacal Percy the benefit of her medical training, help Mary with the new baby, and break up the dysfunctional love-triangle with Mary's stepsister Claire. Along with George Tighe, she would introduce the Shelleys to a new intellectual circle, inspiring them, as she had perhaps once inspired the young Sophia Parnell, with a sense of youthful radicalism.

Given William Parnell's close friendship with Mary Tighe and Margaret Mount Cashell, and Joshua's relationship with William Godwin, it would be almost inconceivable to imagine that Margaret's unconventional life in Italy was not commonly discussed at Portrane House. Sophia, in particular, could not have been left untouched by the intellectual freedom her old friend now enjoyed.

Unable to pursue a political career of her own in this era before women's suffrage, Sophia had, prior to her brother William's death, been content to busy herself improving Portrane Demesne and expressing her political beliefs through charitable donations and whatever influence she could exert upon her husband and brothers. Her interest in marine science had also led her to build a unique collection of Irish seashells and to entertain members of the Geological Society of Dublin who came to Portrane to study the cliffs. To feed her insatiable interest in atheist writers such as Hume, Gibbon, Voltaire and the *Encyclopédistes* she established the fine library at Portrane House that was to be such a comfort to her in her old age. But it was never enough.

Sophia was very much an intellectual of the Enlightenment but she was no writer. She had little to say that hadn't been better expressed by someone else. What she did have, in spades, was the steely conviction and the necessary wealth to indulge her passions.

In the year following her brother's death, word reached Sophia of the death of her old friend, Sophie de Condorcet, and of the birth of Eliza's third child, whom the O'Connors had chosen to name 'George'. As Eliza set out to take up where her mother had left off and publish what remained of her father's writings, Sophia at the same time elected to take up where her brother William had left off, and concern herself with the education of the poor. No longer willing to spend her energies in *inactive and unprofitable sympathy,* she determined to make a difference, even if it had occasionally to be through the proxy of her husband.

Sophia Parnell was no political *ingénue*, but the daughter of one of the most astute political operators of his day. Getting George to put himself forward for public office, however, would not be an easy task. His family history carried a stigma that his marriage to Sophia had only partially erased and it would have been entirely understandable if he was nervous of bringing all *that* back into the public consciousness. It would be January 1824 before he took his first tentative steps towards becoming a public figure, and when he did, it would happen at a Vestry meeting at the Protestant church in Donabate. At this meeting George proposed several motions, the following included:

> *'Resolved. That we entertained sanguine hopes that when an arrangement was made to set to rest the long-agitated question of Tithes, it would not have escaped the attention of the Legislature, that nine-tenths of the People of Ireland profess the Roman Catholic Religion – that, in many Parishes the Protestant Clergyman is exclusively supported by the tithe of the Catholic Farmer, and the Tithe of the potato garden of the Cottier. We entertained hopes that the many would have been heavily taxed to support the religious opinions of the few.'*

It was a small move, and at a local level, but the news still made the national newspapers. As a liberal and fair-minded landlord, and a lawyer who was known to be supportive of secret ballots and totally opposed to the Tories, it was now only a matter of time before someone other than his wife would suggest that he consider standing for parliament. Public image now assumed a far greater importance to Sophia. Family reputation mattered.

Ever since 1813, when Caroline Parnell left her husband, Henry, and fled through war torn France with her children to Switzerland, the Parnell's had been ultra-sensitive about their reputation. The increasingly eccentric activities of Thomas 'Tract' Parnell would not have helped assuage their concerns for such matters and a degree of sensitivity to public opinion was perhaps only to be expected.

Sophia, in all of this had been a loyal sister to her brothers. She had seen herself as something of a maternal force and protector of her brothers and their children. She was, in her own mind at least, the adult in the room, the realist in a family of introverts and romantics. In 1825, these protective instincts led to a dispute with her niece, Emma, who had recently become engaged to Edward Lord Clifton.

During the build up to the wedding, Emma decided that she would prefer to remain at Lady de Vesci's where she had been living for the past two years. But Lady de Vesci, although a cousin of Sophia's, was so closely related to Emma's fiancé that she would have been considered more a part of his family than Emma's. This bothered both Sophia, and Emma's father, Henry. It had echoes of her mother's desertion, of yet another woman trying to distance herself from the Parnells.

Following the engagement, Sophia had been given reason, most likely by Henry, to expect that Emma would come and stay with her until her wedding day, and that she, as the elder female in the family, would be charged with helping to prepare her niece for her impending nuptials. But Emma was happy at Abbeyleix and reluctant to transplant herself to Portrane. She had never been happy in that house, and she and her aunt Sophia had never gotten along.

Insensitive to her aunt's feelings, and to the wider impression that this very public snub would create, she wrote to Sophia, and told her she intended to remain with the De Vesci family at Abbeyleix. Sophia was incensed and wrote a strongly worded letter to Emma and the De Vescis, letting them know of her hurt. It was not received well.

On 2 June 1825, Emma wrote to her fiancé, Edward:

> *'Yesterday we were all a little annoyed by a letter from my aunt Mrs. Evans, in reply to one of mine, telling her I had promised to remain with your dear Aunt. My Aunt seemed vexed about its being so arranged, but as it is settled so, I hope she will soon make up her mind to it. I don't know why I should tell you this however, but only that I could not help seeing that Lord and Lady de Vesci seemed both quite hurt at my aunt's letter, and seemed to wish very much that I should remain where I am.*
>
> *Perhaps I have said a great deal too much about this, and I hope you will forgive me, my dearest Clifton, if I have. But you know you have often told me you liked to know all my thoughts, however far from being wise ones. I cannot tell you how much I love our dear relations Lord and Lady de V. Long before the beginning of our friendship I had been accustomed to look upon them as my dearest and best friends, and I think the last two months have rendered them still dearer to me.'*

Whatever was going on between Sophia and Emma, it would appear that Sophia at least had an ally in Emma's father. Fearing that Sophia's determination would prevail, Emma wrote to her fiancé once again, pleading with him to intervene:

> *'Remember, you are not to let Papa take me away*

from Lady de V. He never minds anything that I say, so I must depend upon you dearest.'

In all of the copious correspondence that passed between Emma and her fiancé, Sophia is hardly mentioned, unlike her brother Thomas, or 'Uncle Tom', who appears to have been in constant personal contact with her. She also, in her letters, appears to have taken a similar dislike to Lady Morgan, a close friend of George and Sophia's, and an equally formidable and independent thinker.

Few details survive of the wedding, which was solemnised on 26 July 1825 in the old church in the grounds at Abbeyleix. From those that do, we know that among those present were Viscount and Viscountess de Vesci, the Earl and Countess of Darnley, the Hon. John and Lady Elizabeth Bligh, and Sir Henry Parnell, his daughter Caroline and the Hon. and Rev. William Wingfield.

Given the traditions of the day it would be unthinkable if Henry had been in attendance, but not his sister, Sophia. Definitely not in attendance, however, was Emma's mother, Caroline. She had chosen to remain in self-imposed exile in Paris.

A few weeks after the wedding, George and Sophia were once again in reflective mood and Sophia suffering a renewed bout of insecurity and self-doubt. That August, from Kilmullan in Co. Laois, George wrote to her:

'I can say with perfect truth that after being in your society 20 years that my desire and affection for you has increased in proportion as years have rolled on; and as that time has enabled me more fully to appreciate your merits.'

Emma and her brother, John, would remain close to her 'Uncle Tom' for the remainder of his life, and John would eventually follow Tom into the missionary life. But though they would continue to visit their Aunt Sophia at Portrane, and to bring their children on the occasional summer visit, they would never be as close to Sophia as their brother, Henry, and his wife, Sophy. In the years to come, it would be young Henry that Sophia would correspond most frequently with, and upon whom she would rely most heavily.

18

SCANDALOUS WOMEN

In NOVEMBER 1825, Sophia returned to Paris. George's sister Mary, now residing on the fashionable Rue de Colombier, had recently been widowed. Her husband, William Lawless, had died the previous Christmas. He was fifty-two.

There was to be no reprieve from her grief this time and George had could only put off visiting his sister for so long. Grateful, for the opportunity, after so many years, to renew her friendship with old friends, Sophia insisted on travelling with him. It would afford her an opportunity to see Eliza and little George, who would now be three years of age.

Her return to Paris was not without a dash of the clandestine. About her person she carried a personal letter from the famous novelist Lady Morgan, author of *The Wild Irish Girl*. She was charged with delivering it personally to Elizabeth 'Betsy' Patterson, ex-wife of Napoleon's younger brother, Jérôme. Morgan, a frequent guest at Mount Evans and a long time

Sydney Owenson, Lady Morgan

correspondent of Betsy's, was reluctant to entrust it to the postal service.

An Irish-American socialite famous for her risqué dress sense, Elizabeth 'Betsy' Patterson had married Jérôme Bonaparte in Baltimore on Christmas Eve 1803. Napoleon, who disapproved of the marriage, demanded it be annulled and that his brother return to France without her. Jérôme ignored his brother and, in the autumn of 1804, attempted to travel with pregnant Elizabeth to his brother's coronation, only to find that Elizabeth had been banned from setting foot anywhere in continental Europe.

Jérôme set off for Italy alone, intending to reason with his brother. Elizabeth never saw him again. Three years later, despite still being married to Elizabeth, he would marry the German princess, Catharina of Württemberg. Elizabeth had little choice but to flee to London, where she gave birth to a son, Jérôme Napoleon, before returning to Baltimore to live with her Donegal-born father.

Following Napoleon's defeat at Waterloo, Betsy returned to Paris to flaunt her Napoleonic connections. Newly-divorced, but not remarried, she was well-received in exclusive circles but found herself constantly watched and her movements monitored. She longed for letters from friends that had not been intercepted by the police and, suspecting that this might well be the case, Lady Morgan entrusted hers to the care of Sophia.

Elizabeth Patterson knew everyone of consequence in continental Europe and her letters to her friends frequently contained gossip of the great names of politics, literature and the royal courts. Not since her youthful meeting with Madame de Staël, however, had Sophia met such a woman, and the visit served only to renew her social aspirations and invigorate her ambitions for her husband. For all of her liberal and intellectual tendencies, Sophia Evans was very much a child of her class.

Elizabeth Patterson Bonaparte

Betsy Patterson was at this time a bitter and isolated woman, anxious for whatever social contact she could get. In her return letter to Lady Morgan, of 28 November 1825, she acknowledged Sophia's delivery of the letter and complained of her loneliness:

'Mrs. Evans has given me your welcome letter; I cannot express to you how much I was delighted at hearing that you had not forgotten me. I passed only a few months in Italy, where I saw the most

beautiful woman in the world, who since died in her husband's palace at Florence, surrounded by friends, and conjugally regretted by Prince Borghese! He buried her in the handsomest chapel in Europe. She left a legacy to my son of twenty thousand francs ...

Do contrive to get a letter to me by une occasion particuliére. I do not like the idea of the police, your readers, receiving what was intended for me ... I have fifty scandalous things to tell you; but I write in haste that I may send my letter to England by a friend. I have been in Paris only a few days; I have seen no one. All the people whom I knew are dead or absent.'

Also living in Paris at this time was another exile, Sophia's sister-in-law, Caroline Dawson-Parnell. For some time now Caroline had been living in humble accommodation and refusing to meet with any of her relatives, even her children, with whom she had kept in constant contact by post. Lest they should learn of her address, she had her post delivered under the pseudonym of Madame Elizabeth Pearson to the Post Office.

It is not known if Sophia made any attempt to find Caroline, but just as it would have been unusual for her *not* to, it would have been equally unlike Caroline to have consented. She was only too well aware of how close Sophia was to Henry, and whose side Sophia would have taken in the entire affair.

It would not be until 1860 that Caroline's daughter Emma would break the veil of secrecy. She would travel to Paris to find her mother living in poor accommodation with only a single attendant, a forty-year-old German journalist by the name of Ferdinand d'Eisenach. Caroline had known Ferdinand since he was a child and, deprived of her own children, had directed all of her maternal affections upon him and paid for his education. It was he, according to Emma, who 'with faithful devotion' now managed her affairs. Emma would find her mother 'a very stout old lady with a large white face, sitting in an armchair, unable to move but full of vivacity and talk'.

It was to prove a brief reunion. Caroline died just seven weeks after Emma's visit. She was sitting before the fire when Ferdinand left her for a few minutes to post a letter. While he was gone, she accidentally set fire to her clothes and was unable to extinguish them before his return. Though not severely burnt, her feeble body could not recover from the shock and she died a few hours later in the arms of her beloved Ferdinand, with whom her daughter would remain friends for life.

The stigma attached to 'fallen women', and the effect of the ensuing scandal on their families, was not a subject that Sophia was exactly unfamiliar with. Apart from Caroline Parnell, she had personal connections to the men affected by the two most scandalous wives of 19th century Ireland, Lady Elizabeth Cloncurry and Lady Caroline Lamb. These women were as intimately known to George's friend, Lady Morgan, as their husbands were to him and Sophia.

Lady Elizabeth Cloncurry was the second wife of Baron Cloncurry, Valentine Brown Lawless. Prior to his marriage, Cloncurry had been known to Sophia through his friendship with her late father, Sir John Parnell. They had been fellow directors of the Grand Canal Company. But it was through her husband that she had come to know him personally.

As a senior United Irishman allowed to return to Ireland after serving three years imprisoned without trial in the Tower of London, Lord Cloncurry had much in common with George Evan's father, Hampden Evans, and throughout the years of Hampden's exile, he and George had shared the difficulties and the challenges of overcoming the stigma of a radical past and dealing with the prejudices and suspicions of the post-Union administration. As a result the pair had become firm friends and regular correspondents. George's sister, Mary, furthermore, was married to Cloncurry's cousin, William Lawless.

Lord Cloncurry would have been a familiar table companion of Sophia's, and it was to be at one of dinner party, at Dublin Castle, on 26 November 1827, that all three of these stories would intersect. At that particular dinner party, hosted by William Lamb, 2nd Viscount Melbourne and Chief Secretary for Ireland, George and Sophia would be joined by fellow guests, Lady Morgan and Lord and Lady Cloncurry (his third wife Emily, and not the object of the aforementioned scandal). Cloncurry and George had been spending a great deal of time together recently, having entered into official discussions regarding a proposal to build a ship canal between Dublin and Galway.

Back in 1806 an old school mate of Cloncurry's, Sir John Piers, had wagered that he could seduce Lady Elizabeth Cloncurry and, despite Cloncurry's best efforts to thwart him, he won his bet. Cloncurry's wife confessed her infidelity and was promptly taken into exile by her uncle. Cloncurry then sued his former friend Sir John Piers, who fled to the Isle of Man.

The lawsuit made Cloncurry a figure of ridicule for many years in Ireland, but throughout it all George and Sophia Evans had remained steadfast friends and confidantes, a relationship that could only have been strengthened by the scandal that accompanied Caroline Parnell's 'desertion' of Sophia's brother Henry in 1813.

The other 'fallen woman' mentioned above, Lady Caroline Lamb, was the daughter of the Anglo-Irish peer Frederick Ponsonby, 3rd Earl of Bessborough. In 1805, at the age of nineteen, she had married the Hon. William Lamb, heir to the 1st Viscount Melbourne, the couple having become 'mutually captivated' during a visit to Brocket Hall in 1802. For many years the pair had enjoyed a happy marriage.

Elected to the House of Commons in 1806, William Lamb was well known to both Sophia's brother Henry, and to their great friend, Lady Morgan (who had been a confidante of Lady Caroline Lamb both before and during the scandal that was to rock British Society). Sophia would have met him on many occasions during the London season.

Back in 1812, Caroline had embarked on a tempestuous affair with Lord Byron and the resulting scandal had been the talk of Britain and Ireland ever since. It was perhaps the only piece of tittle-tattle within Sophia's social circle more salivating to the gossips than that of Caroline Parnell's decision to desert her brother, Henry, and flee through war torn France to Switzerland. In some ways it may even have robbed that particular scandal of much of the attention it might otherwise have received.

The reason the scandal surrounding Byron and the Lambs had lasted so much longer than that of Ladies Cloncurry and Parnell, was Caroline Lamb's decision, in 1816, to publish a Gothic novel, *Glenarvon*, in which she chose to portray both her marriage and her affair with Byron in so lurid fashion as to cause William Lamb even greater embarrassment. Her spiteful caricatures of leading society figures in the novel turned the Lambs into social pariahs in England and forced them to flee to Ireland.

As a loyal and sympathetic sister, Sophia could not fail to see the parallels in William Lamb's predicament and that of her brother, Henry, and to empathise with what he was going through. She and George, therefore, were conspicuous amongst the few who refused to shun him. Though the Lambs had briefly reconciled following the affair, by the time of the dinner party at Dublin Castle they had legally separated.

Throughout the entire affair, Caroline had been in constant correspondence with Lady Morgan. This was especially true during the period after Byron broke things off and her husband took her back to Ireland in disgrace, hoping in vain that distance would cool her ardour for the infamous poet. But Caroline and Byron continued to correspond.

Lady Caroline Lamb

Caroline had shared much of this correspondence with Lady Morgan, who in her turn was a frequent visitor to Portrane. Having had a front row seat at the beginning of this, one of the most infamous scandals in British parliamentary history, Sophia and George were about to have a front row seat to its conclusion.

In November 1827, Caroline fell seriously ill. Her struggle with mental instability, further complicated by abuse of alcohol and laudanum, had caused her body to shut down. Word was sent to William Lamb at Dublin Castle. He received it just before he was due to host the aforementioned dinner party.

Most of the people around the table that night had been touched at some stage in their lives by the type of scandal that had blighted their host. Lady Morgan's career as an actress and novelist hadn't exactly endeared her to the elite of Irish Society, and George and Sophia had known the scandal of her brother's failed marriage and the stigma of having a strain of 'madness' running through her family. The cuckolding of Lord Cloncurry, furthermore, had made him a figure of public ridicule.

Unlike Cloncurry, however, who had since remarried, William Lamb still held deep feelings for his estranged wife and mother of his only son, George Augustus Frederick, who, like Sophia's brother, John Augustus, had been born with severe mental problems. From Sophia Evans at least, William Lamb could always be guaranteed empathy and sympathy, and never more so than in the aftermath of that dinner party, for no-one could help but notice that something was amiss with Lamb that night.

The following morning, 27 November 1827, Lady Morgan noted Lamb's dark preoccupations in her diary:

'Mr. Lamb was in the lowest spirits from the bad accounts that had come of poor Lady Caroline. Poor Lady Caroline, her life was fast ebbing, but she had kind friends round her.'

Shortly after that, on 13 December 1827, William Lamb received another letter, this time from Caroline's doctor, to the effect that he believed Caroline was nearing the end. Abandoning his duties at the Castle,

Lamb made the perilous winter crossing to England and was at her bedside when, just seven weeks later, Lady Caroline died.

William Lamb was not the only attendee at that party to be bereaved so suddenly afterwards. That same month Sophia lost her brother, Arthur, who died suddenly at Mount Avon. Throughout all his time at Mount Avon, Arthur had been privately cared for and his presence kept a family secret. Details of his death were not even published in the newspapers. He was buried in the local cemetery, his headstone referring to him as 'late of the College of Physicians'.

It is not known what became of the Dobsons, to whom Arthur had been so generous in his will, but as they were not mentioned during its final administration of in March 1829, it is likely that the legacies were paid as requested over the course of the previous year, at least to those devisees who were still alive at the time. Twenty years of poverty in disease-ridden London would, by the law of averages, have taken at least one of them since the will was first drafted.

If there was one thing that Sophia and George had learnt from the experiences of such friends as William Lamb and Valentine Lawless, it was that Posterity had a cruel and selective memory. They had never been blessed with children, or felt the pain of parental or marital separation. But they certainly knew what it was like to be the subject of public gossip, and subjected to the type of negative stereotyping that still attached to mental illness, 'impotent' husbands, 'barren' wives, and landed gentry.

With no children waiting to inherit their wealth, and life reminding them annually of the need to leave something positive to Posterity, Sophia decided that the time had come to dedicate at least some of her time and personal wealth to the children of her less fortunate neighbours. The education of the poor, so long a passion of her late brother William, would now become hers.

19

SOPHIA'S SCHOOLS

UP UNTIL 1827, the closest Sophia had ever gotten to facilitating the education of the poor was the odd charitable donation and George's decision to accept a place on the committee of the *Education Society to Establish Free Schools for the Moral and Useful Instruction of the Poor*. That year, however, she and George decided to found and fund two public schools in the Donabate and Portrane area. The schools were to be situated half way between the two villages.

Though George and Sophia would each nominally endow the school of their respective gender, the driving force behind the scheme, and the building of *both* schools, was known locally to have been Sophia and Department of Education records list her as the schools' 'manager'. Frances Power Cobbe records as much in her autobiography:

> *'Mrs. Evans, of Portrane, of whom I shall say more by and by, built and endowed capital*

schools for both boys and girls, and pensioned some of the poorest old people.'

The schools were established according to the Lancastrian system, in which an experienced teacher taught a select group of older children, who then taught the younger or weaker pupils in small groups. They were also, at least nominally, multi-denominational. There were, however, few Church of Ireland children living in the Donabate or Portrane area who would have required public schooling, and the teachers that Sophia employed were both Catholic. In all of this Sophia remained faithful to the work of her late brother, William, whose ideals would subsequently be embodied in Ireland's fledgling system of primary education.

Sophia's schools, a hybrid of traditional primary and vocational education, were provided with half an acre of land on which the students were taught to grow crops. The girls, furthermore, when they reached an appropriate age, were also taught the skill of embroidery. Several 'very elegant dresses and aprons' were worked here, 'one of which was for her Majesty Queen Dowager Adelaide.'[24]   That dress was most likely presented in 1834, when Sophia was presented at a Royal Drawing Room by Mary Parsons, the Countess of Rosse.

George and Sophia Evans were by now known to be passionate and vocal supporters of Catholic emancipation, of the abolition of tithes, of universal suffrage and of the secret ballot. The creation of two schools in Donabate, therefore, was bound not just to reflect their politics, but to be noticed. In 1827, in her book *The O'Briens and the O'Flahertys*, Lady Morgan described George as:

---

[24] Lewis, Samuel. Topography of Ireland (1837).

'... a good landlord, a liberal politician, and one of the few who still hold by the country which gave them birth and subsistence, and reflect back upon it the high benefits of enlightened and well-directed patriotism.'

In December of that same year, Sophia Evans received even greater praise, this time from Daniel O'Connell, who read an excerpt from a letter he had recently received from the parish priest of Donabate to a meeting of his newly formed Catholic Association:

'There is an extensive school for females in Portrane, carried on with liberality and munificence truly characteristic and worthy of the amiable and benevolent lady who has established, and supports it solely at her own expense, unconnected with any other Education Society or Association whatsoever. The mistress is a Catholic, has an annual salary of twenty guineas, house and coals free, with other perquisites. No book, no publication is introduced without the approbation of the Parish Priest.

There are from fifty to a hundred children, all Catholics, instructed in reading, writing, arithmetic, and in all kind of needlework, provided with stationery, and all, this year, handsomely clothed at this Protestant Lady's expense. It is almost impossible to conceive the vast utility, the manifold good resulting from this liberal school. I need scarcely say that this humane and distinguished lady, to whom the parents and the rising generation of this parish owe so much, is Mrs. Evans, wife of George Evans Esq., and sister to Sir Henry Parnell.

The boys' school is not as yet carried on with any kind of system, as we have had the building of a new one in contemplation. The erection of this school-house, forty feet long by twenty wide, Mr.

Evans has kindly and generously taken upon himself, at his sole expense, and has given a commodious site, together with a portion of land, rent free, as an equivalent for the free tuition of the poor Catholic children of this parish....'

O'Connell was not unfamiliar with Sophia Evans, having been in constant communication with her brother Henry on the subject of Catholic emancipation. Having read the Rev. Murray's letter, he moved that Murray be requested to discover an appropriate means of expressing the 'heartfelt gratitude and admiration of the Catholic Association' to Mrs. Evans.

Having dipped his toes in the arena of public service and found that he rather liked it; George Evans accepted another appointment, three years later, as High Sheriff of County Dublin, his first real taste of political power. As the Sovereign's legal representative George became responsible for judicial, ceremonial and administrative duties and the execution of High Court writs. His thoughts were beginning to be exercised by questions of a national nature, as evidenced by the following letter to his good friend, Valentine Lawless:

'Portrane, May 23rd, 1829.

Dear Lord Cloncurry,

Your views do not quite agree with mine. When I differ from a person so distinguished for his attachment to his country, and for his unwearied exertions for its welfare, I should, perhaps, be inclined to mistrust my own opinion and defer to his ; but as yet I am not convinced, and I thus inflict on your lordship a view of my scepticism.

It is an easy task to declaim with warmth and pathetic eloquence on the hardships that the Irish poor endure, and to adduce as further crimes against the Irish landlords the Sub-letting Act and the Disfranchisement of the Forty-shilling Freeholders. To oppose these topics, which naturally excite sympathy, may be invidious, and in some degree difficult, by the excitement produced by the very discussion itself; yet, when so imminent a scourge, as I conceive the Poor Laws to be, are advocated by many well-meaning and influential persons, I did think that perhaps my humble, and, I trust, dispassionate view might not at this time be entirely irrelevant.

I believe that public opinion is running in a current too strong to be well directed, and that we lose sight of the disadvantages attending the introduction of the system, which, from English experience, are not problematical, to adopt what in itself is no way adapted to the civil or political state of the country.

Your society are eagerly employed in furthering what is strictly the work and advantage of the English landlords, who are themselves writhing under the infliction of the Poor Laws. It is certainly not from love and affection that they wish to introduce them into Ireland, but in the vain hope of alleviating their own evils; but I affirm, that they must fail in this, without they are able to impose upon the rental and capital of Ireland a rate equivalent to their own, otherwise the temptation of high wages in England will induce the Irish labourer still to leave the Irish shores.

Now, I should be glad you would pause a little, and calculate what amount would be required to raise the price of labour in this country to a par with that in England, and if you think you can afford the introduction on these terms, why then there is an end to my objection.

But, you will say, we only want the introduction of the system, such as it was in the time of Queen Elizabeth we only want to support the old and infirm. I do not think that many are prepared to go further, and would shudder at the idea of introducing the English system; but let us pay due attention to the opinions of the English, both in and out of Parliament.

They, no doubt, talk of a provision for the old and infirm, but this is only incidental with their other arguments; they do not rest their advocacy on this point; they do not hesitate to declare, that they want to be relieved from the competition, not of the old and infirm, who never emigrate, and who are maintained by the benevolence of their own countrymen, but from the competition of the able-bodied Irish labourer, to whom, if you do not pay eighteen pence or two shillings a day at home, must still enter into competition with the English labourer.

Suppose we are to have the Rates introduced into this country, independent of the expenses I have alluded to, what a system of petty litigation will arise what myriads of small attorneys will people all the villages in the kingdom. I wish some unbiased person would pass the summer months in England, and after visiting the different parts of it, report to your society the blessings of the Poor Rates.

With much esteem, &c.
George Evans.

The appointment as High Sheriff, shared on an annual basis amongst the landed gentry, may well have temporarily satisfied Sophia's hankering for a return to the political milieu of her childhood. But Dublin wasn't London, or even Paris for that matter, reminders of which kept raising their heads. The primary source of such news was Lady Morgan who was still in touch with Betsy Patterson, and who came to stay at Portrane for two days in September of that year 'to get rid of the smell of the paint' while her townhouse was being redecorated.

But Sophia had contacts of her own in Paris and, in October 1829, having doubtlessly heard of George's recent promotion, the Condorcet-O'Connors came calling once again. Their eldest son, Arthur junior, had passed away that year at the age of twenty and their second son, Daniel, having just turned nineteen, was now the legal heir. In order to 'inherit his real property in Ireland' Daniel needed to be naturalised as an Irishman and George, as High Sheriff, agreed to personally hand a letter to Francis Levenson Gower, the Chief Secretary, on their behalf.

George's public profile was slowly rising and by 1830 he was to be found acting as foreman of the Grand Jury of County Dublin and protesting to the Chief Secretary on such diverse and mundane matters as the granting of planning permission for houses without any space for accumulated refuse, and the exorbitant fees being imposed on the County by surgeons in respect of their attendance at coroner's inquests. Slowly, but surely, his legal career was being left behind. Daniel O'Connor's naturalisation would be one of the last legal cases he would take.

The only dark wing to be spread across Sophia's happiness that year was the death of her old friend, Lady Anna Maria Jones. She died at her home in Worting, in North Wales, on 7 July 1829 at the age of 80. Sophia at that time was in dispute with her brother Thomas, and her nephew, John, regarding the will of her late brother, Arthur. In all of this she was being advised, not by her husband, George, who was a lawyer by profession, but by George's brother, Joshua, who had by now assumed the position of tribal oracle on all matters legal. Joshua advised her, in January 1830, that she had nothing to fear from Thomas, and that the claims of her nephew in particular were spurious and ill-advised.

It was against the background of this battle of wills, that Sophia learnt from Anna Maria's younger sister,

Penelope Warren, that the continuing legal wranglings surrounding Arthur's will, were nothing to the trials that now faced Penelope Warren, for the spirited and highly intelligent Lady Jones had allowed herself to die intestate! Her adopted son, Augustus, in a letter to his wife,[25] gives some idea of the mess that had now fallen to her sisters to resolve:

'Dearest, dearest Mia. How providential our marriage took place when it did! Had it been delayed another month, it might not have taken place for years. My aunt, the most methodical of women, and possessing an amount of clear understanding which would have done credit to the best men of business, she, with all her minuteness of detail, has left two wills in the same envelope, and in such a state that it seems clear the second is good for nothing, and the chief question is, whether it invalidates the first. If it does, she has died, intestate; if it does not, her money goes almost entirely (for the greater part of it will certainly go) to the last possible persons in the world she would have wished.

And as for Worting, it is not even named; though she had promised it to Dr Warren, and, it is quite clear, meant to give it him. The last will, which has the signature obliterated, and "this to be burnt" written at the bottom, is dated as far back as 1821. The other is a will of 1809, when my sister was alive, and is chiefly in her favour. .... However, thank God! her life was spared long enough to carry into partial effect, her kind and generous intentions in my behalf.'

There would always be legal disputes surrounding the Evans and Parnell family wills, and Sophia would

---

[25] Hare, August C. *Memorials of a Quiet Life, Vol. 1 of 2* (Classic Reprint), Forgotten Books Ltd., London, 2018.

learn to deal with them with a pragmatic detachment. However, this particular dispute, for some reason that remains unclear, appears to have left a bitter aftertaste, especially with regard to the behaviour of her brother, Thomas. Whatever had gone on behind the scenes, it had left her feeling hurt and betrayed.

20

THE RIBBONMAN AND
THE ALLEY CHILD

PORTRANE WOULD NEVER be seriously affected by any of the outrages of Ribbonism, but that did not isolate the inhabitants of Mount Evans from the effects of it elsewhere.

The Ribbon Society – an agrarian secret organisation whose members consisted of rural Irish Catholics – had been formed in the early part of the century in response to the miserable conditions of tenant farmers and rural workers. The name of the movement derived from the green ribbon its members wore in their buttonholes. Its primary objective was to prevent landlords from evicting tenants, and others from taking the land of the dispossessed. Acts of violence were not uncommon.

In March 1830, quite out of the blue, Sophia Evans received two desperate visitors at her house in Portrane. They carried a written petition, asking her to use her influence with her husband. They wanted George to leverage his influence in the cause of a man facing the death penalty.

A servant took possession of the petition and noted on it that Mrs. Fitzpatrick and her companion, James Lalor, intended to wait for her reply. The letter (preserved in the National Archives in Dublin) read as follows;

'To Mistress Evans, wife of George Evans of Portrane in the County of Dublin, Esqr. – The humble petition of the bearer, Mrs. Anne Fitzpatrick, wife of John Fitzpatrick of Ardlea, in the Queen's County, one of your tenants there. Sheweth –

That Petitioner and ancestors were for the last century your tenants at Ardlea and Clonboyne in said County, and never were in arrear of rent, or committed any fault in said time, but preserved a strictly honest, pure, moral and religious character, which Petitioner presumes with humble deference and respect, makes room for the subject of the present petition. –

That on the night of the 4th February last, John Connor, a nephew of Petitioner, also a sub tenant of yours and James Lalor of Clonboyne aforesaid, was unfortunately found, or purposely made drunk to entrap him, and in such state forcibly pressed into a mob or party of Ribbonmen who put a pistol into his hand and forced him to the attack of Fingleton's house at Ballyknockin in the said County, where he and two others were taken and another that died, with others wounded. –

That said John Connor so taken and tried at the late assizes for the 20th February before Lord Plunkett and pleaded "Guilty" and submitted, whereupon sentence of death and execution on the 2nd of April next was recorded of him, who is the only one of your tenants implicated – and is the first of a large circle of relatives, your tenants, who have never done wrong or troubled your Honour. –

But Petitioner takes this very Journey to beseech your Ladyship, on her bended knees, to intercede to save his life, or commuted (if not otherwise) to transportation as it's the grave and convinced opinion of the Roman C. Clergy and of all intelligent persons, that this vile association is now dissolved and therefore human life, never again to be sacrificed needlessly by the humane Government of Ireland and Petitioner truly grateful will ever pray.

22ⁿᵈ March 1830,
James Lalor & Anne Fitzpatrick.'

Sophia immediately understood the urgency of the petition, and its purpose. The concept of the Royal Prerogative of Mercy had a long tradition in English law, and prior to 1837 the King still had the power of life and death over his subjects. In Ireland, that power was invested in the King's representative, the Lord Lieutenant.

No commoner was ever going to breach the wall of bureaucracy that surrounded the Lord Lieutenant on their own. Mrs. Fitzpatrick's desperate hope was that George, as High Sherriff, would have sufficient access to his secretaries to ensure her petition reached his desk.

Sophia immediately despatched a rider to George's office on Mount Street, and George subsequently made his way to Dublin Castle, where he personally delivered the petition to William Gregory, the Under Secretary. There was a covering letter:

'
No. 3 Lower Mount Street,
Tuesday.

Dear Sir,

I did myself the honour to wait on you this day to hand you the enclosed petition from the neighbourhood of Maryborough. Perfectly aware as I am of the press of business you have to encounter, I should not have requested your attention to it, had it not been a case of life or death ...

If there should be any extraordinary circumstances in the report of Lord Plunkett to his Majesty's Government in Ireland as to Connor's case, I am confident that it will be favourably considered by His Grace, the Duke of Northumberland ...

You will I hope pardon the liberty I take in requesting you will have the kindness to let me present the urgency of this application as Connor's friends are now in town awaiting the decision of the Irish Government.

*I have the honour to be Sir,
Your most humble servant,*

George Evans.'

Anne Fitzpatrick's letter referred to a court case that took place at the Queen's County Assizes during which three men, John Connor, William Delaney and Laurence Shorthall, were indicted on a charge of having assaulted the house of John Hanlon, of Ballyhelan, on the 4 February 1830, and made him promise to give up the land he occupied. The men were also charged with having fired on police at another location later that same night. When the charges were put to the prisoners, Connor pleaded guilty, but Delaney and Shorthall pleaded innocent and the trial continued without Connor.

According to the victim, John Hanlon, a party of men had forced open his door, knocked him down and made him promise to surrender land he occupied at

Ballyknocken, a mile distant from his dwelling house and two miles south of Rathleague. On cross-examination, Hanlon admitted that he had seen his attackers clearly and that none of the accused had been in that party. Another witness, kept in police protection, identified William Delaney as having been among the party of thirty-eight and that he had personally seen someone brandishing a pistol.

The party, having left Hanlon's house had allegedly been on their way to another when they were ambushed by police, at which point shots were fired. The police alleged the mob had fired first, and that they had merely returned fire. They also alleged that in the subsequent chase, sixty-year-old William Delaney had been stabbed in the back with a bayonet and nineteen-year-old Shorthall apprehended as he fled.

Courthouse at Maryborough (now Portlaoise), built 1805.

Since 1823, when parliament passed the Judgement of Death Act, judges had been given the power to reprieve the death sentence in all capital felony cases other than murder. As both men had previously been of good character the judge, Lord Plunket, indicated to the jury that he would be willing to receive a recommendation to mercy if they saw fit to make one. The jury of local landowners, took less than a minute to refuse. All three defendants were sentenced to hang on 2 April 1830. The decision caused a local outcry.

On 28 March, just five days before the executions were due to be carried out, Thomas B. Kelly, the High Sheriff of Queen's County wrote to William Gregory. Such was the present state of feeling in the county regarding the executions, that he feared a riot:

> *'... I conceive an additional military force will be necessary during the executions of Ribbonmen that are to take place in Maryboro' on the first and second of April.'*

Subsequent to the receipt of this letter, Gregory sent word to the Royal Hospital, ordering a detachment of the 7th Hussars to march immediately to Maryborough. The detachment was to consist of a captain, two subalterns and fifty non-combatant officers and privates. They were ordered to arrive in Maryborough by the first of April, and to remain there until ordered otherwise.

Laurence Shorthall's death sentence had already been commuted to transportation for life on account of his young age. But it would appear that there was to be no such reprieve for the man who had carried the pistol and no such person appears among the transportation records for that year. Given the size of the military detachment that had been despatched to Maryborough, not to mention the fact that the order to the 7th Hussars had been issued just three days before the planned executions, it would seem extremely unlikely that the executions would have been cancelled or that the only one of the alleged Ribbonmen to have carried and fired a pistol would have been pardoned. One must assume therefore, in the absence of any records to the contrary, that the intervention of George and Sophia Evans, had ultimately proved fruitless and that John Connor was hanged, as planned, with Delaney at Maryborough.

At about this same time George was also asked to exert his influence with his sister, Nancy Putland, in the famous 'Child of the Alley' case, as related in his memoirs by his good friend, the former magistrate, Frank Thorpe Porter:

> *'Amongst my personal recollections, there is one which I hope to narrate without ruffling or alarming the most sensitively delicate of my readers, although amongst the prominent characters of the scene about a dozen belonged to the most wretched and degraded portion of the female sex, and dwelt in a mean, loathsome, and disreputable locality named Cole Alley[26], which was, and perhaps still continues to be, occupied by denizens of a similar description. I shall apply to them the term adopted by Hood in his exquisite production of "The Bridge of Sighs," and designate them "unfortunates."*
>
> *I had been a magistrate for three or four years, when I was one day informed by the attendant of the police-court that a deputation of females from Cole Alley earnestly besought me to give them an audience. My colleagues were amused at the application, and ironically congratulated me on such an exclusive preference; but I determined to accede to the request, and directed them to be*

---

[26] Now called 'Meath Place' in Dublin's Liberties, off Meath Street.

admitted. About twelve of them entered the court, and amidst the "unfortunates" I perceived a female child of ten or eleven years of age. The spokeswoman of the party led this child forward, and addressed me to the following effect:—

"Yer worship, this poor little girl was born in the alley. She was not quite a year old when the collar (cholera) made a great sweep up there, and took off her mother, who was one of us. The child had no one to care for her, so we agreed to do the best we could for her, and we gave her a bit of food, a rag or two to cover her, and she lived about among us, so that we used to call her our own child. But now, yer worship, we see that she is coming to a time of life when to stay in the alley would be her destruction. We are doatingly fond of her, and it would be a heartscald to us all to think of her ever falling into our course of life. We would beg of you to have her put into some school or institution where she will be reared in decency, and trained to earn honest bread."

I at once stated to "the deputation" that I should do my utmost to realize their wishes, and that they might leave the child to my care. They embraced her most affectionately, and with the warmest thanks for my compliance, they departed. The Poor Law Unions had not been organized at the time, and I sent the child on a remand committal to the worthy matron of Grangegorman Prison, Mrs. Rawlins, with a note explaining the circumstances, and requesting that the little girl should be kept apart from the juvenile delinquents. My wishes were strictly complied with. On the following day, I dined at Portrane with the worthy George Evans. I mentioned the transaction to him, and he communicated it to his sister, Mrs. Putland. That lady was an impersonation of charity, and at once offered to have the "child of the alley" placed in one of the many institutions which she contributed to support. I regret that I am unable to state any further results, having omitted to make ulterior enquiries, but I have always considered the earnest application, perhaps I might fairly term it the supplication, of the Cole Alley "unfortunates" as the strongest acknowledgment, offered sincerely and spontaneously, by Vice of the superiority of Virtue.'

21

GEORGE ENTERS POLITICS

DANIEL O'CONNELL CREATED the pro-emancipation Catholic Association in 1823 as a pressure group against the British government. He followed this up the following year by founding the Catholic Rent, established in conjunction with the Catholic Church to raise funds to finance the Catholic Association. He then stood, in 1828, as an openly Catholic candidate in a by-election in County Clare against William Vesey Fitzgerald, a man who had just joined the British Cabinet as President of the Board of Trade.

Having won the seat, O'Connell was blocked from taking his seat by the necessity to take the Oath of Supremacy, which was incompatible with his Catholic faith. The Prime Minister, the Duke of Wellington, and the Home Secretary, Sir Robert Peel, though opposed to Catholic participation in Parliament, recognised that denying O'Connell his seat could lead to another rebellion or uprising in Ireland and convinced the King that Catholic emancipation and the right of all non-

192

Anglicans to sit in Parliament needed to be established. With the help of the Whigs, it became law in 1829.

In all of this both the Evans and Parnell families had been supportive of O'Connell. In 1826 Henry Parnell had even published his *New History of laws against Catholics.* George's politics, however, lay somewhat to the left of Henry's. But they also lay considerably to the right of his late father's, a fact only too readily observable even at this inchoate stage of formal political engagement, by a letter he wrote to the editor of the Dublin Evening Post:[27]

> *Sir – I had the pleasure of reading the admirable letter of Lord Westmeath, relative to a subscription for the wounded, and the widows and children of those who so nobly distinguished themselves in the late glorious struggle that took place in Paris. I had intended to have remitted my subscription to my friends in France, but wishing also that the subscription should succeed in this country, I take the liberty of placing in your hands £25 for that purpose. Though a humble individual, I feel deeply interested in the success of the Revolution, not merely in relation to France itself, but as necessarily being the precursor of institutions for the well-being of mankind, more in unison with the present state of the civilized world.*
>
> *I have the honour to be your obedient servant,*
> *GEORGE EVANS.*
>
> *Portrane, August 8, 1830.*

The revolution referred to above was the second French Revolution, also known as the 'July Revolution' or 'Three Glorious Days'. It led to the overthrow of King

---

[27] Waterford Chronicle, Saturday 14 August 1830, p.4.

Charles X, the French Bourbon monarch, and the ascent of his cousin Louis Philippe, who had sat in the first Revolution's Convention as 'Philippe Egalité'. The revolution had been triggered primarily by the imposition of the death penalty for anyone profaning the Eucharist and the provision of financial indemnities for properties confiscated by the 1789 Revolution to anyone who had been declared 'enemies of the revolution'.

This second revolution was a landmark in European history for it marked the replacement of the principle of hereditary right with that of popular sovereignty and a constitutional monarchy. It also, quite neatly, marked the boundaries of George's liberal philosophy and political allegiances, at least so far as he expressed them following his marriage to Sophia. Indeed it proved something of a godsend, for it allowed the Reform movement to argue that, unless change was quickly forthcoming, a modern revolution could well happen in Britain. The King, and the Tory prime minister, disagreed, and their popularity evaporated.

George Evans believed that Ireland was economically better off within the British Empire, or rather that she would be exceptionally vulnerable outside of it. It is doubtful that he would have felt comfortable articulating such views while his father, that giant enhaloed monument to family pride, still cast his living shadow over family affairs. But Hampden Evans was dead now, and George was his own man. The solution to poverty, he believed, lay in education and economic growth, the solution to corruption in reform of the electoral system. Everything else was a secondary concern.

By November 1830 Wellington was gone and the first Whig government since the French Revolution took its seats in the House of Commons, elected on promises of parliamentary reform, and led by a prime minister, Charles Grey, who had unsuccessfully attempted a Reform Bill some forty years previous. The

Reform movement, it appeared, was gathering a head of steam, and George Evans was enthused.

The evolution of the Reform movement proved to be an extraordinary development in British politics, and most especially in Ireland where, for the first time since 1798, it managed to unite the middle and working classes, both Catholic and Protestant, around a shared goal of democratising parliamentary representation and challenging the power of the Tory-Anglican local elites. But as the first Reform bill of the new government was defeated in the House of Lords, riots broke out all over the north of England and south Wales and George worried that the movement in Ireland could similarly descend into violence.

With Reform associations and political unions being revived all over the kingdom by middle-class and moderate veterans of the Peterloo period, George decided that it was important for people like him to be represented within the movement and seen to support its aims. He even spoke publicly at the County Dublin Reform Meeting that took place at Kilmainham Courthouse on Saturday, 3 December 1831. Waxing enthusiastically about the non-sectarian nature of the movement, he proposed a motion calling for that continuing to be the case.

Also attending that meeting was Daniel O'Connell, who Sophia's brother, Henry, had recently recommended to public office, suggesting his appointment as Master of the Rolls. Following the passing of the Act of Emancipation, O'Connell, had set his sights on higher goals than simple parliamentary reform. He was now intent on repealing the Act of Union, and returning Ireland to a position of legislative independence under the British Crown, i.e. with an Irish parliament sitting in Dublin and with full Catholic involvement.

While George was broadly supportive of Repeal, the possible economic effects of leaving the Empire at this moment in time worried him. In such a situation, he believed, Reform should take priority and declared that he would only vote for Repeal at the current time should the Reform movement fail.[28] In voicing these opinions, George set himself immediately at odds with O'Connell.

The *Repeal Association* that O'Connell founded proceeded to select candidates to be put forward at the United Kingdom general election of 1832, but in north County Dublin they found themselves faced with a totally unexpected challenge. Sophia Evans had finally managed to persuade her husband to stand for parliament.

'She induced and aided her husband to contest and win the representation of the county from the Tories, and for many years Mr. Evans sat in Parliament, affording on all occasions, loyal help to the Whigs, and now and then a modified support to O'Connell. Mrs. Evans was as a Mme. Roland in all his political work.'

Boston Post, 26 December 1885.

Despite the fact that George was due to take his master's examinations just a month before the polls opened, and the fact that his twenty-one-year-old nephew, William Lawless, son of his younger sister, Mary, had recently been seriously injured in a shooting accident at Portrane[29] – an accident that had caused George to suffer a 'bilious attack' from which he was slow to recover – George proceeded to declare his candidacy. His manifesto was carried in the pages of the *Freeman's Journal*:

'Having neither personal interests to advance, nor any object of ambition to attain, my future actions

---

[28] *Limerick Evening Post* - Friday 07 December 1832, p.4.
[29] *Morning Advertiser* - Saturday 13 October 1832 p.1.

will continue to be guided, as my past have been, solely by what I honestly conceive to be for the advantage of my native country. My watch words of Parliamentary duty will be Education, Economy, and equal rights to all.'

The education of the poor, especially the education of poor females, was Sophia's primary political passion at this time and it is interesting to note that it takes primary place now, in George's election manifesto, ahead of even his own particular bugbears of economy and universal suffrage.

Sophia had been hoping and planning for this for years. As far back as 1816, there is even evidence that she had been directing George in his political education and trying to steer him away from the extreme politics of his father. In letter to her in August of that year George confessed to having been unable to suppress a smile when he came to a passage in a biography of Benjamin Franklin that she had thought 'unfit' for his perusal.

There would have been few women of Sophia's day, who would have read Benjamin Franklin's biography, or any other political biographies for that matter, and just the mention of the fact that she felt there were passages within it that she would rather her husband did not read, would suggest that politics was a subject that was very much a hot topic in their household, and in their relationship. Given her upbringing, it could scarcely have been otherwise.

On George's behalf, though very much motivated by her own ambitions for him, Sophia developed a network of political and journalistic contacts, drew upon her own intelligence and family experience, and helped to manage her husband's campaign. His election agent even began to lobby the new Chief Secretary, Edward Smith Stanley, on the inconvenience to freeholders in north County Dublin having to travel to Kilmainham to register as voters.

For a first-time candidate, and an independent to boot, George's campaign was run with extraordinary professionalism and attention to detail.

There was, however, a fly in the ointment. George was not totally opposed to the repeal of the Act of Union, but there were many local landlords who were, not least his neighbour Charles Cobbe. As voting at this time still had to be made in public, a tenant who voted against the wishes of his landlord could well expect to feel the consequences and George was only too well aware that he needed the votes of his neighbours' tenants to be elected.

George opted, therefore, to sit on the fence and openly declare that, while he was not totally opposed to repeal of the Union, he believed that the country was 'not at present sufficiently united to hazard a separation from England'. That August, O'Connell discussed George's stance in a letter to a supporter:

'I have been sedulously canvassed to volunteer my little services for George Evans who seeks the County of Dublin. The hesitation on his part however to declare for the Repeal has so far compelled me to decline conceding whatever assistance it is in my power to give him. It must be admitted that he is among the best Irishmen of his caste that could be indicated in these or other days and I think his return matter of good certainly.

Numbers of his supporters regret his coquetting (for it may be called so) on the great question but profess their personal attachment to him to be such as to induce them to give him a respite on the Repeal. He takes advantage of Stauntons' 'golden mean'[30] for giving the go-bye to the pledge by offering, when the measure shall be brought

---

[30] An irrational number like pi and e, whose terms go on forever after the decimal point without repeating.

forward, to resign his seat at the 'requisition' of the majority of his constituents provided he shall not decide on supporting it.

This proposal is one in which evasion can obviously be practised with great success. The machinery is cumbrous and how is the question as to the majority to be ascertained? Occur what may, the Anglesey Party rejoice greatly at having such a candidate [Evans] for the Metropolitan County and they at least feel assured of his triumph.'

Supported in his canvass of County Dublin by the Whig peer, Lord Lansdowne, who addressed a circular to his tenants urging that they vote for Evans, George was elected for Co. Dublin on 22 December 1832. Of all his vocal and enthusiastic supporters, there was none more pleased for him than his wife. Perhaps a little too pleased. Observing Sophia's delight, Lady Morgan, on 5 January 1834, recorded in her diary that found Sophia Evans to be:

'a first-rate woman, but, perhaps, too ambitious about her husband's parliamentary career.'

A tad caustic, perhaps, for a woman who in her diary just a few days previous had numbered Sophia amongst her oldest friends:

'January 2. – Kildare Street. We had a cordial household, hospitable time at Malahide – all old friends – the Talbots – the Evans of Portran, my old lover and friend, Edward Moore. The fine old Castle is always my delight.'

George never did become a Repealer and his continuous 'coquetting' following his election managed to so infuriate O'Connell that the spat between them

Daniel O'Connell

soon became intensely heated and personal. But despite O'Connell's campaign of intimidation, George held his nerve and stuck to his guns. His persistent ambiguity may have helped to get him elected, but the storm of criticism it brought upon him did not simply evaporate once the election was over. In January 1834, at a public meeting in Rathmines, O'Connell exposed George's stance to such public ridicule that his remarks were carried in the national press:

> *'I once heard of a woman who, seeing a man executed for forgery, put on a resolution that her eleven sons should never learn to write. Now, it would be well for George Evans if he had not been taught writing, and his mother was not an honest woman to allow him to be instructed. He says he will contribute to the abolition of tithes. So far so well. It is putting his best leg foremost: but I fear he is ham-strung in the other. There is a large class standing up for the continuance of the tithe system – the men who, by peculation and robbery, fatten on the miseries of the poor – and we are not as divided on Repeal as we are on the abolition of tithes.*
>
> *George Evans gives the same reason for opposing the Repeal, and aiding in the abolition of tithes. There's a fellow for you! I think the next time you are choosing a Representative you will discard him. (Cheers) As many as are of that opinion will say 'aye' – the contrary will say 'no' (Loud cries of 'aye'). The ayes have it – carried unanimously. (Cheers and laughter). I verily believe that there never was more folly than in the letter of George Evans; and it is a deplorable and sad condition for the metropolitan county to be represented by one of the Cloncurry clique ...'*

George Evans disliked O'Connell. He considered him autocratic, vainglorious, and more than a little presumptuous in claiming to speak for *all* sections of Irish society. He particularly disliked O'Connell's attitude towards the landed gentry, which he found more than a little hypocritical, given that O'Connell himself was far from underprivileged. Stung by the increasingly personal nature of the attacks, he accused O'Connell of trying to silence 'men of property and education'.

O'Connell, of course, was having none of it. He knew his public and was never afraid to play to the gallery. He dismissed George as nothing more than 'a landlord and a Whig'. Indeed, George could hardly have expected less from a man who could sign his letters as 'Daniel O'Connell, Liberator of Ireland' and who at one time or another had fallen out with almost every other nationalist politician with whom he had disagreed.

Truth be told, the Evans family had always been much more than liberal-minded landlords. George's father, Hampden, had been a member of the Society of United Irishmen and a friend of such revolutionary figures as Lord Edward Fitzgerald, Thomas Addis Emmet, Archibald Hamilton Rowan and Theobald Wolfe Tone.

Like many other Protestants inspired by the French and American revolutions, Hampden Evans had been quick to volunteer and when the Society evolved into a paramilitary organisation. He had not only served in the Rotunda Division during the rebellion of 1798, but had hosted Society committee meetings at his home in Portrane. That rebellion had failed miserably. A French army sent to assist the revolution was overwhelmed by British forces and Hampden was betrayed by a certain Thomas Boyle, who implicated him, along with a Father Teeling of Donabate, in a plot to assassinate Lord Carhampton, the commander-in-chief of the British army in Ireland.

Following his arrest and imprisonment, Hampden had been facing execution when he was granted a last-minute reprieve on condition that he went into voluntary exile in Germany. Later allowed to move to Paris on grounds of ill-health, he set up home with his wife and daughters in a house on the Boulevard des Invalides, where he continued to entertain many of his old colleagues, including the Wicklow rebel, Myles Byrne and Thomas Addis Emmet. Such impeccable patriotic and revolutionary credentials, however, cut little ice with Daniel O'Connell, who was a committed pacifist.

Despite his father's nationalist instincts, George Evans had somehow managed to avoid getting caught up in the rebellion of 1798 and had remained in Ireland to take care of the family estates until 1812, when Hampden was finally given permission to return. He had inherited the estate outright upon Hampden's death in 1820 and from that point onwards had always chosen to express his patriotism and responsibilities as a landlord in an understated and apolitical manner. He was not, and would never be, a risk taker.

George's personal brand of nationalism was always weighted more heavily towards some form of devolved government and constitutional monarchy than independence. There were enormous economic benefits to had from remaining part of the British Empire that he was reluctant to see lost. He also happened to enjoy London society, and the privileged trappings of his parliamentary seat. As did his wife. But for all that, George Evans still considered himself an Irishman and his loyalty remained first and foremost to his country and to his constituents.

At the time of O'Connell's rebuke, George and Sophia were personally financing the education of local Catholic children and pensioning the poorest of the elderly population of Ballisk to prevent them falling into destitution. George was also, privately and confidentially, donating to the building of Catholic churches within the city of Dublin, a confidence that one parish priest felt compelled to break following

O'Connell's attack on his character:

> *'Dear Sir, I feel a considerable degree of reluctance in trespassing on the space of your journal; but gratitude towards a good man compels to seek this favour. This is the third time, within a short space I have had to acknowledge donations of five pounds from Mr. George Evans, of Portrane, towards the building of chapels in this parish. Yet he possesses not a rood of ground in it; nor do I recollect having at any time having done any act to deserve this peculiar attention.*
>
> *The manner of doing an act often enhances its value; and, when I say that Mr. Evans himself was the bearer of his donation, during my absence last week, at the Retreat, I cannot but esteem his act, not merely as a benefit to the parish, but as compliment to the station which I hold. Mr. Evans is a public man. If public men be public property, their private virtues cannot be uninteresting to society. Edification is due from men of station to the public; and. whenever the occasion presents itself, even the private virtues of public individuals should be recorded for the good of society.'*[31]

Though O'Connell knew of all this, and of other acts of atypical liberalism, he still persisted with his personal attacks. George was deeply wounded. 'I belong to no party,' he famously hit back, 'I have no object in view but the happiness and prosperity of Ireland'. He would sooner, or so he claimed with a slyly oblique reference to his family's revolutionary past, 'be doomed to perpetual exile than submit to such a tyranny'.

In her memoirs, Lady Morgan sympathetically recalled George's plight, describing him as:

---

[31] *Dublin Mercantile Advertiser*, Monday 24 July 1837, p.1.

*'the butt and victim of all O'Connell's hatred,
malice and calumny, because he will not crawl
after him and resists his appeal.'*

Such is the nature of politics, however, that just five
months later, George Evans and Daniel O'Connell
managed to put the matter of Repeal behind them,
enough, at any rate, to jointly form the Anti-Tory
Association in Dublin. O'Connell's campaign of public
vilification, however, was never entirely forgotten, at
least not by Sophia.

On 12 May 1835, in a letter to Harriet Grote, wife of
George Grote, the English political radical and
classical historian, Sophia's resentment was palpable:

*'Evans quite agrees with your views, but adds
O'Connell and his adherents to the evils we have
to contend with. Our position makes us more
susceptible of O'Connell's influence than you can
be in England. We feel it is one which blasts and
withers whatever it approaches, and that nothing
good will ever come to maturity near its
pestilence.'[32]*

George, meanwhile, continued to campaign on a
platform of Reform, and in particular the issue of the
secret ballot, which he believed would be essential to
the eventual liberation of tenants from the claws of
their landlords. In the run up to the general election of
1837, speaking at the registration of candidates at
Kilmainham he declared:

*'... I will say this, that I never, since the first time I
went into parliament, ceased to advocate vote by
ballot. I will make a few observations as to the*

---

[32] Grote, Mrs. Harriet. *The Personal Life of George Grote*, John
Murray, London 1873, p.105.

utility of that question. If the ballot was introduced the county electors of England would return Liberal members to represent them in Parliament, and I will explain why.

On the discussion on the Reform Bill, Lord Chandos introduced a clause, enabling every man paying £50 a year rent to vote for members, although he should be a tenant at will; and every man thus situated is completely under the thumb of his landlord, as my footman is under mine. If the ballot were in operation they would vote for their country, but they cannot do so at present.[33]

As George committed himself to national politics, Sophia, too, began to commit herself to the only form of social activism that was available to women of her class – that of supporting charities. Along with George's sister, Nancy, she began to take on committee roles with various charities about the city and to become a dutiful attendee at fund-raising sermons, balls and bazaars. As the wife of an M.P., it would have been expected of her, but it could not have been easy for a woman of her essentially private disposition.

From the moment she had arrived at Mount Evans, Sophia had been as remote a character to her tenants as the abbess of an enclosed order. She had not exactly renounced the world, rather had become extremely selective in her engagement with it. She enjoyed socialising, as long as she was accompanied by George, but so loathed being left too long in entirely female company that she rarely, if ever, accompanied her husband on shooting expeditions, during which the men would be gone for long hours and their wives and daughters obliged to spend extensive periods in idle conversation with each other while they awaited their return.

––––––

[33] *Dublin Weekly Register* - Saturday 12 August 1837, p.7.

In all of her new activity, Sophia's saviour was Nancy Putland. Nancy could always be relied upon to take up the social slack. They grew quite close as a result, each coming to depend upon the other's strengths as a foil for their own shortcomings.

22

THE DARWINS

THE SPAT WITH O'Connell notwithstanding, the years following George's election saw Sophia return to a social circle she had not experienced since her tour of France in 1802. She travelled now on an annual basis to London for the 'season', which took place between the months of February and July to coincide with the sitting of parliament. London was home from home. She still had her house on Welbeck Street.

It was during these trips that Sophia and George became good friends with the Darwin family, and most especially with Erasmus Darwin, older brother of the famous naturalist, Charles. In years gone by George and Sophia had once attempted to get her brother Arthur to attend Erasmus' father, Robert Waring Darwin, at his practice in Shrewsbury, but Arthur had refused to go. The families were not exactly strangers.

Despite a thirty-two year age difference, George Evans and Erasmus Darwin had recently become close, and both George and Sophia enjoyed hearing his

208

reports of his brother Charles' voyage aboard *The Beagle*. Sophia was especially interested in his discoveries, for she was something of an amateur naturalist herself. The voyage of *The Beagle* seemed of a type with the adventures that Lady Jones was wont to describe to her from her time in India; adventures that Sophia herself would have loved to have undertaken.

> *'One of her pursuits was conchology. She succeeded in making a unique collection of Irish shells, in specimens of which her beautiful shore was singularly rich.'*
>
> Boston Post, 26 December 1885.

Through their friendship with Erasmus, Sophia and George would also become good friends of his sisters, Caroline and Catherine. Caroline was the second eldest of the Darwin sisters, and Catherine the baby of the family, ten years Caroline's junior. In her early teens, Caroline had taken charge of Charles and Catherine's education and the younger pair had once competed for her affection. Following their mother's death, in 1817, Caroline had more or less become a surrogate mother to them.

Caroline Darwin was a formidable woman, made older than her years by her teenage experience of child-rearing. At thirty-three years of age, she was perhaps more in tune with fifty-year-old Sophia, than her twenty-two-year-old sister Catherine. In contrast to their more libertine brother, Erasmus, the Darwin sisters were extremely moral and pious, not exactly the type of company in which Sophia could discuss or debate her privately held beliefs. But they got along famously, and would remain friends for years.

As a result of these friendships Sophia and George would often find themselves mentioned in letters received by Charles Darwin aboard *The Beagle*. In the

Caroline Darwin

first of these, sent by Caroline on May of 1833, she mentions that Erasmus is spending quite a lot of time in their company.

'We heard from Erasmus who seems very happy & seemingly leading a dissipated life for him. Mr. & Mrs. Evans of Portrane are in London & he sees a good deal of them. Mr. Evans is in Parliament for the County of Dublin.'

Caroline Darwin, 1 May 1833.

Erasmus Darwin was part of a social set that included the likes of Charles Dickens, Robert Browning and George Everest, and his free time in London was generally spent making the rounds of the type of intellectual or literary dinner parties that George and Sophia Evans had long since become accustomed to in Dublin. But it was not Erasmus' literary friends that were occupying the minds of his friends and family at this time, rather his unusually intense friendship with his first cousin's wife!

In May of 1833, Catherine Darwin and her thirty-one-year-old sister, Susan, paid a visit to London and took lodgings on Regent Street, to be close to Erasmus. During this visit Catherine wrote to Charles about her eldest brother's love life. Erasmus, she claimed, had been 'carrying on' with Fanny Wedgwood, wife of their first cousin, barrister and etymologist, Hensleigh Wedgwood. In this same letter, she also took the time to mention George and Sophia Evans.

> *'We see a great deal of Erasmus now, as our lodgings are not very far from his, and he is good natured and pleasant, we enjoy it very much ... He seems to be more in love than ever with Fanny Hensleigh, and almost lives at Clapham. Papa has long been alarmed for the consequences, and expects to see an action in the papers ...*
>
> *Do you remember the Evans of Portrane in Ireland? Mr. Evans is Member for the County of Dublin, so they are in London, and are very nice friends for us. We are going with them and a large party down to Richmond by steam on Saturday, dine there, and return in the Evening. – Mrs. Evans enquired very much after you, and said that she could not conceive any thing she should enjoy more than your Voyage.'*

Catherine Darwin, 29 May 1833.

In August of 1833, the Italian composer and virtuoso violinist, Niccolò Paganini, came to London to play a series of concerts and all of London society flocked to see him. Tickets for the concerts were highly prized and such was the demand that an extra concert was hastily added. It took place on Thursday, 8 August at the Theatre Royal.

Amongst the most memorable pieces he played that night, and which the young Emma Wedgwood, sister of the married woman with whom Erasmus was currently involved, recorded in her diary, was his single-string *Variations 'St Patrick's Day' sur un Theme Irlandais,* reason enough on its own for the Irish in London to flock to see him.

Immediately following that Thursday night concert, Sophia Evans and a certain Mrs Amelia Warren announced their intention to travel to Surrey the following Saturday morning to visit Beulah Spa. As they had an almost empty carriage at their disposal, they invited Emma Wedgwood to join them (Amelia Warren and her husband Charles had been friends of Emma's parents for almost thirty years). There was a considerable age gap between Emma and the two old married ladies who had issued the invitation, but the offer was too good to turn down and the journey could be made all the more enjoyable had she someone closer to her own age to chat with. And so Emma invited the author, Harriet Martineau, to join the party. Harriet had been an occasional visitor to the Dawson's home since she arrived in London and was well known to Emma's cousin, Erasmus Darwin.

Harriet Martineau was thirty-one when she first began to orbit the Evans' social circle in London. Sophia was fifty-three. They were hardly peers, but while everything points to their first introduction having been made by Emma Wedgwood, who had been acquainted with Harriet Martineau since at least March of 1833, it could so easily have been via a

Emma Wedgwood (later Mrs. Charles Darwin).

number of other routes, not least through Sophia's brothers William and Henry, who were, like Martineau, well-acquainted with Thomas Malthus, or even through Sophia's husband who, as an Irish pro-Reform M.P., Harriet would have had much to speak about at that time.

Sophia and Harriet may even have met before, Harriet having spent the summer of 1831 in Dublin visiting her brother James and his wife, Helen. James was at that time ministering as co-pastor at the Eustace Street Unitarian Chapel in Dublin.

Harriet Martineau was something of a celebrity. Having begun her literary career in 1821 writing anonymous articles for the *Monthly Repository*, amongst which was her feminist treatise *On Female Education*, she had since been forced by financial necessity to dip her toes in the waters of economics. Her first commissioned book, *Illustrations of Political Economy*, was a fictional tutorial written in the form of parables and intended to help the general public understand the ideas of Adam Smith. It had only been published in February of the previous year, but was already out-selling the work of Charles Dickens. Harriet had also, as luck would have it, recently worked herself into a state of poor health as she struggled to satisfy the demands of her publisher.[34] She needed a break.

Beulah Spa was a natural saline spring that had become one of the great tourist attractions of the Victorian age. Just an hour's drive from London by horse and carriage, it was said to have water that was more pure than the West Country spas, and to contain more salts than the health-improving waters of Cheltenham. But like many spas at the time, Beulah could not rely entirely on the proceeds of the 'taking of the waters' and since 1831 it had been simultaneously operating as a place of entertainment.

The gardens at Beulah had been designed by Decimus Burton and the scenic views that were to be had from various locations about the thirty acres of grounds had been enhanced by the construction of many 'rustic edifices'. There was also a circus ring, a rosery, an upper and lower lake with water fowl, a maze, an 'orchestra' and a *camera obscura* with a telescope powerful enough to see Windsor Castle thirty miles away.

---

[34] Emma Wedgwood-Darwin's diary. CUL-DAR242. Aug 9-10, 1833.

Beulah Spa, Norwood. Image courtesy of Wellcome Collection.

Entertainments, which were controlled by the clerk at the entrance lodge, included minstrels who serenaded lovers, concerts daily by military bands, dancing, astrology, acrobatics, archery (bows and arrows provided), fireworks and illuminations with myriads of polychromatic lamps. Beulah was, in many respects, the Disneyworld of its day; a perfect place for respectable young ladies to meet eligible young gentlemen. Given the thirty year age gap, it is more than possible that Sophia and Amelia acted as chaperones.

But if Harriet Martineau intrigued Sophia Evans, it was nothing to the effect she had on Erasmus Darwin. They had much in common. Both had suffered greatly with childhood illnesses, and both continued to suffer from the consequences, Harriet having lost her sense of taste and smell, and much of her hearing as a child. Erasmus, for his part, was so prone to illness and lethargy that he was thought incapable of holding down a profession and had been 'retired' on a pension just four years previous, at the age of twenty-six. His more famous brother, Charles, described Erasmus as a man possessing:

> '... a remarkably clear mind, with extensive & diversified tastes & knowledge in literature, art, & even in science. For a short time he collected & dried plants, & during a somewhat longer time experimented in chemistry. He was extremely agreeable, & his wit often reminded me of that in the letters & works of Charles Lamb. He was very kind-hearted; but his health from his boyhood had been weak, & as a consequence he failed in energy. His spirits were not high, sometimes low, more especially during early & middle manhood. He read much, even whilst a boy, & at school encouraged me to read, lending me books.'

Erasmus, on the face of it, would seem to have had far more in common with Sophia Evans than her husband George and, truth be told, Erasmus had always been more relaxed in female company than male, especially educated, stimulating and empathetic female company. Sophia, for her part, had suffered a debilitating and life-threatening illness as a child and in all probability understood Erasmus better than his own family, there being a sense of collegiality to be found in the sympathetic affinity of pasty-faced invalids. The pair, crucially, also shared a sense of humour that has been variously described as 'dry' and 'cynical'; a subversive trait that may well have had its roots in the same field.

On 1 September 1833, Caroline wrote to Charles on *The Beagle*. Once again the news was all about Erasmus, and about Sophia and George Evans, who at that time were planning to take a holiday in Scotland and trying to encourage Erasmus to come with him (in an attempt, perhaps, to wean him from his attachment to Fanny Wedgwood). Erasmus refused to bite. He was, he declared, not overly enamoured with the company that Sophia Evans was keeping:

'We staid at Osmaston about 10 days & when we came back Erasmus came home and has been with us ever since. I think he will go no expedition this summer but return to London when he leaves us. Mrs. Evans of Portrane wanted to persuade him to go with her into Scotland, & I believe he would if he had not discovered there were to be some young ladies of the party who he disliked. He is very constant to Mrs Hensleigh Wedgwood & thinks her the nicest of women – She and Hensleigh were staying here last week with their baby who they are very fond of, & Erasmus with all his horror of babies plays with the little thing and watches it for any length of time...'

Caroline Darwin, 1 September 1833

The young ladies referred to above were almost certainly the 'Misses Warren', daughters of Mrs. Charles Warren of Sundridge in Kent, for they would be listed among the Evans' tour group when they booked into the Royal Hotel in Inverness later that September. The father of the Misses Warren, Charles Warren, was a Commissioner of Bankrupts and a colleague of George's brother, Joshua. He was also a brother-in-law to Sophia's friend, Penelope Warren, younger sister of Lady Jones.

Harriet Martineau in 1833.

In order to prevent an 'action in the papers' attempts were made to pair Erasmus off with Emma Wedgwood, but little came of this ill-conceived matchmaking and Emma would eventually marry Erasmus' younger brother, Charles. As the summer drew to a close, however, Erasmus developed a new romantic interest, in Harriet Martineau, a woman considered by many today to have been the first ever female sociologist.

Harriet would go on to become quite famous for her journalistic contributions on a vast number of controversial issues that engaged Victorian society and during the time Sophia spent in her company, she would have guaranteed lively and stimulating conversation of a kind that must surely have reminded Sophia of Sophie de Condorcet. Harriet's radical stances on such issues as education, women's rights or the abolition of slavery, were not a million miles away from those of the Parisian *salonnière*.

At the time she met Sophia, Harriet was just about clinging to the remnants of her Unitarian faith. Thirteen years later, however, following a trip to the Middle East to study the evolution of religions, she would become increasingly sceptical of religious beliefs, including her own liberal Unitarianism. Her avowal of atheism in the *Letters on the Laws of Man's Nature and Development* (1851) that she co-authored with Henry George Atkinson, would scandalize Victorian Society almost as much as Charles Darwin's *On the Origin of Species* eight years later.

Martineau's ability to earn enough through book sales to support herself – a rare enough feat for a woman of her day – was not something that was universally lauded in polite society. Her incipient radicalism, furthermore, did not sit well with the pious Darwin sisters, and they considered her a bad influence on their brother. Sophia, doubtlessly, viewed things differently, but she kept her opinions to herself and the Darwin sisters, in consequence, would remain friends and continue to visit with her until at least April 1840.

In October 1836, *The Beagle* returned to England and Charles Darwin returned for a while to Cambridge before settling in London, where he proceeded to share a house with Erasmus. Charles Darwin had only visited Ireland once before, in April 1827, when he travelled to Belfast and Dublin, shortly after

Erasmus Alvey Darwin

Reproduced with permission from John van Wyhe ed. 2002-. The
Complete Work of Charles Darwin Online.
(http://darwin-online.org.uk/)

abandoning his medical studies in Edinburgh. But he had not met with either George or Sophia Evans on that occasion, and they would have had little reason to call on him unannounced, or to issue an invitation for him to visit.

But things were different now. George and Sophia had developed a close friendship with Erasmus, and with his sisters, Caroline and Catherine. Desperate for an introduction, they saw in Catherine the better instrument for achieving it, for Erasmus had by then more or less disappeared from their social set. Using the excuse of passing on some news of Charles, received from Mrs Warren, they pleaded for an introduction. In February 1837, in a letter to Charles, Catherine attempted to procure one for them:

> '*I want you to see the Evans sometime; they are at Ibbotson's Hotel and Mr. Evans talked much about you, and how much he wished to see you; he had heard of you from Mrs. Warren[35], who had heard again from Mr. Lyell[36]. – Pray write us an account of your London trip, when you return to the quiet of Cambridge.*'

Catherine Darwin, 16 February 1837.

It is not known whether George and Sophia ever got to meet Charles Darwin, either formally or informally. What we do know, is that by the time Catherine wrote her letter, Erasmus had forsaken the usual round of intellectual dinner parties to spend morning, noon and night with Harriet Martineau. In a letter to his sister,

---

[35] Unidentified. Possibly the wife of Charles Turner Warren, or Penelope Warren, sister of Lady Jones and wife of Dr. Pelham Warren, fellow of The Royal Society. Most likely the former, with whom Sophia had travelled to Beulah Spa in 1833.
[36] Charles Lyell, pioneering geologist and Secretary of The Royal Society.

Charles Darwin

Caroline, on 9 November 1836, Charles would describe the couple's somewhat hectic and oddly intense relationship as being more akin to master and slave than husband and wife:

> *'Erasmus is just returned from driving out Miss Martineau.— Our only protection from so admirable a sister-in-law is in her working him too hard ... How pale & woe begone he will look.— She already takes him to task about his idleness— She is going some day to explain to him her notions about marriage — Perfect equality of rights is part of her doctrine. I much doubt whether it will be equality in practice.'*

Two years later, in April 1838, Charles would be describing Harriet Martineau as 'frisky lately as a rhinoceros'. It seems likely, therefore, that Erasmus no longer had much time to devote to his Irish friends, or that an invitation was likely to be forthcoming from that quarter and, as his relationship with Harriet deepened, he began to drift apart from his old friends, George and Sophia Evans included.

The following summer Martineau's health broke down during a visit to the continent. Fearing a tumour she retired to solitary lodgings in Tynemouth near her brother. In Erasmus' absence her ardour cooled, and while they would remain friendly, they too eventually drifted apart.

If George and Sophia's desire to meet with Charles Darwin was never satisfied, Sophia could at least harvest some consolation from the privileges that attached to being the wife of an Irish M.P. As part of the 'London Season' she would make occasional visits to St. James' Palace for those 'Drawing Room' occasions at which women of the nobility and gentry would be presented to the Queen.

Sophia had been presented to Queen Adelaide in May 1834 by the Countess of Rosse and she returned, in October 1836, to present a Mrs J. Wood. Two years later again, she would be presented to the youthful and hopeful Victoria by Hester Catherine Browne, the Marchioness of Sligo. Such grand occasions served only to stoke Sophia's ambition or, more accurately, her ambition for her husband. Her father and eldest brother had been knighted and had achieved high office. Why not George?

Her beloved husband, belatedly ambitious at the grand old age of age of sixty-six, was still as handsome as ever. The passage of time had been kind to him, exaggerating rather than diminishing his patrician features. He was as much in love with her as ever, and she still strangely insecure. In October 1837, while on a hunting trip to Dinwiddie Lodge near Lockerbie, he replied to one of her letters:

> *'It is now upwards of 32 years since I had the happiness of joining you and never in all that time had I a day's uneasiness as far as relates to you, or one hour's regret. Your society has been a consolation to me in every shade of life.'*

23

HENRY'S SUICIDE

DESPITE THE FACT that O'Connell would make funds from the Repeal Association available to George Evans for the general election of 1841, George would ultimately lose his seat to the Tory candidate. It probably did not help his broader appeal that in a letter to the *Freeman's Journal* – on July twelfth of all dates – he had described Queen Victoria as 'The Queen of Ireland'. His last-minute appeal to the Tory heartland failed to convince and an increasingly polarised electorate struggled to understand what George actually stood for.

Subsequently appointed to the Privy Council of Ireland and the Central Loan Fund Board of Ireland, George now found himself on the fringes of political life. But whatever disappointment Sophia may have endured as a result of her husband's demotion, it quickly paled against the tragic events that followed.

On the morning 8 June 1842, Sophia's brother, Sir Henry Parnell, while in residence at his Chelsea

225

Sir Henry Brooke Parnell

townhouse at Cadogan Place, failed to come down to breakfast following a visit from his hairdresser. A couple of minutes after midday, afraid that something was amiss, his valet, Isaac Manning, went up his bedroom to enquire on him. He found him hanging from his bedpost by his cravat in what appeared to be an act of suicide.

Manning called John Parnell, Henry's eldest son, who was in the dining-room and the body was hastily cut down. A surgeon was sent for, and arrived ten minutes later. Bleeding was attempted, but Henry was quite gone. At the subsequent inquest, John Parnell explained that his father had become delirious on 1 April, and that his servants had been so worried that they had sent for him. He had arrived on 7 April:

'As soon as I came here, I found that a strict watch was required in his room, and that he was not to he left to himself; if I went away the servant was to be there or my brother. Someone was to be in his room continually. I did not, for several days, understand why this was. But in a few days, when my father got better, he wished to be left by himself.

When Dr. Bolton found that this was the case, he told my father that he could not allow it at all. This caused my father to make an explanation with my brother, and my brother explained to me why this close watch was observed.

From my brother, Henry Parnell's, account of the matter, it appeared that, at the commencement of the attack, my father had presented to his mind the thought of self-destruction; he communicated this to Mr. Bolton, his medical attendant; and the result was that Mr. Bolton took with him my father's razors from the house, and gave injunctions that he should not be left by himself at all.'

Henry had been suffering from insomnia. When asked about his feelings, his constant answer was that he felt 'very low.' He would occasionally try to read, only to quickly give up and occupied his time in going for long walks. Eventually he lost interest in everything.

Henry was, by all accounts, a very reserved man. According to Manning he would never speak to a servant except to give orders. In the weeks leading up to his suicide, however, he had appeared so much better that he had resumed the management of his household, which for some time had been entrusted to his eldest son, John.

Henry's death devastated Sophia, and her grief was only matched by her anger at the physicians who had been caring for him. She was particularly incensed at the actions of the aforementioned Mr. Bolton, a charismatic character that Sophia believed to be little more than a quack, and to whom Henry's personal physician appeared to have ceded control.

Her anger was not assuaged by the fact that the inquest jury decided to neither call nor question Bolton, despite the fact that Henry's son-in-law, Mr. Edward Henry Cole, had stated that he believed Henry's extreme melancholy and weakness had been caused by the immense quantity of medicine that he had been made to take, and which had reduced him 'from a stout man to a mere skeleton'.

On 24 June 1842, Sophia wrote to Henry's second son, Henry William, regarding the prosecution of the inquest. Her anger and distress are only too evident:

'Before I left London I wished for my own conscience sake to ascertain more of Mr. Bolton, that if I wronged him I might endeavour to mitigate my feelings against him. I enquired of him from two physicians whose truth and honor I believe may be depended on, and the result was such as I feel justifies us in the cruel belief that to

*him we may attribute our affliction, and I cannot
exonerate Mr. Chambers from lending his sanction
to him, though he might not have been aware of
the system which had been so long carried out to
enfeeble the mind as well as the physical powers
for the purpose of plunder or enriching himself as
the expense of his victim. This is a most painful
subject, yet I derive consolation from it. It is to us
the most satisfactory way of accounting for the
dreadful event.*[37]

Following the reading of Henry's will, proved under
£7,000, the residue of Henry's estate would pass to
Henry William, the eldest son and successor to the
barony, John Vesey Parnell, having 'renounced' it, for
reasons which remain unclear.

Henry junior was by this time a retired navy
lieutenant who had seen more than his fair share of
adventure. He had been present as a midshipman on
the *Shannon* at the capture of the *U.S.S. Chesapeake*
in 1813, and also aboard the *Glasgow* at the battle of
Navarino in 1827. He had a thirst for adventure that
was most un-Parnell-like and, if he did not quite
resemble his late father in all of that, he did at least, to
some degree, resemble his aunt, to whom he was
extraordinarily close.

Following the inquest, Sophia returned to Portrane
where her consolation, in all of her suffering, had
always been the beauty of the sea and surrounding
'country' that even today can lift the heaviest heart.
That landscape had always been her refuge, her
resolutely secular chapel-of-ease. And it was to prove
no different now. On 29 June she wrote to Henry from
Mount Evans:

---

[37] In the margins of this letter Henry would later at the following
comment: '*This is quite true. I firmly believe that Mr. B. and Mr. C.
were the chief causes of my Father's suicide. H.P.*'

'I have found the quiet and solitude I can enjoy in this place of great use to me, & in a little time I hope again to be able to enjoy many things which used to give me pleasure.'

Seeking some small remembrance of her brother from the things he left behind, Sophia asked Henry for some of her brother's books; preferably those in which he had made some personal notes. She also asked him to follow up on a winter cloak she had wanted made for George, who had not been in the best of health of late. Old age, and years of adherence to the old saw 'Eat at pleasure, drink by measure' had finally caught up with her husband and he had fallen prey to 'flying gout', a variation of the disease that manifested itself in migratory pains up and down the body. He was not looking forward to the coming winter.

24

GEORGE'S DEATH

SOPHIA HAD NO sooner returned from her brother's funeral when grief once again spread its dark wing over Mount Evans.

In the early hours of Saturday, 2 July 1842, her husband was taken ill. Gripped, perhaps, by a portent of impending doom, George had gone for a long walk the day before, surveying all that he owned and all that he would leave behind. Between two and three of the following morning he became so alarmingly ill that his wife, convinced he had been struck down with cholera, sent a carriage to fetch his physician, Dr. O'Grady, from his home near Malahide.

O'Grady remained with George until 3pm the following day, at which point the patient was looking so much better that the good doctor left his bedside. George called for a drink and Sophia presented the cup to his lips. Having taken a sip, he fell backwards and died. His death was attributed to 'an attack of flying gout to the heart'.

Sophia's own heart, not long surrendered to one

sorrow, was now called upon to endure a second. It was almost more than she could bear.

The following Monday, the *Freemans Journal* printed a brief obituary:

> *'The right hon. gentleman was a Whig of the most popular school, and his influence in the county of Dublin, which, both on account of his station and property, as well as character, was considerable, and always exercised in furtherance of the cause of reform. He was a good and indulgent landlord, and as far as a Whig might be, a good Irishman. He was thoroughly and determinedly opposed to Toryism; he was a good and indulgent landlord, and fully recognized the rights of freedom of election...'*

At fifty-nine years of age, Sophia could share her double grief with only her nephew Henry, with whom she was in constant correspondence, and with her mother-in-law, Margaret, now in her nineties. But Margaret had become an infrequent visitor to Mount Evans by now, preferring to spend most of her time at the family townhouse on North Great George's Street. Here she could seek solace and consolation in her religiosity without an eyebrow being raised against the florid dictates of her faith; a faith that was so directly opposed to her daughter-in-law's more natural and deistic approach to life.

For Sophia, grief was not a trial sent by God to test her faith: it was a natural part of life, a burden to be endured, survived and conquered; however long it might take. Grief also had its own plan. It would not depart solely according to the movements of her will. She simply had to wait it out.

In the immediate aftermath of her brother's suicide, Sophia had confessed to her favourite nephew, Henry, that while she had been struggling to find the joy in anything for a while, the beauty and solitude of the countryside about Portrane had given her the strength to cope. But that had been *before* George died.

With whom was she to share that beauty and seek consolation now? How was she to face the daily grind of a world in which there was no George Evans, and she bereft of his comfort? How could she listen to the plangent sighs of the sea and not feel a tide of grief rising in her breast? On August 13 she wrote:

> *'I am still my dear Henry only less wretched when I dwell on the hope that my separation from my beloved husband cannot last long. I endeavour to keep myself occupied and to fatigue myself sufficiently every day to induce sleep. These are the physical remedies that have certainly alleviated the sufferings I have undergone.'*

Unable and unwilling to face down the inevitable tide of consoling platitudes, no matter how sincerely intended, Sophia refused to receive any and all visitors to Mount Evans and sank for a short while into a dolent and discomfiting aboulia that must at times have been only too painfully reminiscent of the early stages of her late brother Henry's demise. In her desolation she battled daily to recover the beauty she had always found at Portrane and which just a short time ago had been so effective a balm against her fraternal loss.

But the scenery about Mount Evans was now so fully associated with her memories of George that she simply could not bear to share them with anyone. And so she gave herself over to the silence and the small sounds that in the past had never intruded upon even the softest conversation, but could now only too easily intrude upon her doleful introspection. It would take several weeks before she could even begin to darn her frayed composure and foresee the beginnings of a future without him:

'I have suffered so much that I scarcely yet can bear to think of my sad bereavement, but I am more composed than I was and will do all in my power to struggle with my afflictions for the sake of him who is gone and who I trust still watches over me.'

Without George, daily life lost all definition and Sophia soon wearied of the struggle. Her customary responsibilities proved no bulwark against her grief, and she slowly wilted under the burden. George's mother was of little help. She had her own sorrows to tend to.

For several weeks it appeared as though Sophia was destined to spend her first winter without George at Mount Evans in solitary contemplation of her loss. But then, out of the blue, she received a letter from Penelope Warren, sister of Lady Jones, the latter of whom had passed away in 1829. Penelope offered to spend the winter with her in London, if Sophia was willing to make the journey.

It was a generous gesture, but it served only to highlight her future predicament. Penelope's visit would be fine for her first winter of widowhood, and would help to dispel the foggy lassitude of the loneliest hours, but it was not, in any sense of the word, a solution, and it necessitated a winter crossing of the Irish Sea.

A more enduring, heartfelt, and neighbourly friendship would be built over the succeeding years with Edward Breton Wolstenholme, a former magistrate and close friend of Sophia's late husband, George. Wolstenholme, who was married to Sophia's cousin, Arabella Ward, daughter of Edward Ward of Castle Ward in Co. Down, had for some time nurtured a deep affection for Sophia. Just two months after George's funeral, and at a time when she could tolerate no visitors at Portrane, Sophia went to spend a few days at his estate at Newberry, near Carberry in Co. Kildare.

This was no casual friendship, and what Sophia Evans and Edward Wolstenholme subsequently grew to feel for each other, though never venturing beyond the platonic, could only be described as love. But even platonic love is fraught with pitiful complications when one or other of the parties is married.

In many ways, Edward Wolstenholme became as dear to Sophia as her brothers Henry and William had once been. She would mention Wolstenholme frequently in her letters to her nephew, Henry, but not once in all those letters would she ever mention his wife, Arabella. Wolstenholme would also quickly replace Joshua Evans as her legal advisor of choice.

In the aftermath of George's death, Sophia's primary problem was her tenants. Her farm workers she knew intimately, for she was happy enough to be the giver of money, but she baulked at the responsibility of having to demand it. *That* had always been George's job. Had she been fortunate enough to have had children, the responsibility for that unpleasantly feudal task would now be her son's. Anxious to please her, Wolstenholme offered to take on the responsibility.

Wolstenholme's advice and friendship notwithstanding, Sophia would have been lost at this time without the love and assistance of her favourite nephew, Henry. George's death had left her with many financial burdens that could not be cleared until George's will had successfully navigated the choppy waters of probate and as a result she was forced to borrow money from several people, Henry included. Once the will had been through probate, she paid everyone back and then set her imagination upon matters of legacy and memorial.

By tradition Sophia had two years of official

mourning to mull over her future: two years in which widows were expected to abstain from entering society and to passively observe the running feet of time; two long years in which she would have to content herself with the visits of sympathetic neighbours, nephews and nieces; two years in which to browse the limited possibilities of an empty and pottering widowhood.

But she didn't need constant reminding of the extent of her loss, or particularly want to face the relentless tide of sympathy. What she needed was an outlet for her still considerable energies. She needed a project.

'Left with a large sum of money (£60,000 it was reported), beside her good estate of Portrane and her house in Eaton Square, Mrs. Evans devoted herself to the improvement of her property and neighbourhood. She built two handsome schools and gave the children who attended them a little garden. She planted extensively, made fine walks and built great greenhouses.'

Boston Post, 26 December 1885.

As the bewigged and green-suited 'Liberator' travelled the country, invoking all manner of Celtic symbolism and holding monster meetings at historic sites, it must have seemed to Sophia as if George's discreet patriotism and charitable works, not to mention his family's role in the 1798 rebellion, were about to be erased from history by a growing tide of Catholic nationalism that seemed hell bent on appropriating the country's history as a solely Catholic tradition.

Something had to be done. While others of their class had vacillated, her husband's family had put their lives on the line in the quest for Irish freedom. While others of their class had sat in *inactive and unprofitable sympathy*, George Evans, like her brother

William, had put himself forward for election and had fought for electoral and legislative equality. People needed to be reminded of all that, now more than ever. But what was to be done? How could people be *made* to remember? A monument of some sort was called for; a monument that would be visible for miles; a monument built consciously for posterity and which spoke to both George's goodness *and* his patriotism.

Just two years had passed since the founding of the Archaeological Society in Dublin and interest in Ireland's 'Celtic' heritage was becoming increasingly fashionable, especially amongst the landed gentry. A revival of interest was similarly underway in Ireland's round towers, triggered in no small part by the decision of the Royal Irish Academy to hold an essay competition on their purpose and origins. With George Petrie, the eventual winner, promoting his theories through the pages of the Dublin Penny Journal the towers had become a subject of topical public debate.

If a fit mode to mark her husband's passing was to be found, Sophia judged, it would inevitably be in the shape of a monument. And if that monument was to make a lasting impact on the landscape, and on the denizens of a peninsula he had worked so hard to fairly represent, then it simply *had* to be a tower.

George had been buried with his father, Hampden, within the roofless ruins of Saint Catherine's, the old Church of Ireland parish church in Portrane. The memorial tower that his wife commissioned in 1843 would be built on a hill that overlooked that grave from the south. Designed by the architect George Millar, at the exorbitant cost of £1,240, it would be obtrusive and magnificent, and incapable of being ignored. It would also, significantly, be the first round tower to have been built on Irish soil since the Norman invasion. It would be Sophia's very own, and very Irish, Taj Mahal.

Some expertise was obviously called upon in the

tower's design, for it made every effort to conform to historical proportions, the architect allegedly using as his model the round tower at St. Brigid's Cathedral in Kildare town. But Sophia wasn't content to simply build *a* tower, it had to be *George's* tower and so, at the same time as the tower was being constructed, she commissioned the sculptor Christopher Moore to make a marble bust of her husband to sit in the doorway of the round tower, from which she could imagine him looking down upon her whenever she strolled past. The plinth that supported the bust would carry the following dedication:

'To the memory of George Evans M.P., an honest man, firm friend and true patriot. This monument, a revival of the ancient architecture of his country, is respectfully, affectionately and mournfully dedicated.'

The Plinth. Photo courtesy of Bruce Ross-Smith.

Notice, if you will, the deliberate selection of the third person possessive: *his* country. Notice also the qualifying adjective in *true* patriot.

Despite the ecclesiastical history of the ancient towers, the word *Christian* was never even alluded to. Her husband may have been Protestant, but Sophia

Bust of George Evans.
Image courtesy of John Evans-Pritchard.

herself had issues with all of that. Privately sceptical of organised religion, but still a firm believer in the afterlife, Sophia Evans had never been a regular visitor to the small Anglican Church in Donabate, attending only when compelled to do so by societal requirements or when accompanying house guests who wished to attend. As a result, she was not on good terms with the local vicar who, on one occasion, even dared to 'read' her from the pulpit:

> *'Naturally Mrs. Evans, holding the opinions we described (though keeping them much to herself), was not a regular attender at the village church. Carriage loads of her guests, however, were frequently set down at the gates on Sunday, and sometimes she accompanied them herself to her large old-fashioned pew'.*

> Boston Post, 26 December 1885.

While attending a Sunday service with some house guests, a large dog that may or may not have been her own, followed Sophia into the church and lay down at her feet. Sophia made no attempt to shoo the animal outside and no-one dared to approach her on the matter. During the service, the constant rapping of the dog's tail during his sermon so infuriated the venerable gentleman of the pulpit that he interrupted his reading to turn on Sophia Evans.

'Turn out that dog if you please!' he raged, 'it's extremely wrong to bring a dog into a church!' This irreverent farce so amused one young local woman that she made a note of it in her diaries. But she never recorded what happened next. It was scandal enough for Frances Power Cobbe that Sophia Evans had had the temerity to enter a church with a dog.

That same year, round about the first anniversary of George's death, Edward Wolstenholme invited Sophia to take a break from the empty chairs and beds, and the poignant striking of clocks in empty halls, to come stay with him as his house guest at Newberry. While she was there, the Wolstenholmes were joined by another guest, newly arrived from England; a certain James Johnson, the former Physician to the King.

James Johnson M.D.

A native of Ballinderry in County Derry, Johnson made for an interesting house guest. He was well-educated, well-spoken and well-travelled. A former naval surgeon he had accompanied the expedition against the French forces in Egypt, but was forced to return to London invalided. He had subsequently served in the North Sea aboard the HMS Driver.

During the peace of 1814 Johnson had had the good fortune to be serving aboard the HMS Impregnable as the Duke of Clarence conveyed the Emperor of Russia and the King of Prussia to London. Having attended the Duke for a slight attack of fever, the two became friendly and following the Duke's accession to the throne, in 1830, Johnson was invited to become his physician extraordinary.

During his three day stay at Newberry Hall, Sophia invited Johnson to visit with her on his return journey and, four months later, in November 1843, he duly arrived at Mount Evans, where he became quite excited about the 'Widow's Tower' he found currently under construction. He noted particularly how it had fallen to a lady of noble birth to:

> *'... conceive the idea of a monument to the memory of her deceased lord, that would survive the Pyramids themselves, and transmit their joint names to the latest posterity – in the perfect model and dimensions of the ancient Irish Round Towers'.*

In her audacious choice of a round tower as a memorial for a liberal Protestant politician, Sophia Evans had both reclaimed that part of her husband's heritage that so many appeared determined to deny, and found herself setting in train a fashion for the building of memorial round towers that would endure long after her death. Five thousand years hence, Johnson believed:

> *'... the Tower of Portrane will probably be the only surviving representative of that ancient family of Round Towers, whose origin and pedigree have*

puzzled the antiquarian literati for nearly a thousand years past.'

25

THE DONABATE CHARTISTS

THE WINTERS WERE cruel and quiet, and under their dark shadows Mount Evans became akin to a mausoleum, swollen sadly with the memory of familiar sounds. By the time spring came around Sophia would be so desperate for company that she would pack her trunks and head to England, or to continental Europe, to visit friends and relatives. Travelling was no hardship to her. Sea voyages excited her. She was, by now, something of an 'old salt'.

An intelligent woman denied an outlet for her intellect by societal restrictions, Sophia loved to travel and loved to read. Her 'holidays' to mainland Europe were frequently as much about her 'studies' as the novelty of seeing new places. She would often return with new books, and new interests.

Every September or October, she would enjoy at Mount Evans the occasional visit from nieces and nephews who would bring their families for short stays. But all too soon the stables and coach houses would empty, the carriages would roll up in front of the house, and her guests would be borne away to the sound of crunching gravel and shouted farewells. They had families of their own to care for and would hunker down for the winter in their own, far distant, homes.

Her mother-in-law would come out to Mount Evans occasionally, to spend time with her children and grandchildren, but only when the townhouse on North Great George's Street became too small to accommodate their number. Once winter arrived, the steady flow of guests to Mount Evans became the drip of a hanging icicle, until the following year, when the vernal thaw set in.

The darker months at Mount Evans were not entirely devoid of compensations, however, and one of the few comforts of Sophia's early widowhood would be the unlikely friendship that she managed to strike up with a young local lady in her early twenties, the daughter of a former political adversary of her husband, who lived just up the road on the Swords side of Donabate.

Three score years and change lay between Frances Power Cobbe and Sophia Evans, and political differences between Frances's father and Sophia's husband had long served to keep the two families at arm's length. Following George's death, the Cobbes reached out to Sophia in her grief and isolation, and she and Frances quickly became, in Frances's words, 'pleasantly intimate'.

This unlikely friendship was forged, initially at least, in a shared and fruitless opposition to the new Dublin to Drogheda railway line that was planned to run through the village of Donabate. Not everyone saw the railway as a thing of beauty and modernity; for some it was the iron horseman of the apocalypse, the technological personation of death ripping up the natural beauty of the countryside and spoiling its splendour and peace. Charles Dickens, in his novel *Dombey and Son*, the first instalments of which were published in 1846, described the shriek of the railway whistle as:

'a shrill yell of exultation, roaring, rattling, tearing on, spurning everything with its dark breath.

There was no stopping progress and the railway was forced through the village and onwards up along the coast, heading for Drogheda. The battle to stop it however made comrades-in-arms of the Cobbes and Sophia Evans and following the opening of the line, an agreement was reached between the two families to share the annual cost of establishing a post-office in the village.

Sophia and Frances had much in common. Both had grown up as the only daughter in a brood of brothers; both were voracious readers and largely self-educated; and both were non-conformist in matters of religion and privately resentful of the privileges accorded by right to their male siblings. When Cambridge University finally opened its doors to women, in 1869, it would be partly on account of the restless campaigning of Frances, who famously presented a paper to the Social Science Congress of 1862 titled *Female Education, and How It Would be Affected by University Examinations.*

For years previous to the birth of this unlikely friendship, Frances had deflected her parents' attempt to turn her into a young society lady. Truth be told, she was not an overly attractive young woman and she would always feel more at home in the woods than in the ballroom. She never made any great effort to make herself attractive to men and was vehemently opposed to the wearing of corsets and the female invalidism she believed them to cause. She would often joke about having been born into a body which 'however defective ... from the aesthetic point of view', had been so robust and healthy as to be 'a source of endless enjoyment' to her. The botanist, Joseph Dalton Hooker, in a letter to

Charles Darwin, once referred to her, somewhat unkindly, as a 'disenchanting mountain of flesh'.

Frances was also, crucially, a lesbian; a fact she had yet to fully come to terms with in 1845. In sixty-five-year-old Sophia Evans, however, she found the tolerance and understanding she could never fully enjoy at home: a fellow victim, perhaps, of the nods and winks of the local gossips.

Frances Power Cobbe at 72.

One autumn evening in 1845, as Frances, who in after years would achieve fame as a suffragette and early animal rights campaigner, was travelling from Donabate by coach to seven o'clock dinner at the home of her 'very kind old friend', Mrs Evans, she passed a field of potatoes. Observing the leafy display, she remarked to her companions on the splendid looking crop. Three or four hours later, as she returned home in the dark, a dreadful smell wafted from the same field.

'Something has happened to those potatoes,' someone in her carriage exclaimed, 'they do not smell at all as they did when we passed them on our way out.' They had just witnessed a pivotal moment in Irish history. The potato crop had been hit by blight. Over the coming years it would cause widespread famine and disease and more than a million people would lose their lives.

The failure of the potato crop heralded great hardship for the tenant farmers of the Portrane peninsula, but for some it represented something of a political opportunity. Patrick Ryan, the Parish Priest of Donabate, had been converted to Chartism while working as a priest amongst the Catholic miners and linen workers of Bradford and Barnsley in West Yorkshire. On his return to Ireland he had established a small Chartist organisation in Donabate and joined it to the national body, the freshly formed Irish Universal Suffrage Association.

The membership of the IUSA consisted mainly of artisans, tradesmen and £40 freeholders who had lost the vote in 1829. Their president, Patrick O'Higgins, was a wool merchant. Only in Donabate was the membership dominated by small farmers and farm labourers. That was entirely down to the charismatic leadership of the Rev. Patrick Ryan.

The Chartists were a parliamentary reform movement that had been founded in 1837 according to the principles of a manifesto called *The People's Charter*. It called for universal suffrage for men, equal electoral districts, voting by secret ballot, abolition of property qualifications for MPs, and annual general elections. Their primary strategy was to use petitions and mass gatherings to put pressure on politicians and their methods were largely peaceful and constitutional, apart from occasional insurrectionary outbreaks, most notably in South Wales and in Yorkshire.

In 1839 and 1842, the Chartists managed to present petitions signed by millions of working people to the British House of Commons. That level of support, however, was never replicated in Ireland, where the movement was opposed by Daniel O'Connell. His 'Repeal' movement was the dominant political force amongst Catholics in Ireland and intolerant of any other movement that might dilute or weaken it. In October 1841, in response to an allegation by O'Connell that the Chartists were essentially an English organisation dominated by Orangemen and Tories, the Catholic Chartists of Barnsley wrote an open letter of appreciation to Father Ryan in Donabate, in order to:

> '... remove the unfavourable impression which such imputations are calculated to make upon the minds of our unhappy brethren in Ireland'.

Ryan attempted to get this letter, signed by over one hundred of the most prominent Catholic members of the movement in England[38], printed in the *Freeman's Journal*, but was refused on the grounds that it was an advertisement and would have to be paid for as such. The letter was subsequently printed in the pages of the *Northern Star*, a north of England newspaper that was effectively a Chartist periodical.

Father Ryan was very much the driving force behind the Chartist organization in Donabate and the *bête noire*, not just of the local Repeal Association, but of his archbishop. In choosing to join the Chartist movement Ryan had broken ranks from the official

---

[38] Burland, John Hugh. MS Annals of Barnsley, pp 186-188.

CHARTIST DEMONSTRATION!!

"PEACE and ORDER" is our MOTTO!

TO THE WORKING MEN OF LONDON.

Fellow Men,—The Press having misrepresented and vilified us and our intentions, the Demonstration Committee therefore consider it to be their duty to state that the grievances of us (the Working Classes) are deep and our demands just. We and our families are pining in misery, want, and starvation! We demand a fair day's wages for a fair day's work! We are the slaves of capital—we demand protection to our labour. We are political serfs—we demand to be free. We therefore invite all well disposed to join in our peaceful procession on

MONDAY NEXT, April 10,

As it is for the good of all that we seek to remove the evils under which we groan.

The following are the places of Meeting of THE CHARTISTS, THE TRADES, THE IRISH CONFEDERATE & REPEAL BODIES: East Division on Stepney Green at 8 o'clock; City and Finsbury Division on Clerkenwell Green at 9 o'clock; West Division in Russell Square at 9 o'clock; and the South Division in Peckham Fields at 9 o'clock, and proceed from thence to Kennington Common.

Signed on behalf of the Committee, JOHN ARNOTT, *Sec.*

Chartist Demonstration Flyer

church position and caused a bit of a stir. The majority of the Catholic hierarchy were hostile to Chartism, and Chartists had frequently been denounced from the altar. Some priests even tried to intimidate Chartists by refusing to baptise their children and withholding the sacraments until they had withdrawn from the Association and surrendered their membership cards to them.

The enmity between the two movements was extreme. The Leicester Chartists dubbed O'Connell 'one of the vilest traitors and political apostates recorded in the annals of delinquency'. The Halifax Chartists declared him to be 'Satan amongst the Angels of Heaven' and the Chartists of Hull organized public burnings of his portrait. O'Connell and his supporters were no less scathing. They labelled the Chartists variously as 'wretched', 'miscreants', 'violent and unthinking', 'the worst enemies of Ireland', and 'evil'.

Ryan, like the Chartists themselves, was at his most politically potent between 1841 and 1844, when he became active in the organisation of petitions. The first of these, drafted in 1842, was titled *Chartism and Repeal*, and argued for an alliance between Irish Repealers and English Chartists. The second, in 1843, was called *Civil and Religious Liberty*, and dealt with the persecution of Irish Chartists by Daniel O'Connell and the Irish Clergy. Very much a maverick within his own church, Ryan quickly managed to split his own community.

In Donabate, there were now two opposing Catholic factions, the Repeal Association and the Chartists, who actually supported many of the same causes, *including* Repeal. How many people had actually joined the IUSA in Donabate is difficult to assess: it is unlikely to have been large, but at the same time it was significant enough for the population to consider a request for extra police when the enmity between the two groups became heated.

A measure of that enmity can perhaps be gleaned from a letter that the Rev. Patrick Ryan wrote to the *Freeman's Journal* shortly before he decided to join the IUSA in 1841:

'It is melancholy to observe the diabolical spirit of ill-will and hatred which, has been recently infused into the minds of some ignorant persons in this city. I have, I regret to say, experienced this personally.

A man, whose name I shall now forbear to mention, but who is the same person to whom the "Loyal National Repeal Association," promised its protection against the legal consequences of his violence and misconduct, told me to my face, after he had been informed by myself that I was a Catholic priest—that if I should presume to take the chair at a meeting of the Irish Universal Suffrage Association, he would seize me by the neck, and drag me out of it, even if I were clothed in my robes.

Now, Sir, permit me to ask you when such a threat has been made to a priest, what is a layman to expect from such characters, particularly when they are encouraged in it by an association upon whose protection they rely with the most implicit confidence?

I am your obedient Servant,
P . Ryan .
Donabate, August 12, 1841.

Sophia Evans had never involved herself overly much with her husband's tenants and had rarely allowed the world beyond the borders of her demesne to overly intrude on the largely self-contained life she lived within it. The farm, and the house, were her kingdom and her laboratory, and within their lofty confines she had been largely content and happy, finding a collegiality and authority in the running of the farm that she thoroughly enjoyed. Family assets beyond the house and farm, however, had always been George's domain. She had rarely, if ever, sought to trespass on that.

The shopping lists, the servant's salaries, the steward's accounts, the poor rates, the school expenses and teachers' salaries, the butcher and gas company accounts, the lawyers, bankers, painters, plumbers and decorators, the taxes and estate correspondence, the charitable committees; all of these she could cope with, because she was happy to be the giver. But rents and leases, these were troublesome matters, and unpleasantly feudal. She hadn't the stomach for that. *That*, had always been the sole responsibility of her husband. *That* had always been man's work.

Following George's death, the task of setting and collecting rents still had to be done, and as her land steward, William Kelly, a man known to have Tenant Right and Repeal sympathies, was considered unwilling, or unsuited, to doing it, she had turned for help to Edward Wolstenholme. It was to prove one of the biggest mistakes of her life, for he had set himself to the task with an almost reckless enthusiasm.

In late January 1846, the Rev. Patrick Ryan allowed a 'Tenant Right' petition to be placed on a table at the door of the parish church in Donabate, where many of Sophia's tenants were alleged to have signed it. At this point in time tensions between various factions in Irish politics were approaching boiling point. Chartists within the Repeal movement were very much engaged in an internal struggle that was leaching working class support away from O'Connell, and the country was just six months away from the Young Ireland expulsion from the Repeal Association for their refusal to renounce the use of violence. Editorials in the *Nation* newspaper, furthermore, were growing ever more militaristic in tone.

On hearing of the petition, Edward Wolstenholme, whose personal politics lay somewhat to the right of his old friend, George Evans, was so incensed that he set out to discover who, if any, of Sophia's tenants had signed it. When he discovered, or at least was led to believe, that a teacher at Sophia's boys' school had done so, he promptly fired him and issued threats against any other tenants who might be thinking of signing that, or any other, Chartist petition.

The teacher, who may or may not have been a member of the local Chartist organisation, had been employed by Sophia for seventeen years without any cause for concern or complaint and was well regarded locally. His sacking for having merely exercised his constitutional right to sign a petition to parliament, caused all manner of upset and excitement in the village, and the temperature was hardly lowered when it was later alleged that the teacher hadn't actually signed the petition.

The atmosphere in the village now became so volatile and dangerous that the schoolhouse had to be closed and enquiries were made regarding the availability of extra police to keep the peace should cooler heads not prevail. In Sophia's absence, Wolstenholme had overstepped the mark, not just of his agency, but of propriety.

At the height of this bad feeling, one opportunistic tenant decided to try and land William Kelly, Sophia's land steward and a prominent member of the local Repeal Association, in hot water. Despite his Tenant Right and Repeal credentials, Kelly was not universally popular with Sophia's tenants, especially those resistant to his efforts at persuading them to modernise their agricultural practices.

For a long time many of these tenants had been arguing for rent reductions on the basis that the land they were leasing was poor land when compared to land elsewhere on the peninsula. But Kelly was undermining their case by achieving record yields on the same land and winning regular prizes at the Royal Dublin Society for his employer. Seen very much as Sophia's right-hand man, there was bound to be a reaction when the petition crisis broke. It came in the form of a poison-pen letter:

'Madam,

The kindness which I often experienced at the hand of your late excellent husband combined with a high personal regard for yourself, compels me at the risque of great pecuniary loss to put you on your guard with respect to a low cunning insidious man of the name of Kelly a member of this association (the Repeal).

He has recently boasted the he will ere long host a Repeal meeting in your drawing room and his plan of operation is to sow dissension between you and your tenantry so as to force you to leave Portrane and let the domain and house to him. He has compelled most of your tenants to become subscribed to the Repeal fund and of course associates. Just question them quietly upon this subject and then examine Kelly himself.

A friend.'

Kelly began to fear for his life, convinced that he was being set up to take the flak from both Wolstenholme and those angry tenants who felt he was too loyal to the woman they were now accusing of having directed Wolstenholme's actions. To add further fuel to the fire, Wolstenholme was being touted by some as being a German, even though his family had been settled in Ireland for several generations and had come from old Anglo-Saxon stock. Wolstenholme was further accused, in the pages of the Northern Star, of having lured the tee-totalling schoolteacher into a pub on the pretext of paying him his salary while his bailiffs emptied and took possession of his cottage.

As the rhetoric ratcheted up, William Kelly applied for a licence for two pistols to defend himself and his wife, and was refused. Feeling isolated and vulnerable in his cottage at Middlefield, he wrote to Sophia indicating that he would have to leave and take his wife to a place of safety if their security could not be guaranteed at Portrane. Losing Kelly was not something that Sophia could afford to do right now, so she hopped on the first boat back to Dublin, intervened on Kelly's behalf and got Kelly his licence.

When Sophia heard about Wolstenholme's treatment of her long-serving schoolteacher, she attempted to remedy matters. But the teacher had had enough and left with a year's salary in lieu of wages. The exact nature of his departure is unclear, but what we do know is that Sophia Evans had never, either before or after this incident, shown any intolerance of socialist philosophies, especially when couched in democratic and non-violent principles. The fact that O'Connell was so vehemently opposed to the Chartists might even have provoked a degree of sympathy for their cause. Just three years later she would be writing quite admiringly to her nephew, Henry, about the ideas of the French utopian socialist, Henri Blanc.

The whole affair was subsequently, and somewhat blindly, put down to a misunderstanding. It did little to diminish Sophia's affection for Wolstenholme, whatever about her trust. It did, however, prove something of a momentous epiphany. She had lost a valued teacher and almost lost her steward. From here on in, she quickly realised, she needed to take closer control of her estate. She had been avoiding her responsibilities for too long. This was not what George would have wanted. It had done little to serve his memory. She must, and would, do better.

The death, on 13 March 1846, of ninety-six-year-old Margaret Evans left Sophia, who had returned from London just days beforehand, alone in a large twelve-bedroom house with just her servants and her books for company. But she was mistress of the estate now in a way she had never been before. There were no longer anyone else's opinions or feelings to consider. She could pretty much do as she pleased.

Well, almost. Financially, Sophia was in some difficulty. The cost of building the tower had taxed her severely: her generosity to her tenants during the continuing famine had taxed her even more. And if all that wasn't enough, she now had the added stress of dealing with her brother Thomas, who was slowly falling out with all of his former friends and becoming increasingly difficult to deal with.

Explaining her difficulties to her nephew, Henry, she complained that she would do anything to make Thomas happy, except allowing him to spend all she was worth 'in that wasteful extravagance which he calls serving God'. It was all becoming too much for Sophia. She needed to get away from Portrane and, over the following months, would become increasingly desperate to do so.

The Chartist movement would more or less fizzle out in Ireland over the following years and, in 1848, the Chartist Priest, Patrick Ryan, would be granted permission to retire as the parish priest of Donabate on a pension of £20 a year. The grounds for his retirement would be given as 'infirmity'. He would be replaced by Fr. John McCarthy.

26

VACCINATION

Sophia evans' zeal for modernization did not just apply to agriculture; she was equally forward looking with regards to medicine. In April 1845, for example, she entered into a debate with her nephew, Henry, who was procrastinating about allowing his son, William, to be vaccinated against smallpox. Smallpox was a devastating disease that on average killed three out of every 10 people who contracted it. Survivors were usually left with scars, which were often severe. A certain anxiety persisted in conservative circles, however, regarding the wisdom of allowing animal diseases to enter the human bloodstream.

The scientific basis for vaccination against smallpox had only begun in 1796, when an English doctor named Edward Jenner observed that milkmaids who had contracted cowpox did not show any symptoms of smallpox after variolation. Following several experiments to test the theory, Jenner published his treatise *On the Origin of the Vaccine Inoculation*, in

1801. But his discovery was not universally welcomed. The rationale for criticism was wide and variegated, absorbing all manner of sanitary, religious, scientific, and political objections.[39]

Edward Jenner vaccinating patients in the Smallpox and Inoculation Hospital at St. Pancras: the patients develop features of cows.

For some parents, the smallpox vaccination itself induced fear and protest on account of the inevitable scarring (the vaccination process involved scoring the flesh on a child's arm and inserting lymph from the blister of a person who had been vaccinated about a week earlier). For some objectors, clergy included, the vaccine was seen as 'unchristian' because it came from an animal, while for others their discontent mirrored a general distrust in medicine. Many people, like Henry

---

[39] Durbach, N. They might as well brand us: Working class resistance to compulsory vaccination in Victorian England. The Society for the Social History of Medicine. 2000;13:45-62.

Parnell, remained nervous of inoculation and, concerned for the health of Henry's children, Sophia wrote to him, enclosing a copy of a letter by Pope Pius VII endorsing vaccination, and asking him to reconsider.

Edward Jenner vaccinating a child

'I send you the Pope's letter and am anxious to know how little William is today. Do you not incur a great responsibility in not averting an evil when it is in your power to do so by vaccination? And is not the virus of the smallpox a much more fearful poison to permit to enter the blood than that antagonist the cowpox. I wish you would be convinced that you are not doing justice to your children by withholding their being vaccinated, with the infection of smallpox about them. I know that you act from a sense of duty, and only would

261

wish that you could view it in another light.'

That concern for the immunisation of her grand nephews and nieces was, quite obviously born of a personal experience of deadly disease, but it was also to prove somewhat prophetic. Not long after Sophia had written, Henry's wife fell ill. The nature of her disease is never explicitly mentioned in the letters that passed between them, but it would appear that having resisted vaccination for so long, Henry's wife had now contracted smallpox. Sophia was full of advice:

'Your letter gave me pleasure as it contained a much better account of dear Sophy than I expected. If no organic disease has taken place, you have reason to hope that you can save her, but I am convinced that an immediate sea voyage is the remedy that will restore her & that your plan of taking her to Malta is the best you can adopt.

I should like to be of your party. I have suffered so much from officious kindness that I am unwilling to inflict it, but if Sophy would venture to try me she would find me never in her way. I am so good a sailor that I feel that without intruding on the wish which I am sure she feels to receive assistance & care only from yourself, that I could be a comfort to you both & you know how fond I am of the sea.

I should of course defray my share of the expenses, whatever they may be on sea or on land & do my dear Henry gratify me by accepting this offer and prevail on dear Sophy not to be alarmed at the idea of a troublesome companion.

'Mr Evans, a friend whose opinion I rely on, insists on my leaving Ireland, but this your uncle Tom is not aware of as he might perhaps insist on my never returning to it, which I intend to do when the feverish excitement which is now

uncomfortable has subsided. No one knows my motive for travelling but two or three whose discretion I can rely on. I am going to Germany if I do not accompany you.' ...'

Leaving Mount Evans for such a prolonged period meant leaving the managing of the farm, as distinct from the tenants, to someone she trusted, and there was no-one she trusted more than William Kelly. What action, if any, Sophia took regarding the poison pen letter accusing him of using her home to host Repeal Association meetings while she was abroad, is unknown, but a later letter to Henry suggests that at least some disciplinary measures were being considered:

'I am glad to say that Kelly got off very triumphant, but I am obliged to make such changes in consequence of misconduct that I have no wish to stop at Portrane for another month or two, till the excitement is over.'

What Kelly was triumphant about is unclear, perhaps it had something to do with clearing his name with Wolstenholme, or perhaps it concerned some minor legal case that he had won, but it is clear from her letter that Sophia was pleased for him. She liked, and depended, on Kelly, and any changes she subsequently made did not involve firing him. In fact, the very tenants who had so recently complained about him would very soon have ample reason to be grateful that she had not.

In the end Henry's wife, Sophy, did not survive long enough to make the trip abroad and she died on 5 April 1846 at their house at 13 Bryanston Square, Marylebone. On hearing the news Sophia wrote to Henry again:

'I cannot say, dear Henry, how shocked and

afflicted I am. I wish I was with you. Would you come abroad with me and bring your children? I would go anywhere you liked. My original plan was Germany. There are many reasons which make me wish to leave Portrane for a few months and I am sure you should not remain just for now at Bryanstone house. In October we could all return together to Portrane. Dear Henry, do not let affliction overpower you. She has left you but for a while, and those pledges of mutual love which remain to you, demand from you an unbroken spirit ...'

27

THE GREAT HUNGER

BACK IN 1831, when Sophia hired William Kelly, he had been employed as land steward and gardener to a Mr. James Pratt of Farmhill, in south County Dublin. Kelly would have been seen as an unusual choice to replace Doherty, the old steward at Mount Evans. He had never managed an estate of this size before and, unusually for the time, he was a Catholic; a former graduate of the short-lived Bannow Farm School.

The post of steward at Farmhill had been several steps beyond the level of gardeners and ploughboys that so many other graduates of Bannow had gone on to become but, while there, obsessed with efficiency and scornful of waste, Kelly had nonetheless managed to achieve something of a reputation as a talented agriculturist on the back of a pamphlet he had written on the management of what at that time were called 'villa farms', i.e. medium-sized estates of ten to twenty acres used primarily as the Dublin residences of wealthy judges, high ranking law officers and professional or mercantile gentlemen.

If there was anyone in the county likely to have

read William Kelly's ground-breaking work on villa farms, it was Sophia Evans, a largely self-educated woman with a keen interest in politics, philosophy and the natural sciences. As a member of the Irish Horticultural Society, she had even presided as a judge at some of the exhibitions at which William Kelly had hitherto competed. Whatever references or recommendations had been made on Kelly's behalf, they must have been powerful for, despite his lack of experience in managing estates of this size, Sophia hired him to modernise her husband's estate.

We need to exercise some historical imagination here to understand the scale of this achievement, and what it would have meant for a non-university educated Catholic to have taken on so large an estate just four years after the granting of Catholic Emancipation. This was no simple head-gardener position. The Evans estate offered an opportunity for Kelly to test his methods, and his mettle, on an industrial scale. From a villa farm of just thirty-six acres, Kelly was now expected to take charge of an estate over *sixty* times that size. Not having managed anything quite so grand before, it was a daunting prospect that required, not just an advanced level of skill and education, but an unshakeable belief in his own ability.

Garrulous and loquacious at times, Kelly had a wry and grim sense of humour that occasionally bordered on self-parody. But behind the bucolic charm there was always a degree of humility and self-deprecation that made people want to listen. Spreading his knowledge and know-how amongst those tenant farmers willing to listen, Kelly had worked hand in glove with Sophia, who had by then pretty much taken over of the modernisation of the estate while her husband, George, concentrated on his legal and political career in Dublin. Sophia had, in fact, already begun to re-design the grounds according to her personal preferences when Kelly arrived, but she had always been open to new ideas, especially those with a proven basis in science.

The success of the land reclamation efforts at Bannow would have been well known to George and Sophia as reports on the project had been ordered and compiled for the British House of Commons, where George Evans had sat as the member for County Dublin. In her younger years, furthermore, Sophia had come under the influence of the agriculturalist, Arthur Young, whom she had met in Paris, and she had long desired a steward of similar calibre to turn her farm into a profitable business.

Kelly, too, had read Young, and in after years would quote him at length in his letters to the press. Like Young, Kelly, was also capable of rhapsodising on such subjects as manure and the need for agricultural modernization, though his sympathy for, and understanding of, the countryside economy was far more empathetic than Young's for having been raised in a community of smallholders reduced to wage labour by modernization.

Like Young, Kelly saw himself, not as a common 'salt of the earth' farmer or rustic savant, but as an agricultural scientist, a potential educator, a man who could help to modernise the farming practices of a backward nation and make a reputation for himself in the process. To realise his ambition, he needed an employer liberal, wealthy and willing enough to grant him the land and the time to complete his experiments. In Sophia Evans, it appeared, he had found one, and throughout her estate he turned bad land into good and poor yields in record ones.

The failure of the potato crop that autumn (1845) would lead to a rapid spread of smallpox throughout Ireland and when the 75% of the potato crop that had been lost in Fingal in 1845, was followed by an almost complete loss in October of 1846, local tensions and resentments rose even higher. As the tenant farmers of Ireland relied heavily on the potato for food, the result for most parts of the country was famine and disease, most notably smallpox.

Between the years 1841 and 1851 the surrounding agricultural areas would see their populations fall by 12-20%. On the Donabate-Portrane peninsula, however, it would fall by 0.8%, i.e. from 1170 people in 1841, to 1160 in 1851. This was in part due to Sophia Evans taking charge of her own accounts and advancing loans to her tenants with little hope of ever being repaid. By 1846 these loans averaged out at five weeks wages per person and were often accompanied by 'gratuities' that she ordered be paid to her labourers for as long as food prices remained unreasonably high.

When added to the cost of building her round tower, the effect on her finances proved so severe that Sophia suddenly decided to apply to the National Education Board for a grant to help cover the cost of running the two local schools she had founded and for which enrolment had recently escalated. For fifteen years she had resisted making such an application, despite being perfectly entitled to do so. Mistrustful of government commitment to standards, she had preferred to run the schools independent of outside interference. In her application for funding she was still, at the age of sixty-seven, listed as the schools' manager and, despite her schools' independent status, she was granted 100 school books and the salary for a teacher. Famine or no famine, the children would stay in school.

Another reason that the famine was not felt more deeply in Portrane was the radical land management practices of Sophia's steward, William Kelly. Before the famine, Sophia had already ordered the bogs surrounding her estate to be drained and reclaimed, providing much needed work for local labourers and extra land for her tenants to grow alternative crops. When the famine struck, in the autumn of 1845, Kelly had acted quickly. He had stabled his machinery and reverted to manual labour, providing much needed extra employment in the area. He had even found work for the children of the labourers in the manual dibbling of seeds[40] and prepared the area like no other to face the imminent apocalypse.

And he didn't stop with providing employment. During the famine, the most cost-effective means of providing food relief, it was quickly found, was to import cheap poor-quality maize or 'Indian meal' from Britain's Indian colonies. Daily survival rations were set at a pound of meal per day for adults, and half a pound of meal per day for children. The meal was generally ground and added to warm water.

Kelly, his attention having been drawn by Sophia to a recent article she had read concerning the experiments of a Viennese baker with wheat and beetroot, suspected the meal could be more effectively used and began to experiment; mixing varying quantities of Indian meal with cheaper crops. The crop he finally settled on was mangelwurzel, a type of beet grown primarily for livestock feed.

This plant had begun life in Germany as *mangold-wurzel*, literally 'root of the beet', but this was apparently misheard as *mangel-wurzel* or 'root of scarcity'. The latter translation made its way to France as *racine de disette* and, in the previous century, an English translation of a French work by the Abbé de Commerell had introduced this plant to the English-speaking world by the same name. Drawn by the etymologically suspect nomenclature to the possible use of the plant for human consumption, Kelly had acted with the irresistible urge of the visionary and his bread proved so popular on the peninsula that within weeks it was in 'extensive use'.

The sense of emergency having imbued her with fresh energy and confidence, Sophia recovered her enthusiasm for her little schools and, on Monday 14

---

[40] See Ronan, Gerard. William Kelly of Portrane, Fingal County Council, 2019.

Champion Orange Globe Mangel Wurzel.

December 1846, she attended the half-yearly examination of teachers-in-training at the National Board of Education, having hitherto visited several National Schools throughout Dublin. She still believed that education was the only true way out of poverty. Whether her attendance was indicative of a desire to educate *herself* regarding current teaching standards, or a precursor to allowing her schools to be taken over by the state, it represented a renewed commitment to getting things done. Her period of official mourning was well and truly over.

Sophia was not the only person to be energized by the horror of the famine. Just two days earlier, on 12 December 1846, Kelly had offered samples of his mangelwurzel bread to the Practical Agricultural Association, and then again, seven days later, to the Royal Dublin Society. Within days the national newspapers were carrying a description of the bread. With the potatoes rotting in the fields and the wheat and oats that would normally go to pay the landlord now being consumed by his tenants, this new type of bread eased the burden on tenant farmers by reducing their consumption of expensive wheat in favour of a cheaper crop.

Kelly also knew, from practical and experimental experience at Portrane, that better land management and a reduction in reliance on the potato could prevent the famine from recurring. He began, therefore, to campaign for change. On the 8 December 1846, a paper by him was read to the weekly meeting of the newly formed Farmers' Club or Practical Agricultural Society, at Northumberland Buildings in Dublin, and reported five days later in the *Leinster Express*. In this paper Kelly advised as to the type of crops that should be grown during the current emergency and gave instructions on the most efficient way to grow them.

So successful, in fact, were Sophia Evans and William Kelly in mitigating the effects of the famine in their own locality that Kelly was even invited by The Irish Farmers Association to share his methods with the country at large. His *Irish Small Farmer of 1847; Containing Ample Directions for the Cultivation of the Soil During the Present Crisis* was published in January of 1847, and aimed at helping tenant farmers move away from their reliance on the potato and teaching

THE
IRISH SMALL FARMER

OF

1847;

CONTAINING AMPLE DIRECTIONS

FOR THE CULTIVATION OF THE SOIL

DURING THE PRESENT CRISIS.

BY WILLIAM KELLY.

STEWARD TO MRS. EVANS, PORTRANE, COUNTY DUBLIN.

Author of "A Treatise on Villa Farms," &c.

Published at the request of

"The Irish Farmer's Association."

DUBLIN:

CUMMING & FERGUSON, LOWER ORMOND QUAY,

Agents for the Sale of the JOURNALS of

"THE ROYAL AGRICULTURAL SOCIETY OF ENGLAND;"
"THE HIGHLAND SOCIETY OF SCOTLAND;" ETC.

TWO PENCE.

them how to cultivate alternative crops and maximise their yield.

Kelly's book took a revolutionary, modern and organic approach to subjects such as economy of labour; food resources; land reclamation and drainage; manure making and application; tillage and deepening of the soil; systems of crop rotation; crop management; the comparative merits of crops for cattle and people; calf rearing and cow feeding; dairy management; garden crops; bee keeping and cottage economy. It even dealt with hygiene and the recycling of human waste. Just four months later many of his ideas would already be finding their way into other publications and quoted by other 'experts'. In their work together, Sophia Evans and William Kelly had placed Portrane at the heart of an agricultural revolution; a revolution that was passing almost unnoticed because another revolution happened to be taking place at the same time.

The Paris revolution of February 1848, in which Louis Philippe had been overthrown in an almost bloodless revolution and a poet, Alphonse de Lamartine, installed as head of the provisional government of the Second Republic, had raised unrealistic expectations across famine-ravaged Ireland, where the sudden collapse of established regimes across Europe had given fresh impetus to the divided and dispirited Repeal movement in which Kelly was very much involved at a local level.

Sophia had been feeling increasingly vulnerable in the house on her own. A recent burglary had seen all of her gowns stolen in a single night. The thief, she joked, had at least had the decency to leave her a single dress gown to wear 'which was very considerate', but her maid's watch had also been stolen, a fact that appeared to have upset her far more than the loss of her gowns. Sophia had only avoided meeting the burglars because she taken to sleeping again in a guest bedroom close to the servants quarters.

It was the last straw. She'd had enough. In July of 1847, she left Portrane for London with little idea, if any, of when she might return.

28

THE THIRD REPUBLIC

HAVING INITIALLY PLANNED to go on to Germany from London, Sophia went first to visit Henry, only to find him unwell. Not wishing to overstay her welcome, she left early, for France, travelling from Calais to Paris in the company two English gentlemen who dared to talk politics in her company only to find that she revelled in it:

> *'I had a very pleasant journey with two gentlemen and their wives, one a conservative, the other a radical. We fought all the way, which made the journey very agreeable.'*

Sophia arrrived in Paris on 17 March 1848, just three weeks after the end of the February Revolution and three days before the first copies of Karl Marx's *Manifesto of the Communist Party* hit the streets. Not having arranged accommodation in advance the sixty-eight-year-old widow found herself struggling. The hotels were all full.

Running about the town for an entire day as though miraculously resistant to the debilities of old age, it

275

seemed as if Sophia would have to settle for unfurnished accommodation and furnish it herself, only to find a modest furnished apartment at the last minute at 102 Rue du Fauberg St Honoré, in the 8th *arrondissement*. The building had recently housed a day school run by a certain Mr. Murray, but that had moved out two years ago. It was more than sufficient for a widow and two married servants.

102 Rue du Fauberg St Honoré.

It was perhaps a measure of her desperation to stay away from Portrane that Sophia decided to visit Paris at a time of even greater unrest and uncertainty than existed in Ireland. But then she had many happy memories of the place, and friends currently resident in the city, not least of whom were George's sisters, Nancy Putland and Mary Lawless. Mary would often travel up from Tours whenever Nancy was in town.

Accompanying Sophia on this trip were her servants, Mr and Mrs Fisher. They were making their first trip to Paris and Sophia was keen to share her knowledge of the city with them. Once the trunks had been unstrapped and unpacked, she aksed them what they would like to see in Paris. But of all its many delights Mrs Fisher only wanted to see one thing: 'the house where the murder was.' What Mrs Fisher was referring to was the murder of the Duchess de Choiseul-Praslin, which had been front page news for several weeks the previous year.

The Duke and Duchess had only just returned to their home in Paris on the night of 17 August 1847 when, between four or five in the morning, the Duchess de Choiseul-Praslin rang the servants' bell. Madame Le Claire, the Duchess' *femme de chambre,* went to assist her and found her door locked. Le Claire immediately sought assistance and by the time she and the other servants entered the room they discovered the boudoir open and reeking of gunpowder and the Duchess was lying in a pool of her own blood with several deep wounds to her throat. Surgeons arrived quickly but there was nothing they could do. The Duchess died two hours later.

The police were now called and the Prefect took everyone into custody. Having interrogated those present, and searched the house for clues, they determined that no robbery had been committed, or even attempted, and that the garden was in so pristine a state as to render it impossible that anyone could had entered or left by it. They subsequently learned that the Duchess had been madly in love with her husband and recorded as much in her diary But they had enjoyed a rather volatile relationship. Numerous violent confrontations between the two had recently been witnessed by staff, the most recent concerning the children's governess, Henriette Deluzy-Desportes, with whom the Duchess believed her husband was having an affair and planning to elope.

The Duchess had also come to suspect that Henriette had been hired by her husband to estrange her from her children. She had threatened to leave her husband, which would have ruined him socially and had fired Henriette. Henriette, however, had yet to leave.

The Hotel Choiseul-Praslin.

The evidence against the Duke was overwhelming: the bloody trail that led from the Duchess' room to his own; his pistol found at the scene with fragments of the Duchess' flesh on it; and a fresh blood-stained dagger handle found hidden in his room. Several pieces of bloody cord were also found in the pocket of the his dressing gown.

Urged by the magistrates to account for his actions, the Duke's answers proved so contradictory and improbable as to all but amount to a confession. Transferred to the Luxembourg Palace pending trial, he proceeded to commit suicide in his cell by taking arsenic. The hotel had since become something of a tourist attraction and for Sophia's maid, this was the only real attraction in Paris; a sight that didn't require a knowledge of French or European history to appreciate and which would be readily understood by her peers on her return to London.

Sophia quickly settled into to her new apartment, but popular uncertainty about the liberal foundations of the provisional government quickly began to surface following the national elections on 23 April 1848, and she could feel the atmosphere changing. Despite agitation from the left, the French voting public had elected a moderate and conservative National Assembly. Feeling the pace of change was too slow, and in danger of grinding to a bureaucratic halt, the radicals began to protest against the government. Sophia, in a letter to Henry, confessed to being worried:

> *'Everyone agrees that there must be another revolution, the result is predicted according to the wishes of the Prophet, but I fear there is still more distress to be inflicted on this country. The town looks the same, but if you go into a shop you find the change, nothing but poverty and discontent.'*

The 'Prophet' above, is not a reference to Islam, but to Robespierre, a man regarded by many in France as a *true* prophet. In their eyes, Robespierre had stood alone among the political class in defending the prospect of true brotherhood for a politically united France: a France united by evangelical love. Robespierre was the heir to Jesus, and to the apostle Rousseau: the truth of his utterings making him a 'true prophet'.

One man who believed Robespierre to have been a prophet, but whose more gentle form of utopian socialism Sophia found intriguing, was Louis Blanc, a polititian renowned as both an orator and a historian.

Socialism was only beginning to find its feet in Europe, and Paris was at the centre of its development and evolution. Sophia would not have been alone amongst her class in being curious and Louis Blanc's name would already have been familiar to anyone who read *The Spectator*.

Louis Blanc

Blanc, currently a member of the provisional government, was very much a leader of the moderate wing of French socialism, and something of a maverick in his advocacy of socialism *without* revolution. His legacy today is enshrined in article 23.1 of the Universal Declaration of Human Rights, which enshrines the 'right to work'. The phrase owed its existence to Blanc's *Droit Au Travail,* a treatise first published in February of 1848, just weeks before Sophia arrived in Paris.

In his writings Blanc had likened the sufferings of Robespierre to the Passion of Christ as the revolutionaries turned their back on Revolution.[41] But the Prophet's message had now been passed on to a new generation and it was up to them to see to it that the Revolution reached its inevitable fulfilment. Hence, according to 'the prophet', another revolution was inevitable.

Against this backdrop of increasing political tension and uncertainty, Sophia found herself being invited to all manner of official functions in the run up to the opening of parliament, not all of which impressed her. The country had changed so much since the second Revolution and she did not care much for what she saw of the new Republic, or, for that matter, of its president, Louis Napoléon Bonaparte, nephew of the Napoléon.

That April she wrote to Henry that she was expecting an invitation to meet the President. She intended, she said, to refuse. She had seen all that she wished to see of the second republic at the Embassy and the Prefecture. But then, in a remarkable *volte face,* Sophia suddenly accepted an invitation to attend the opening of the new French Assembly. It took place on 4 May 1848.

---

[41] Jacouty, J.-F. (2003). Robespierre viewed by Louis Blanc: The Christianlike prophet of the French Revolution. Annales historiques de la Révolution française. 103-125+220.

Amongst all the speeches Sophia heard that day, none impressed her more than that of the Socialist minister of state, Louis Blanc, a passionate orator who called, in the face of much vocal opposition, for the creation of state-funded cooperatives in order to guarantee employment for the urban poor, an initiative he intended should ultimately be controlled by the workers themselves.

The French National Assembly on 4 May 1848.
Sophia viewed proceedings from a first floor gallery.

Was it a coincidence that Blanc was due to speak? Or had Sophia been invited specifically to hear him? It is not impossible that she had already met Blanc during her earlier social engagements at the embassy and Prefecture, but however it came about, Blanc's moderate and pragmatic Socialism impressed her. On 8 May 1848, she wrote to Henry:

'My dear Henry,

It seems a long time since I have heard from you. I hope you are quite recovered and that I shall soon [see] you here. The town is so <u>unquiet</u> though there has been yet no disturbance, that I think it likely that I may not remain my month out. I would on no account run the risk of finding myself in a revolution & therefore I wish you would pay me a visit soon. I have this apartment until the 3rd of June if I remain ...

I have just got the account of the poor rate I am to pay, amounting to within a few shillings of £40. Our Electoral Union contained 12 paupers when I left home last July ...

I was at the Chamber of Deputies a few days ago, it is an amusing Bear Garden.[42] A Socialist made a very eloquent and well-delivered speech. He was as well-dressed as any of the other Deputies, but was a mason. The right attempted at first to silence him, on which he folded his arms and waited till the noise was over to begin again, presently the benches on both sides were filled and at last he was listened to with great attention.

The subject discussed was the Budget. He said that he would propose a large increase to it, and urged the Government to restore <u>Order,</u> not by the Bayonet & the interference of the Police, but by giving work to those in distress, & that Government should undertake large and extensive works in all parts of France to employ

---

[42] Contemporary metaphor for a place of tumult and disorder.

*workmen and the Class to which he belonged –
that it was false to say that the Socialists were
the enemy of the people, or that the rich were the
enemies to the poor, we were all brothers, but
poverty created the gulf that separated the
classes, and now destroyed the happiness of
France.*

*Ever my dear Henry,
Very affectionate,
S. Evans.'*

When Sophia referenced 'the Prophet' in her earlier
letter, she betrayed a familiarity with the history of the
French Revolution, perhaps even Blanc's *Histoire de
dix ans : 1830-1840*, a monumental work that had
been published as far back as 1842. That the allusion
did not have to be explained, suggests that Henry, too,
was familiar with it. Blanc's name, furthermore, had
over the course of the last year been a familiar one to
readers of *The Spectator*.

Even if by some chance Sophia had never
encountered the name before, she had heard Blanc
speak, and had heard him introduced, probably more
than once as his speeech had been disturbed. His
name would also have been mentioned several times
by his detractors during the course of that debate. So
why was she so coy about naming him? Could it be
that she wanted Henry to consider Blanc's ideas free
from any prejudice his name might invoke?

A week to the day after Sophia sent that letter, on
15 May 1848, Parisian workmen, feeling that their
democratic and social republic was slipping slowly
away, invaded the National Assembly and proclaimed a
new Provisional Government. This attempted coup on
the part of the working classes was quickly suppressed
by the National Guard and the leaders arrested. But it
was the last straw for Sophia. She packed her bags
and fled to Calais. She would be followed soon after by

Louis Blanc, who had to flee for his life. Escaping on a false passport to Belgium, he too would end up in London

Sophia sailed from France on May 26th, but not before Nancy Putland had made a last ditch effort to convince her to stay a little longer. Had Nancy actually succeeded in getting her to stay, they would have found themselves swept up in the turmoil of the June Days revolution which took place from 22 to 26 June of that year. But she didn't, and the pair were safe in London by the time that particular disturbance kicked off. Later that summer, having had enough adventure for one year, Sophia left London for Portrane.

Invasion of the National Assemby, 15 May 1848.

The new French government, valuing good relations with Britain, refused to lend its support to Irish nationalism and, as the Paris revolution degenerated into the bloody violence of the 'June days', it was only a matter of time before the idea of a peaceful revolution was similarly abandoned in Ireland. In July 1848 the romantic idealists took up arms.

But like the June Days Revolution in Paris, the Young Ireland rebellion turned out to little more than a brief and violent farce that was quickly subdued. In its aftermath, attention quickly returned to the more pressing matter of the famine and that September, the front page of the *Irish Examiner* carried an article that waxed lyrical on work of Sophia Evans and William Kelly:

> *'Ballyphehane, if reclaimed,' the contributor stated, 'is capable of producing as good crops of every kind as those grown on similar land by Mrs. Evans of Portrane, in the county Dublin. The name of Portrane is now associated with the history of the improved agriculture of Europe, aye, and America, too. Cannot government, or a public body with a suitable staff, do that which a widow lady did by the aid of one practical Irishman?'*

Sophia and William's fame even spread to Canada where the Lower Canada Agricultural Society noted in its journal Sophia Evans' successes, in November 1848, at the Royal Dublin Society:

> *'The same lady got the first prize for the yellow globe mangel, cultivated in the same way, and having the same produce. Both were sown in the second week of May. She also obtained the first prize for carrots, of which the produce was over 60 tons to the Irish acre : manure, 3cwt of guano to the acre; cultivation, beds in rows twelve inches apart, plants 5 inches apart – sown 2nd May. Crop tilled exclusively with the spade, and the report states "the crops on the head lands which would be waste if the plough was used, would remunerate for the entire labour employed."*
>
> *The lady took four prizes (all that were offered)*

> *for very great crops of beans and peas, which is a very good estimate of what a lady can do in the way of farming, and against such competitors as the Duke of Leinster, the Earls of Claremont and Meath, and many others of high rank.'*

Having survived those difficult years, Sophia took some time out to visit her English solicitor, William Whiteside, at Lincoln Inn Fields and, on 28 March 1849, she finally drafted her will. Sophia was, in general, mistrustful of solicitors, and would often joke with her nephew, Henry, about the difficulty in finding an honest one.

To those who would advise her against such frequent travel by sea, Sophia would often boast of being a very experienced sailor and of never fearing a sea voyage. Over the course of the following years she would spend time in Paris, but would also take that long promised visit to Germany and Belgium. In July 1849, she travelled up the Rhine as far as Frankfort by boat. The journey inspired in her a new passion and she soon after wrote to her bookseller to order the complete works of Alfred Lord Tennyson, and four volumes of works on the subject of architecture and classical Greece by Thomas Hope[43].

She was still in Germany when she began to fret about the health of her close friend Edward Wolstenholme. Hearing he was in poor health she had written to him, but had received nothing by way of reply from either Edward, or indeed his wife, Arabella. In the absence of news she became seized with a premonition of grief. She wrote to Henry, half-hoping that he had better news. She was, she wrote, concerned for a:

---

[43] *Household Furniture and Interior Decoration* (1807), *Costumes of the Ancients* (1809), *An Historical Essay on Architecture* (1835), and *Anastasius, or Memoirs of a Modern Greek, written at the Close of the Eighteenth Century* (1819).

'... most valued friend who deserves from me all the friendship I can feel for him and such as at my time of life I can scarcely hope to replace. There was no person that Evans had a greater regard for. But I hope I am anticipating evil where none is likely to exist. However, it occupys my thoughts and makes me defer everything from day to day.

I think I must get a letter before Monday as on that day I have fixed to leave here for Dresden where I calculate to remain till the 3rd of August and then to go to Berlin. I hope to hear from you Poste Restante Dresden, as I wish very much to know how you and your dear children are getting on – if you have found a governess you like and if you have formed any plan of spending the hot weather out of town. You know that I consider that you and the children and governess are engaged to me in October at Portrane.'

Dresden Opera House after the uprising. May 1849.

Sophia was now sixty-nine and, despite her age, still

hale and spry. But age was an undeniable fact and perhaps it was that sense of time running out that imbued her with a sense of invulnerability. The previous year she had travelled to Paris at a time of social upheaval and had only just managed to get out before another revolution started. Now she was heading for Dresden, where an uprising had taken place just two months beforehand, and from which the battered city was still recovering.

Wolstenholme, it turned out, had not died, but it was October before he had recovered sufficiently to be moved. By this time Sophia was back in Portrane. She immediately arranged to have him transferred to her home at Mount Evans, so that the sea air could expedite his recovery.

How Wolstenholme's wife, Arabella, felt about her husband rising Lazarus-like from his sick bed to be carried to the house of another woman, is anybody's guess; but, even if she travelled with him, the optics were not good and, despite the fact that she was a relative of Sophia's, Arabella was never mentioned in Sophia's letters to Henry:

> *'After some weeks more of great anxiety, Mr Wolstenholme's strength of constitution has enabled him to survive his dreadful illness. When able to move he came to Dublin in a bed carriage ten days ago, and is now here, walking a little, driving a good deal on a jaunting car, and his mind is as strong and his spirits as cheerful as ever, however, quite safe.*
>
> *We fear dropsy[44] but I trust the symptoms are only the usual results of such an illness and that in a few weeks more he will be perfectly recovered. I have reason to be grateful that his life is spared, the loss of such a friend would be one which I could never replace ...*

---

[44] Archaic term for oedema.

This country is quite quiet, but Ireland is in an awful state, there is no knowing what may happen, but I trust nothing bad. Good and ill is always exaggerated. My farming concerns are most prosperous and are a counterpoise to the bill I am filing in chancery against Mr Evans and which will be in court next month, after making another effort since I saw you to make it unnecessary.'

Sophia was now in dispute with Joshua Evans regarding unpaid interest that he and Eyre Evans had claimed was due to them under Hampden Evans' will. Effectively, what they were claiming was a part interest in the Portrane Estate that George had left in its entirety to Sophia. The case, in which she would be represented by Edward Wolstenholme, would drag on for years, being decided in Sophia's favour just a year before her death,[45] though even then Joshua and Eyre would appeal the decision. The appeal would fail in February 1853 and costs would be awarded against the Evans brothers.

The prosperous farming concerns that were making Sophia's reputation as a shrewd agri-businesswoman, were down almost entirely to her excellent working relationship with William Kelly. But it was not always a harmonious relationship, Kelly being particularly exercised in recent years about her desire to winter her cattle outdoors in the mild climate of the peninsula. She discussed the matter in a letter to Henry:

'You have been lucky in sheep and I am glad to hear that you like going to fairs, as you need not

---

[45] English Reports in Law and Equity: Containing Reports of Cases in the House of Lords, Privy Council, Courts of Equity and Common Law; and in the Admiralty and Ecclesiastical Courts, Including Also Cases in Bankruptcy and Crown Cases Reserved, [1850-1857], Volume 19, Evans v Evans, p.533.

then employ others to spend your money for you. I have laid in my stock at 24 shillings which as times go is reasonable, but the sheep I had to sell were fat sheep for which there was no demand. Had they been lean instead of fat they would have brought four or five shillings a head more. I only got 20 shillings for them and lean sheep of their size were bringing 33 to 34 shillings a piece.

I am struggling on my new plan to keep my cattle on grass instead of in the yards all the winter. I have all Kelly's polite opposition to contend with. As yet they have required neither hay nor turnips, and are looking in great health; but as yet we have had no winter weather and therefore the system has had no trial. If it succeeds I shall make my fortune. Good old experienced Grangier, whom I have consulted, assures me it is the right method to follow to make money, but there is no vanity to be gratified by it, and therefore all stewards hate it.'

Kelly had already proven himself as an agriculturalist, and much of his reputation had been made on the winter feeding of cattle indoors and the management of crop rotation to allow this to be done cheaply. But the market had changed, and there was now more profit in cattle than grains and Sophia was determined to face down her renowned steward who would always in his heart be a tillage farmer. Despite Kelly's reservations, her scheme appeared to work. She would later write to Henry that:

'I have all my cattle out on grass, not a beast in the stalls, and both the cattle and myself are thriving wonderfully on the new system. I shall sell in Autumn, instead of Spring, but the beast will have cost me only his grass.'

Sophia, in the management of her farms was finally proving herself the equal of the great titled landowners, and in a role not unlike that of the modern managing director of a small to medium sized enterprise. She was doing it, furthermore, when few other women had done so, and no married woman *could* do so while a living husband controlled the purse strings. She began, in consequence, to cultivate a notion of herself as a force in the world, and was no longer inhibited about making difficult choices to enhance it.

Ireland was still in the grips of the famine and Sophia's multiplicity of charitable labours notwithstanding, by the spring of 1849 things had gotten so bad in north County Dublin that the tenant farmers of the district finally roused themselves from their fatalistic slumber and began to act. Following a public meeting in Swords, they became the first tenants in the country to attempt to 'bring the landlords to a sense of the altered state of things' by means of a campaign of public embarrassment.

In the hope of forcing their landlords into a fair abatement of rents, they published their plight and resolutions in the newspapers. The strategy proved successful and modest reductions were subsequently offered by many of the local landowners. Sophia Evans, however, broke ranks, her generosity proving so exceptional that it merited special mention in the London Express:

> *'Mrs. Evans of Portrane, whose charities to the poor have been so constant and liberal during the distress, has made an abatement of 20 per cent to her tenantry.'*
> London Express, 24 November 1849.

This was grist to the mill of the begrudgers: a woman reacting emotionally and throwing away money. That type of generosity was not without risk. She could be seen by more than just her tenants as a soft touch. She might even bankrupt the estate before she was done.

The Irish Famine – Scene at the Gate of a Workhouse.

It never came to that, but it could so easily have done. Kelly's decision to resort to manual labour on her farms had been a risk, and dependent upon his calculations of the increased cost being offset by greater yields. It required confidence, and competence, to take that risk, and there would have been little recovery from it had it failed. That it had succeeded had been entirely due to Sophia's trust in Kelly, and her willingness to take that risk.

But she was struggling now. The introduction of the Poor Laws in 1838 had meant that many tenants were struggling to pay their rents. The 'Gregory Clause' in the Poor Law Extension Act (June 1847) had added to that burden by making landowners responsible for all the landholding tax on any holding valued at under £4. The prices being paid for grains, furthermore, had fallen sharply since the introduction of free trade. It had driven many landlords to clear their lands of smallholders to avoid paying taxes, and driven many more bankrupt. She had done neither. Her portfolio was sufficiently diverse to absorb the shock, in the short term at least.

But she *was* worried. She despaired of a solution ever being found and, having had to economise because of the financial difficulties the famine had placed upon her (relative to how she lived before rather than how her tenants now lived, it must be said), she decided that there was no longer any virtue to be found in concealing the fact:

> *'There is nothing at this moment but misery in the world, whichever way you look. We must wait with patience for the result and bear public ills so long as we are exempt from individual misfortune. The loss of property, where there are large families to support, is an affliction, but it may still be met by economy and prudence and an example of economy is, I consider, now a virtue, as it lessens the foolish shame of being poor & those who could afford to spend should now hoard for the use of the really distressed. I see no hope for Ireland as long as the Free Trade and Poor Laws exist, and when can we expect that they will be altered? It is all very melancholy and very hopeless.'*

Kelly's agricultural papers were so widely published that his influence on Irish agriculture may well have been greater than anyone has ever realised. None of that would have been possible without the active endorsement of Sophia Evans. The land and money, after all, were hers; and rent reductions dependent upon her direction. Kelly's innovations, however, were quickly forgotten once the famine had passed, except for one solitary paragraph in pages of *The Farmer's Gazette* in August 1856:

> *'He who writes the history of Ireland's social condition and progress, during the dark days to which we refer, will leave his task unfinished if he omits from his pages the name of William Kelly'.*

William Kelly would go on to play a pivotal part in the Tenant Right, Home Rule and Land League movements, but it is arguably in his partnership with Sophia Evans at Portrane that he made the biggest difference to people's lives. It had taken a famine to shake Sophia out of her grief, but she had been determined to make a difference and, with Kelly's help, she had.

At the end of the day, however, Sophia Evans was still a landlord, and William Kelly was still her steward. Their efforts were not always as recognised by her tenants as they were by other landowners, who understood the risks she had taken and the costs she had to have incurred in doing so. It could all so easily have been very different.

29

VICTORIA

IN 1849, IN the final months of the famine, Queen Victoria decided to visit Ireland, a much neglected part of her Empire. An estimated one million Irish people had recently perished from disease and starvation, the workhouses were still full, and Asiatic cholera was still cutting a brutal swathe through their population. The preceding years had also seen the rise of the Repeal movement and the Young Ireland rebellion was barely twelve months suppressed. It was, on the face of it, an act of extreme hubris, and destined to end badly.

But it did not. Far from it! Her eleven-day visit to Cork, Dublin and Belfast went rather swimmingly, and inconveniently, for those who would have wished it otherwise. She was greeted with enthusiasm wherever she went. People thronged the streets and cheered. Banners were even flown that read 'Hail Victoria, Ireland's hope and England's glory.'

The royal yacht had arrived in Cork from the Isle of Wight on 4 August 1849. The town of Cobh, renamed "Queenstown" by the Queen during her visit, and the nearby city of Cork gave her so rapturous a welcome that she recorded the details in her diary.

> *'We drove through the principal streets; twice through some of them; that they were densely crowded, decorated ... with flowers and triumphal arches .... that our reception was most enthusiastic ... Cork is not all like an English town ... the crowd is a noisy, excitable but a very good-natured one, running and pushing about, and laughing, talking and shrieking. The beauty of the women is very remarkable ... such beautiful dark eyes and hair, and such fine teeth.'*

Victoria travelled on to Dublin, arriving on 6 August and staying for six days. On 7 August she drove into Dublin with her ladies and visited some schools, the old Parliament House, and Trinity College, before returning to the Viceregal Lodge[46] to rest, read and spend some time with her children. That evening she drove into Dublin again to visit some of the older parts of the city, to find the crowds that greeted her as large and enthusiastic as ever and no doubt with teeth just as fine as their southern compatriots! For Sophia's extended family, however, there was no need to line the streets. They were due to meet her in person.

The intricately ritualised 'Court Drawing Rooms', which were usually held in London every year – two before Easter and two after – were something of a beacon for ambitious social climbers. Usually a mother or mother-in-law would present her daughter or daughter-in-law to the Queen, but influence was occasionally traded by families in order to get their daughter presented in order that future generations could be presented by family members.

But it was not all about the *debutantes*. Older women and married women who had not hitherto had the privilege could also be presented at Court. Sophia

---

[46] Now Áras an Uachtaráin.

Evans, for example, would be presenting both.

Queen Victoria by Franz Xaver Winterhalter (1843).

From the moment the date of the Dublin drawing room was announced, letters had poured into the Lord Chamberlain's office suggesting the names of ladies for presentation. Every lady who had kissed the Queen's hand before was automatically entitled to nominate another for presentation, and Sophia Evans had kissed the hand of a Queen of England on no less than three previous occasions. She had even met Victoria once before, having been presented to her back in 1838 when the eighteen-year-old had first ascended the throne. This occasion, would be different. The drawing room would be in Dublin, and she would be able to nominate some of George's family, who had never had the privilege extended to them before.

It wasn't guaranteed that every, or indeed any, name submitted would be accepted. The list underwent careful scrutiny by both the Lord Chamberlain and the Queen; Her Majesty only receiving those who 'wore the white flower of a blameless life'. But as the widow of a recently deceased member of parliament, Sophia had sympathy on her side. Three weeks before the drawing room was due to take place, she received a court summons granting her permission to present George's youngest sister, Sidney, Sidney's daughter Anna Sophia, and sister-in-law Martha.

The summonses were sent out early to allow the recipients ample time to practice the complicated court curtsy and to order from their dressmaker the highly regulated costume prescribed by the Lord Chamberlain's Office. White dresses were obligatory if the lady to be presented was unmarried, but it was also the fashion for married ladies to wear white on their presentation unless age or bereavement rendered their doing so unsuitable.

And it wasn't only dresses that had to be ordered. It was also compulsory for ladies to wear plumes. If married the lady's court plume would consist of three white feathers mounted as a Prince of Wales plume and worn towards the left hand side of the head. If unmarried, the plume would consist of just two feathers. Only white feathers were admissible. Amongst the wider Evans family, therefore, there was much to be done in preparation, and the sense of anticipation swelled with every passing parade and newspaper report.

On the evening of 9 August Victoria drove from the Phoenix Park to Dublin Castle. Waiting to be presented at this, her first drawing room in Dublin, were over 1600 excited and excitable society ladies of city and county, each resplendently rustling in their finest raiment, the royal visit having provided a welcome and unexpected boon to the dressmakers, seamstresses and farthingale makers of the capital. Some ladies carried bouquets; some carried a fan and a lace pocket handkerchief. Very few carried nothing.

Dublin Castle Throne Room. Photo © Joseph Mischyshyn.

The formalities were due to begin at nine o'clock, but long before that, as Sophia and her guests joined the long queue of carriages that stretched to College Green and beyond, the streets surrounding Dublin Castle had become densely packed with onlookers. Public buildings had been specially illuminated by gas fittings for the visit to ensure that everyone could have a clear view of the Queen, and those lucky enough to be proceeding to the drawing room could do so with an enhanced and memorable sense of occasion.

At precisely nine o'clock the approach of the royal carriages was announced, and almost immediately afterwards the royal party, escorted by two troops of the sixth carabineers, drove up Parliament Street, where the Queen, accompanied by Prince Albert, was loudly and enthusiastically cheered. Behind them, in the other carriages, there followed the Marquis of Lansdowne, Sir George Grey, Lord Fortescue, and several members of the royal household.

As the Queen's carriage entered the gates of the castle, the waiting ladies-in-white flocked in a swish of silks and satins to the windows to watch a military band play the national anthem. They had been waiting in these improvised ante-chambers in sweltering conditions and without refreshment or relief, for hours.

Formal welcome complete, Victoria and Prince Albert then alighted from their carriage to a raucous cheer from the street-side multitudes, who rushed forward to catch a final glimpse of the royal couple as they were conducted to the throne room. It was only now that the waiting ladies at the windows caught sight of her dress – pink poplin, embroidered with shamrocks.

Ladies were presented in order of social status, the wives and daughters of the aristocracy going first. These titled ladies would be afforded the privilege of being kissed by the Queen. The rest – the wives and daughters the lesser gentry, clergy, naval and military officers, professional and merchant classes, and of course, politicians – would have to satisfy themselves with kissing the Queen's hand.

It was to be a busy night for Sophia. She had several visits to make to the throne. The first, her own presentation, was made by the Countess Fingal. Having returned from that, she had then, in her turn, to introduce, amongst others, the Countess Donoughmore, Nancy Putland, George's aunt and niece, Sidney and Anna Acton, and Sidney's sister-in-law, Martha.

On each and every occasion, carrying her train over her left arm, she would make her way through various groups of attendants to the corridor where one of the lords-in-waiting, would spread out her train and that of her companions, before escorting them to the Throne Room. As her name was announced, each lady would curtsy before the Queen, so low as to almost kneel, and kiss the extended royal hand, placing her own un-gloved right hand beneath it.

The Queen's Drawing Room – Dublin Castle 1849.

After passing Her Majesty, the ladies would retire backwards in a succession of curtsies until they reached the threshold of the doorway. Here an official would replace their trains upon their arms, marking the end of the presentation.

It was a long and tiring night – one in which the Queen certainly earned her crust – and it was to be Sophia's last encounter with royalty. She was fast approaching her seventieth birthday and the weight of a long forestalled senescence was finally beginning to fall upon her. She would not live to witness Victoria's equally triumphant return in 1853.

30

LAST DAYS AT PORTRANE

Following her mother-in-law's death, Sophia would pass the short days and long nights of winter alone among her books, surrounded by her old servants and the occasional new one that never quite lived up to the mark. She frequently despaired of finding a good 'upper servant', of the type she could confide in. Such people could be found in England, but few, if any, were willing to travel to Ireland for work.

Every spring and summer, as had become her habit, she would go travelling. The less time she spent at Portrane, the less she had to deal with her brother Thomas or, more pointedly, to refuse him money. Her younger brother, in recent years, had become something of a pitiable nuisance. She was rarely unhappy to have an opportunity to put some distance between them.

Despite her advanced age, Sophia had lost little of her old energy or her love of travel and she would often accompany her sister-in-law, Nancy Putland, who had been widowed just a year before Sophia, on her trips to Paris. Sophia had been leaning on Nancy a lot for social interaction since George died, and Nancy, in her turn, had come to depend on Sophia for financial advice.

Though she had been married to a man of the cloth, Nancy's was not the florid faith of her mother's, a woman who had allowed thoughts of death and resurrection to so dominate her life that she had perhaps neglected to live it to the full. Nancy, by way of contrast, lived for the day. She was fond of the finer things in life and loved company, the more the better. Open-hearted and generous, she was often far too concerned with the pleasures of this life to worry overly much about the next.In both Dublin and Paris she had become famous, some might say infamous, for the lavishness of her parties, several of which attracted the attention of the Dublin press.

Sophia was fond of Nancy and, despite her well-known fondness for peace and quiet, was not averse to a good party herself. Indeed such activities appear to have assumed a greater significance in her social calendar since the death of her husband than they had ever done beforehand. Her dancing days had long since passed, but Sophia was still a regular attendee at the Castle balls, and more than capable of throwing a lavish party herself, not to mention engaging in elaborate practical jokes at the expense of her guests. In her latter years, she had become quite renowned for the subversive and offbeat nature of her humour.

Sophia had long nurtured a romantic nostalgia for the powerful women she had met in France and loved nothing more than to scandalise the more conservative of her dinner guests with stories of their 'outrageous' behaviour. One of her favourite stories was that of her first meeting with the ineffable Madame de Staël. The story, as she told it, was that at one memorable dinner party, as the ladies retired to the drawing room to pass the interval before the men came back, each endeavoured to seat themselves apart from the infamous Madame de Staël, while she in turn glowered upon them in a pellucid display of boredom and disdain.

After a short while, de Staël, tiring of the relentless tide of delicate conversation and doe-eyed blandness, rose from her seat and, without bothering to seek the consent of the mistress of the house, rang the bell and ordered a footman to instruct the gentlemen, who would have been just then settling down to their cigars and brandies, to come up. The reaction of the prim and pursed French ladies to de Stäel's effrontery made such an impression on young Sophia that as an old woman she would delight in teasing her female guests when confronted by that same debilitating feminine delicacy.

Her most notorious prank took place at the base of the cliffs near Tower Bay, where she had organised a *fête champêtre* of *tarte aux pigeons et champagne* in a sea cave that was lit from above by a shaft. The party had proceeded in high spirits until someone noticed that the tide had turned. There was, Sophia insisted, no need to be concerned. They had plenty of time. Mollified, the party continued.

Among Sophia's guests that day was Frances Power Cobbe. Frances had, by this time, effectively made herself her invalid mother's stay-at-home housekeeper in order to pursue her self-directed studies of history, literature, geometry, astronomy, philosophy and writing. She had also, quite recently, abandoned all interest in orthodox Christianity, leaving her with what she called 'a *Tabula Rasa* of faith'. She described herself at the time as an agnostic and, of all those present on that day, she was perhaps the only lady with whom Sophia could share a joke, or indeed a confidence. On this occasion, however, even the redoubtable Frances had been kept in the dark.

Taking their host at her word regarding the turn of the tide, the meal continued for another half hour, until somebody wandered towards the mouth of the cave and discovered that the tide was now 'beating at a formidable depth against both sides of the rocks which shut in the cave'. In the ensuing panic the men searched for a ladder and at one stage even considered climbing the shaft to the upper cliff to get help.

Caves at Portrane. Photo by Mark Devine (CC BY-SA 2.0).

As the water crept further into the cave the entire ensemble slowly began to entertain the prospect of drowning or of having to spend the night. But then, as if by telepathy, Sophia's boat appeared at the mouth of the cave. The whole incident, apparently, had been planned by Sophia who, according to Frances Power Cobbe, could never resist the temptation of infusing a little 'wholesome excitement' among her country guests.

It was a reputation for practical jokes like that, that earned Sophia a place in James Joyce's *Finnegan's*

Wake, a novel heavily haunted by the figure of her grandnephew, Charles Stuart Parnell. In chapter I.2, the following passage is found:

> '*Our sailor king, who was draining a gugglet of obvious adamale, gift both and gorban, upon this, ceasing to swallow, smiled most heartily beneath his walrus moustaches and, indulging that **none too genial humour** which William the Conk on the spindle side had inherited with the hereditary whitelock and some shortfingeredness from his **greataunt Sophy**, turned towards two of his retinue of gallowglasses ...*'

The figures of William IV, William the Conqueror, William Gladstone and Charles Stewart Parnell have all melded in Joyce's imagination to form the figure of the king. But the sense of humour that is famously being referenced here is that of Parnell's great aunt, Sophia Evans.[47]

By 1853 Sophia's health had so seriously declined that she departed for France to seek expert medical care. She was accompanied on the journey by Delia Stewart. Nancy Putland had died in 1851.

In her youth, Delia Stewart had been an ambitious Boston socialite, infamous for her ability to spend other people's money. While her husband, the American admiral, Charles Stewart, was away at sea, she had allegedly become romantically involved with a neighbour, one Joseph Bonaparte, brother of Napoleon and deposed King of Spain.

Delia's third daughter had since married Sophia's nephew, John Henry Parnell, the only son of Sophia's brother, William. Since the wedding not only had Delia Tudor-Stewart come to live at Avondale, but the

---

[47] McHugh, Roland,"Recipis for the Price of the Coffin: Book I,chapters ii-iv", in~ Conceptual Guide to "Finnegan's Wake", p. 26.

political atmosphere had apparently changed too. John Henry's new wife was believed, at least by Sophia, to possess a virulent hatred of all things English and to be prone to giving offence to her Unionist neighbours. Worried for her nephew's reputation, Sophia complained to Frances Power Cobbe that:

> *'There is mischief brewing! I am troubled at what is going on in Avondale. My nephew's wife has a hatred of England, and is educating my nephew, like a little Hannibal, to hate it too!'*

Despite Sophia's reservations about the younger Delia, old age and nostalgia for all things French had obviously brought the families closer over the years, and Sophia had even been asked to stand as godparent for one of the younger Delia's short-lived children. She embarked on this last trip to Paris with the older Delia more in hope than expectation.

> *'During the winter months she was wont to live much alone in her country house, surrounded only by her old servants. When, at last, she found herself attacked by mortal disease, she went to Paris to profit by the skill of some French physician in whom she had confidence, and there, with unshaken courage and calmness, she passed away.'*

Boston Post 26 December 1885.

Following Sophia's death, her favourite nephew, Henry Parnell, hastened to Paris to arrange for her body to be returned to Portrane. Despite the body being in a lead coffin, her little terrier, according to local legend, somehow sensed her presence and fell into such a frenzy of grief that his hysteria spread to the other dogs. For fear of rabies all six of them were shot. Sophia's coffin was carried to St. Catherine's

Church and the grave that had separated herself and George for a little over a decade was finally opened and the couple reunited.

In her will, Sophia left a gratuity of £70 to William Kelly and stipulated that £1,000 be invested in specified stocks from which the annual interest would be used to help run the local primary schools that she had founded. A small amount continues to be paid to this day. Sophia also left Thomas, who had since converted to Methodism, a small annuity to be paid to him, as Frances Power Cobbe described it, 'in dribbles by trustees, lest he should spend it at once and starve if he received it half-yearly'.

Thomas continued to work on his texts in his grimy office on Sackville Street. Old friends who had known him in their childhood would call in occasionally to invite him to their homes, but he would only ever respond by exhorting them to repent, give up good dinners and help him with his texts. He condemned them all to eternal damnation for living in handsome parks while mud villages existed at their gates 'like a velvet dress with a draggled skirt'.

On 25 September 1867, the porter of the building on Sackville Street, whose duty it was to shut up the office, entered the room to find 'Old Tom' sitting quietly in his chair. He had died, as he had lived, searching for answers amongst his tracts. Despite his many privations and unorthodox lifestyle, he had survived his sister by fourteen years.

After Sophia's demise, the lands being on an expiring lease, the estate eventually passed out of the family hands and into the ownership of the Board of Control for the Erection of Lunatic Asylums, an ironic turn of events given Sophia's family history. The site was given over, in 1896, for the construction of St. Ita's Mental Hospital, with Portrane House initially serving as the home of the Medical Superintendent, before being demolished in the 1950s. The tower that Sophia built for George, however, outlasted them all, and stands today, neglected and forgotten.

No mention remains, either on or near the tower, of the man in whose memory it was built, of his family's United Irish past, or of the indefatigable woman whose profound love for her husband drove her to have it commissioned in the first place. The dedication to George Evans disappeared with the bust and plinth and no plaque recalls the tower's status as the first of the replica memorials. The tower's sole identifier is an untitled family crest with three boars' heads and a fading motto of 'Libertas'. The Evans' family gravestone lies similarly forgotten, in the grounds of Saint Catherine's church.

The Evans Family Grave Today.

It was perhaps a blessing that Sophia never lived to see Daniel O'Connell's tower become something of a tourist attraction while her husband's was left to decay on a patch of wasteland, abandoned by his fellow Fingallians behind an unsightly concrete water tower that only served to heap further indignities upon her husband's historic memorial.

Better too, perhaps, that she never learnt how her husband's bust was eventually taken from the tower by Sir Edward Evans-Pritchard, a professor of social anthropology at Oxford University. Evans-Pritchard, a descendant of George's brother Eyre, who had famously converted to Roman Catholicism in 1944, did at least give the tenants of the estate a chance to view the bust before its removal to Oxford.

Sophia Evans had met two Queens, the divorced wife of a King, and possibly even the Emperor and Empress of France; she had met the influential Madame de Staël and befriended the radical feminist Margaret King-Mount Cashell; she had been a close friend of both the Darwin and Condorcet families and a daughter and sister to three of the most able Irish politicians of her day. She had also founded two primary schools in Donabate and had helped in no small way to mitigate the effects of the Great Famine in her locality. And she had been a friend and mentor to another freethinking young local woman who would go on to achieve fame within the embryonic animal rights and English suffragette movements and lead the fight for equality in education.

Her achievement in reviving a tradition of tower building that had lain dormant for seven centuries lies similarly unmarked and unremembered and yet, were it not for her example, it is possible that the replica and memorial towers that now grace such diverse locations as Glasnevin, Ferrycarrig, Larne, Melbourne, Massachusetts and Flanders might never have been built, let alone the curious wooden replica that was famously constructed on Dublin's College Green for the duration of the Eucharistic Congress of 1932.

The tower at Portrane is hardly the Taj Mahal, but even as a posthumous love token, or as local landmark treasured for many years as a navigational aid to local shipping, surely it deserves a better fate than dereliction, for in many respects it stands as a greater monument to the formidable lady who built it than it ever did to her devoted husband.

Sophia Evans' signature.

Bibliography

Manuscripts

Illustrations

Index

BIBLIOGRAPHY

Advertiser Notes and Queries, Volume 2, 'Advertiser' Office, Cheshire, England, 1884.

Akenson, Donald Harman. 'Discovering the End of Time: Irish Evangelicals in the Age of Daniel O'Connell', McGill-Queen's University Press, 2016.

Almanach du Commerce de Paris, des Départemens de l'Empire Francais, J. De la Tynna, Paris, 1814. p.1024.

Blanc, Louis. *Pages de l'histoire de la révolution de 1848*, Brussels, 1850.

Boston Post, page 3, 'Remarkable characteristics of Thomas Parnell's Sister', 26-Dec-1885.

Burtchell, George Dames & Sadlier, Thomas Ulick. 'Alumni Dublinenses: a register of the students, graduates, professors and provosts of Trinity College in the University of Dublin (1593-1860)', Alex. Thom & Co. Ltd., Dublin, 1935.

Caldwell, John Edwards. 'Christian Herald', Volume 6, J. Gray, 1819

Cappock, Margarita. "The Royal Visits to Dublin." Dublin Historical Record, vol. 52, no. 2, 1999, pp. 94–107. JSTOR, www.jstor.org/stable/30101221. Accessed 6 Feb. 2020.

Chapmen, John Henry and Armytage, George John. *The Register Book of Marriages Belonging to the Parish of St. George*, London, 1896. Marriage of Dr. Pelham Warren to Miss Penelope Shipley 3 May 1814.

Cheng, Vincent John, Devlin, Kimberly J. & Norris, Margot. *Joycean Cultures, Culturing Joyces* University of Delaware Press, 1998

Chester Chronicle, p3. Death of Anne Parnell, May 1ˢᵗ 1795.

Cobbe, Frances Power. 'Life of Frances Power Cobbe', Houghton, Boston 1894.

Colburn, Henry. 'A Genealogical and Heraldic Dictionary of the Peerage and Baronetage of the British Empire', p.816, 1839.

Conner, Clifford D. 'Arthur O'Connor – The Most Important Irish Revolutionary You May Never Have Heard Of', iUniverse Inc., New York, 2009.

Cust, E & Pelham E.G. 'Edward, Fifth Earl of Darnley and Emma Parnell, His Wife', Richard Jackson, Leeds 1913.

Darwin, Charles; Burkhardt, Frederick & Smith, Sydney. *The Correspondence of Charles Darwin: 1821-1836*, Cambridge University Press, 1985.

Dictionary of Irish Architects. 'Miller, George', retrieved 23/12/2018. https://www.dia.ie/architects/view/3469/MILLER-GEORGE.

Donovan, Julie. 'Sydney Owenson, Lady Morgan and the Politics of Style,' Academica Press, LLC, 2009.

Dublin Evening Post, 'New Catholic Association', 11 December 1827, p.4.

Dublin Evening Post, 'Tithe Commutation Bill'. 31 January 1824; p4.

Dunne-Lynch, Nicholas. 'Hugh Ware - A Kildare 1798 Rebel in the Service of France', in Journal of the County Kildare Archaeological Society (JKAS) XX (Part II) 2010-11, 99-141.

Ervine, St John. 'Parnell: His Family', Ernest Benn Ltd., London 1925.

'Evans v. Evans', in English Reports in Law and Equity: Containing Reports of Cases in the House of Lords, Privy Council, Courts of Equity and Common Law; and in the Admiralty and Ecclesiastical Courts, Including Also Cases in Bankruptcy and Crown Cases Reserved, [1850-1857], Volume 19, Edmund Hatch Bennett, Chauncey Smith, Charles C. Little and James Brown, 1854.

Fagan, Patrick. 'Infiltration of Dublin Freemason Lodges by United Irishmen and Other Republican Groups.' *Eighteenth-Century Ireland / Iris an Dá Chultúr*, vol. 13, 1998, pp. 65–85. *JSTOR*, www.jstor.org/stable/30064326.

Feldman, Paula R. and Cooney, Brian C. 'The Collected Poetry of Mary Tighe', JHU Press, 2016.

Finns Leinster Journal, Birth of John Augustus Parnell, 20 May 1775, p2.

Finns Leinster Journal 1771-1828, Queen's Birthday Ball, Dublin Castle, 27 February 1782, p2.

Fisher, D.R. 'Parnell Hayes, William (?1777-1821), of Avondale, Co. Wicklow', in *The History of Parliament: the House of Commons 1820-1832*, ed. D.R. Fisher, 2009

Fitzpatrick, William John. 'The Life, Times and Contemporaries of Lord Cloncurry', James Duffy, Dublin 1855.

Freemans Journal, Deaths, 04 July 04, 1842; p2.

Freemans Journal, Deaths, Saturday, 19 Dec 1846; p4.

Freeman's Journal. 'Died on the 13th inst, aged 96 years, Mrs Evans relict of Hamden Evans of Portrane', 15 March 1844.

Freemans Journal, 'Paris, aged 73 years, Sophia, widow of the Right Hon. George Evans, M.P., of Portrane, county Dublin,' Thursday, May 5th, 1853, p4.

Freemans' Journal, 'Royal Dublin Society', 19 Dec 1846, p12.

Geoghegan, Patrick M. 'Liberator – The Life and Death of Daniel O'Connell 1830-1847', Gill & McMillan, 2010.

Griffith, Richard. 'An address delivered at the ninth annual meeting of the Geological Society of Dublin, on the 12th of February 1840', Hodges and Smith, Dublin, 1840.

Groves, Henry. 'Not of the World, Memoir of Lord Congleton', John F. Shaw & Co., London, 1884.

Hibernian Journal, Dublin, 20 July 1774 – Marriage of John Parnell to Miss Laetitia Brooke.

Holland, Evangeline. *The Court Presentation.* Edwardian Promenade, 7 December 2007.
http://www.edwardianpromenade.com/etiquette/the-court-presentation/

Huey, Edmund Burke. Backward and Feeble-Minded Children: Clinical Studies in the Psychology of Defectives, With a Syllabus for the Clinical Examination and Testing of Children. Baltimore, Warwick and York, Inc., 1912.

Hughes, Marie. 'The Parnell Family; Dublin Associations.' *Dublin Historical Record,* vol. 16, no. 3, 1961, pp. 86–95. *JSTOR,* JSTOR, www.jstor.org/stable/30102706.

Irish Examiner, 'From the Farmer's Gazette', Monday, 20 September 1847, p1.

Jarrett, Simon. 'Disability in Time and Place', English Heritage Disability History Web Content, 2012.

Johnson, James. 'A Tour in Ireland; With Meditations and Reflections'. S. Highly, 32 Fleet Street, Dublin 1844.

Jones, Anna Maria. The Poems of Anna Maria. Calcutta: Thomson & Ferris, 1793.

Joyce, James. *A First-draft Version of Finnegan's Wake,* UW-Madison Libraries Parallel Press, 2002.

Keenan, Desmond. 'The Grail of Catholic Emancipation 1793 to 1829', Xlibris Corporation, 2002.

Kelly, William. 'The crops proper to be grown at this emergency, and their culture', *Leinster Express*, 12 December 1846; p.4.

Kelly, William, 'The Irish Small Farmer of 1847; Containing Ample Directions for the Cultivation of the Soil During the Present Crisis', Cumming & Ferguson, 1847.

Kerry Evening Post, 'Death of the Right Hon. George Evans', Saturday, July 09, 1842, p.1

Lewis, Samuel. 'A Topographical Dictionary of Ireland', S. Lewis & Co., London, 1837.

London Express. Sophia Evans' generosity during the famine, 24 November 1849.

Loughlin, Dympna. 'Women and sexuality in nineteenth century Ireland' in *The Irish Journal of Psychology*, pp 266-275, 1994.

Mavor, Elizabeth (ed.), 'The Grand Tours of Katherine Wilmot: France 1801-3 & Russia 1805-7, Weidenfeld, 1992.

Mitford, John. 'A Description of the Crimes and Horrors in the Interior of Warburton's Private Mad-Houses at Hoxton, Commonly called Whitmore House', Bennow, London, 1825.

Morgan, Lady 1783-1859. Lady Morgan's Memoirs: Autobiography, Diaries and Correspondence. Copyright ed. Leipzig: B. Tauchnitz, 1863.

Moylan, Thomas King. 'The Peninsula of Portrane: Part I.' *Dublin Historical Record*, vol. 16, no. 1, 1960, pp. 22–33. *JSTOR*, JSTOR, www.jstor.org/stable/30102698.

National Register, London. 'Death of John Augustus Parnell', p16. 16 Aug 1812.

Ó Cathaoir, Brendan. *John Blake Dillon, Young Irelander*, Irish Academic Press, Dublin, 1990.

O'Connell, Maurice R. Ed. 'The Correspondence of Daniel O'Connell, Volume IV, 1829-1832' Dublin Stationery Office for the Irish Manuscripts Commission, 1977.

Otago Witness, 'The Parnell Family'. Issue 1793, 3 April 1886.

Parnell, William. 'An Enquiry into the Causes of Popular Discontents in Ireland, &c. &c.' 1804.

Porter, Frank Thorpe, Twenty Years' Recollections of an Irish Police Magistrate, Hodges, Foster, and Figgis, Dublin, 1880.

Public Ledger and Daily Advertiser, Death of Hampden Evans, 1 May 1820.

Purcell, Mary. "Dublin Diocesan Archives: Murray Papers (5)." Archivium Hibernicum, vol. 40, 1985, pp 35-114. JSTOR, www.jstor.org/stable/25487460. Accessed 8 Feb. 2020

Reaney, Bernard. "Irish Chartists in Britain and Ireland: Rescuing the Rank and File." *Saothar*, vol. 10, 1984, pp. 94-103. *JSTOR*, www.jstor.org/stable/23195891. Accessed 8 Feb. 2020.

Reid, T. *An Essay on the nature and cure of the Phthisis Pulmonalis,* London, 1783.

Roberts, Matthew. 'Daniel O'Connell, repeal and Chartism in the age of Atlantic revolution.' *The Journal of Modern History,* 90(1), 1-39.

Saunders' Newsletter 19 November 1783, p1. Death of Lady Laetitia Parnell.

Saunders' Newsletter, 27 May 1789, p.2. 'Bills which received Royal Assent on Monday', including private act disinheriting John Augustus Parnell.

Star, Susan Leigh and Bowker, Geoffrey C. *Of Lungs and Lungers: The Classified Story of Tuberculosis.* University of Illinois, 1996.

'Testamentary Counsels, and hints to Christians on the right distribution of their property by will. By a retired solicitor'. Thomas Ward & Company, 1835.

The Gentleman's and Citizen's Almanack, John Watson Stewart, Dublin 1815, p.209.

The Court Magazine & Monthly Critic and Lady's Magazine: Volume 5, Dobbs & Co., London, 1834.

The Court Magazine & Monthly Critic and Lady's Magazine: & Museum of the Belles Lettres, Music, Fine Arts, Drama, Fashions. & c. united ser, Volume 8, Dobbs & Co., London, 1836.

The Court magazine and Monthly Critic, Volume 12, Dobbs & Co., London, 1838

The Northern Star and National Trade's Journal, Vol X. No. 432, London, 21 February 1846. 'Atrocious Outrage and Illegal Interference with thye Sacred Right of Petition', p.3.

Tighe, Mary. *'The Collected Poems and Journals of Mary Tighe'*, University Press of Kentucky, 2015

Tighe, Mary. *'The Collected Poetry of Mary Tighe'*, JHU Press, 2016.

Todd, Janet. *'Mary Wollstonecraft: A Revolutionary Life'*. Weidenfeld & Nicolson, London, 2000.

Venn, John. 'Alumni Cantabrigienses, Vol. 5: A Biographical List of All Known Students, Graduates and Holders of Office at the University of Cambridge, From the Earliest Times to 1900' (Classic Reprint) Paperback, 2019.

Virtue, George. 'The Royal Court Guide, and Fashionable Directory, 1842, with a list of subscribers to Finden's Ports, Harbours, and Watering-Places', London 1842.

Walker, J. *An inquiry into the Causes of Sterility in Both Sexes with Its Method of Cure*. (Ph.d. diss., University of Pennsylvania, 1797), esp. 7-8, American Collection, New York Academy of Medicine, New York.

Weber, Paul. '*On the Road to Rebellion: The United Irishmen and Hamburg, 1796-1803*'. Four Courts Press, 1997.

Warren, C.M. *The Life and Adventures of Jeremiah Grant, commonly called Captain Grant*, Dublin 1816.

Yeldham, Charlotte. '*Maria Spilsbury (1776-1820): Artist and Evangelical*', Routledge, New York, 2016.

Young, Arthur. '*A Tour in Ireland*', Cambridge University Press, 2013.

MANUSCRIPTS

CONGLETON LETTERS - SOUTHAMPTON.

MS64/5 Letters patent appointing Sir John Parnell, second baronet Chancellor of the exchequer of Ireland 22-Sep-1785.

MS64/13/12 Letter from Madame de Brissac to Henry Brooke Parnell regarding a parcel he delivered. 28-Jan-1802.

MS64/17/1 Memorandum by Sir Henry Brooke Parnell about a conversation with Daniel O'Connell and others about presenting a Catholic petition to Parliament, 23-Apr-1815.

MS64/17/2-3 Letters to Sir Henry Brooke Parnell from Daniel O'Connell concerning Catholic emancipation. 13-Jun-1815.

MS64/17/6 Letter from Daniel O'Connell to Rev. William Dunn asking him to Support Henry Brooke Parnell as a parliamentary candidate.

MS64/20/3 Letter to Henry Brooke Parnell from Bishop of Kildare acceding to support O'Connell. 17-Dec-1816.

MS64/20/6 Letter from William Parnell to Henry Brooke Parnell concerning Catholic emancipation, c. 1817.

MS64/20 Letter from A. Fitzpatrick to Sir Henry Brooke Parnell acknowledging Henry's pamphlet on Catholic emancipation. 13-Sep-1813.

MS64/26/4-6 Letters from Sir H.B. Parnell to Sophia Evans.

MS64/34/2 Memorandum of conversation between Henry Brooke Parnell and Lord Anglesey suggesting Daniel O'Connell's appointment as Master of the Rolls in Ireland. 7-Oct-1831.

MS/62 Letters from George Evans to his wife

MS64/86/7 Letter from Sophia Evans to H.B. Parnell.

MS64/90-106 Letters from Sophia Evans only

MS64/109/3 Letter from Sophia Evans to Henry William Parnell.

MS64/344/7 Deed of separation of Sir Henry Brooke Parnell and Lady Caroline Parnell.

MS64/378/1 The degree of John Parnell, from TCD 6 February 1739.

GLOUCESTERSHIRE ARCHIVES
Uncatalogued collection D2624.

Copy will of Hampden Evans 1811

Will of George Evans

Agreement dated 1843 for building a tower in Deer Park at Portrane between Sophia Evans and George Millar.

List of Deeds and Papers between Sir H S Blane, Bart and Mrs Evans, 1847

BRITISH NATIONAL ARCHIVES, KEW.

PROB 11/1753/197 - Will of Arthur Parnell, formerly of the Royal College of Physicians, London of Mount Avon, Wicklow

C 211/20/P124 - Arthur Parnell, merchant, formerly of the College of Physicians, Warwick Lane, London, now residing at Whitmore House in the parish of St John, Hackney: commission and inquisition of lunacy, into his state of mind and his property.

PROB 11/2172/454 - Will of Sophia Evans, Widow of Portrane, Dublin.

NATIONAL ARCHIVES, DUBLIN.

CSO/RP/1829/1409 – Letter from C Condorcet O'Connor, [Dublin], relating to naturalisation of Arthur O'Connor's son

CSORP/1830/434 – Letter from Thomas B Kelly, High Sheriff, Kellyville, Stradbally, [County Laois], recommending an increase in the military force at the time of the execution of Ribbonmen at Maryborough in April.

CSORP/1830/446 – Letter from [Gen Sir Frederick] Stovin, [Military Secretary], Royal Hospital, Dublin, about sending a contingent of the 7th Hussars, to [Portlaoise, County Laois], for the upcoming executions there

CSORP/1830/478 – Petition by Anne Fitzpatrick, wife of John, Ardlea, Queen's County [County Laois], presenting the case of her nephew John Connor, who was pressed into a mob of Ribbonmen and has been sentenced to death

CSO/RP/1830/1320 – Letter from George Evans, foreman, Grand Jury of County Dublin, Swords, [County Dublin], enclosing resolution against the current practice of building houses without any space for accumulated refuse

CSO/RP/1830/1321 – Letter from George Evans, foreman, Grand Jury of County Dublin, Swords, [County Dublin], calling government's attention to the high charges imposed on the County by coroners in fees to surgeons

CSO/RP/1832/4736 - Letter from Dillon McNamara, agent for George Evans, a parliamentary candidate, 51 York Street, [Dublin], concerning the difficulties facing freeholders who wish to register.

PPC 3532 – Petitioner petitioning on behalf of convict, Laurence Shorthall, requesting a reprieve of his sentence. Address given at Abbeyleix, Queens Co.

SPP 130 – Hampden Evans request to move to Hamburg.

Rebellion Papers 620/15/3 – Correspondence between Sir Francis Burdett and Arthur O'Connor.

Portrane Primary Schools, National Archives, ED/1/29/12-13.

ILLUSTRATIONS

CHAPTER ONE – FAMILY HISTORY

The Right Hon. Sir John Parnell, 2nd (1744-1801) by Pompeo Girolamo Batoni (Lucca 1708, Rome 1787), courtesy of The National Trust, Public Collections, no restrictions, Image No. 987120.

Sir John Parnell's Bed (now at Castle Ward), by Andreas von Einsiedel courtesy of The National Trust, Public Collections, no restrictions, Image No. 987120.52571

Lady Parnell née Laetitia Charlotte Brooke holding a Grecian vase (c.1783), by Hugh Douglas Hamilton, photo courtesy of Whyte's auction House.

Thomas Parnell. Frontispiece to his collection of poems 1801. Public domain via Wikimedia Commons. https://upload.wikimedia.org/wikipedia/commons/0/00/Po rtrait_of_Poems_by_Thomas_Parnell%2C_D.D_%284672662 %29.jpg

Parnell Bridge, Dublin by CraftyCadeus via Wikimedia Commons, licensed under the Creative Commons Attribution-Share Alike 4.0 International license. https://commons.wikimedia.org/wiki/File:County_Dublin_- _Parnell_Bridge_-_20160106121003.jpg

CHAPTER TWO – THE WALLED GARDEN

Rathleague Lodge Garden Wall - from the R425. Photo by Gerard Ronan.

Rathleague Lodge today - photo © Alec Silke

CHAPTER THREE – EDUCATION

The Governess, by Paul Lacroix, from tableau of Chardin, engraved by Lepicie 1739. Courtesy of Wellcome Collection. Retrieved under Creative Commons Attribution (CC BY 4.0).

CHAPTER FOUR - THE ROMANTIC DISEASE

Extract from Limerick Chronicle 20-Oct-1799. Public Domain.

A young girl convalescing in an armchair is visited by her dog. Etching by H. Formstecher after H. Bacon. Credit: Wellcome Collection. Attribution 4.0 International (CC BY 4.0)

A Cidade de Lisboa, no final do século XIX/início do século XX. Editora Belém & Companhia. Public Domian, via Wikimedia Commons. https://commons.wikimedia.org/wiki/File:Gravura_da_Cidade_de_Lisboa_-_Editora_Bel%C3%A9m_%26_Companhia.png

Portrait of Anna Maria (Shipley) Jones, Lady Jones, courtesy of Beinecke Digital Collections, call no. Osborn fc82.

Sir William Jones by Edward Smith (engraver). Courtesy of Llyfrgell Genedlaethol Cymru – The National Library of Wales, under Creative Commons license 1.0. http://creativecommons.org/publicdomain/mark/1.0/

CHAPTER SIX – THE FRENCH CONNECTION

'Physionotrace portrait of Lady Mount Cashell' by Carl H. Pforzheimer. Collection of Shelley and His Circle, New York Public Library Digital Collections. 1801. http://digitalcollections.nypl.org/items/7581b872-4f4e-6993-e040-e00a180628a2

La parc de Bagatelle Paris. Photo by Patrick Giraud via Wikimedia Commons under Creative Commons Attribution-Share Alike 1.0 Generic License. https://lb.m.wikipedia.org/wiki/Fichier:Paris_Bagatelle_01.jpg

Self portrait of Sophie de Condorcet, née de Grouchy (1764-1822) [Public domain] via Wikimedia Commons.

CHAPTER SEVEN – GEORGE HAMPDEN EVANS

45 Welbeck Street. Photo courtesy of Mark Philips, Edward Charles & Partners LLP.

CHAPTER EIGHT – PORTRANE HOUSE

Portrane House. Photo courtesy of Peadar Bates.

CHAPTER NINE – ARTHUR AND THE ASYLUM

Royal College of Physicians, Warwick Lane, London, in 1841. Wellcome Library no. 23763i. Courtesy of Wellcome Collection gallery (2018-04-02). https://wellcomecollection.org/works/jscr6f98 CC-BY-4.0

Robert Waring Darwin, seated in an armchair: beside him a letter-book, pen and ink on a table. Mezzotint by T. Lupton, 1839, after J. Pardon. Shrewsbury: John Eddowes; London: Ackermann & Co., 1 February 1839. Wellcome Library no. 9898i. Courtesy of Wellcome Collection gallery (2018-04-01): https://wellcomecollection.org/works/h4bnea28 CC-BY-4.0.

Balmes House. Illustration from Old and New London: Volume 5, Cassell, Petter & Galpin, London, 1878. Public Domain

Bethlem Hospital, London: the incurables being inspected by a member of the medical staff, with the patients represented by political figures. Drawing by Thomas Rowlandson, 1789. Credit: Wellcome Collection. CC BY.

CHAPTER TEN – THE EMPTY CRADLE

The Invalid, by Louis Lang. Public domain, via Brooklyn Museum online collection.

Conservatory at Portrane House from photo courtesy of Peadar Bates.

CHAPTER ELEVEN – LITERARY CONNECTIONS

Portrait of Mary Tighe, public domain, via Wikimedia Commons. Frontispiece from Psyche, with Other Poems. 5th ed. London: Longman, Hurst, Rees, Orme & Brown, 1816. https://commons.wikimedia.org/wiki/File:Mary_Tighe_crop.jpg

Thomas Moore, from 'Portrait gallery of eminent men and women of Europe and America: with biographies / by Evert A. Duyckinck; illustrated with highly finished steel engravings from original portraits by the most celebrated artists.' Johnson, & Wilson, New York, 1873. Public domain, via Wikimedia Commons.

Avondale House. Photo by Sarah777 via English Wikipedia Public domain.
https://commons.wikimedia.org/wiki/File:IMG_AvondaleHouse0148_1.jpg

CHAPTER TWELVE – OF WILLIAM AND GOD

William Parnell Hayes, by John Comerford (1770-1832), NGI 2649, P2419. Photo © National Gallery of Ireland. https://nationalgalleryimages.ie/search/?searchQuer y=William+Parnell+Hayes

CHAPTER THIRTEEN – THE O'CONNORS

Roger O'Connor, via the NPG, engraving T. Lupton, published by Abraham Wivell 1822 (1830 reprint). Public Domain via Wikimedia Commons. https://commons.wikimedia.org/wiki/File:Roger_OConnor_v ia_the_NPG.png

Arthur O'Connor. Image extracted from page 424 of volume 1 of Historic Memoirs of Ireland; comprising secret records of the National Convention, the Rebellion, and the Union; with delineations of the principal characters connected with these translations, etc., by Barrington, Jonah - Sir. Original held and digitised by the British Library. Public domain via Wikimedia Commons. https://commons.wikimedia.org/wiki/File:barrington (1833)_p1.424_arthur_o%27connor,_esq.jpg

CHAPTER THIRTEEN – A FAMILY SCANDAL

Napoleon's Military Carriage. Photograph from The Romance of Madame Tussaud's by John Theodore Tussaud, George H. Doran Company, New York, 1920.

CHAPTER FIFTEEN – POLITICAL AWAKENINGS

The Peterloo Massacre by Richard Carlisle, engraving. Public domain, via Wikimedia Commons. https://commons.wikimedia.org/wiki/File:Peterloo-1819-R-Carlile_(partial).jpg

CHAPTER SIXTEEN – THOMAS TRACT PARNELL

Emmanuel College, Cambridge. Public domain, via
Wikimedia Commons. Diliff [CC BY-SA 3.0
(https://creativecommons.org/licenses/by-sa/3.0)]

Grant and his companions attacked by the military, from
*The Newgate calendar : Comprising interesting memoirs of the
most notorious characters who have been convicted of
outrages on the laws of England since the commencement of
the eighteenth century ; with occasional anecdotes and
observations, speeches, confessions, and last exclamations of
sufferers,* J. Robins and Co. London, 1826. Public Domain.

CHAPTER SEVENTEEN – EMMA

Emma Parnell, from engraving by Arlett, after Sir Thomas
Lawrence, of Countess of Darnley, aka Hon. Emma Jane
Parnell, (wife of 5th Earl of Darnley). Public domain via
Wikimedia Commons,
https://upload.wikimedia.org/wikipedia/commons/6/6b/E
ngraving_after_Sir_Thomas_Lawrence_of_Countess_of_Darnl
ey%2C_aka_Hon._Emma_Jane_Parnell%2C_%28wife_of_5th_
Earl_of_Darnley%29.jpg

CHAPTER EIGHTEEN – SCANDALOUS WOMEN

Lady Morgan. Stipple and line engraving by Robert Cooper,
after Samuel Lover, 1825. Public Domain, via Wikimedia
Commons.
https://commons.wikimedia.org/wiki/File:Lady_Morgan.jpg

Elizabeth Patterson Bonaparte via Wikimedia Commons
https://commons.wikimedia.org/wiki/File:Elizabeth-
Patterson-Bonaparte_Gilbert-Stuart_1804.jpg#file

Lady Caroline Lamb, from Wives of the prime ministers,
1844-1906 published by Elizabeth Lee, 1918. Public domain,
via Wikimedia Commons.
https://commons.wikimedia.org/wiki/File:Lady_Caroline_La
mb_in_her_page%27s_dress.png

**CHAPTER TWENTY –
THE RIBBONMAN AND THE ALLEY CHILD**

Courthouse at the Main Street, Portlaoise, designed by Sir Richard Morrison in 1805. Photo by Andreas F. Borchert, via Wikimedia Commons. Photo licensed under the Creative Commons Attribution-Share Alike 3.0 Germany license. https://commons.wikimedia.org/wiki/File:Portlaoise_Main_Street_County_Courthouse_2010_09_01.jpg

CHAPTER TWENTY ONE – GEORGE ENTERS POLITICS

Daniel O'Connell, engraving by Thomas Kelly. Public domain. https://commons.wikimedia.org/wiki/File:Daniel_O%27Connell._The_great_Irish_liberator_LCCN2003662860.jpg

CHAPTER TWENTY TWO – THE DARWINS

Caroline Darwin, by anonymous painter. Public domain, via Wikimedia Commons. https://commons.wikimedia.org/wiki/File:Caroline_Darwin,_age_16.jpg

Emma Wedgwood, from page 130 of *Emma Darwin, a century of family letters, 1792-1896*, London, J. Murray, 1915.

Erasmus Alvey Darwin, Reproduced with permission from John van Wyhe ed. 2002-. The Complete Work of Charles Darwin Online. (http://darwin-online.org.uk/)

Beulah Spa, Norwood, Surrey. Line engraving. Credit: Wellcome Collection. CC BY

Harriet Martineau in 1833, from Harriet Martineau's autobiography (1879). Public Domain, via Wikimedia Commons, https://commons.wikimedia.org/wiki/File:Harriet_Martineau%27s_autobiography_(1879)_(14781956142).jpg.

Photograph of Charles Darwin; frontispiece of Francis Darwin's *The Life and Letters of Charles Darwin* (1887) Public Domain.

CHAPTER TWENTY THREE – HENRY'S SUICIDE

Henry Brooke Parnell, by H.B. Doyle, 1832. Public domain. https://commons.wikimedia.org/wiki/File:HB_Parnell,_Lord _Congleton_by_HB_Doyle.jpg

CHAPTER TWENTY FOUR – GEORGE'S DEATH

George Evans Memorial Tower © Gerard Ronan

Bust of George Evans. Photo courtesy of John Evans-Pritchard.

Plinth of Evans' bust. Photo courtesy of Bruce Smith-Ross.

James Johnson M.D. by J. Wood. Courtesy of U.S. National Library of Medicine Digital Collections. Image I.D. B015593, Public Domain.

CHAPTER TWENTY FIVE – THE DONABATE CHARTISTS

Frances Power Cobbe – image copied from 'Life of Frances Power Cobbe by Herself', Bentley, London, 1894. Public Domain.

Chartist Demonstration Kennington Common Flyer 1848, Public Domain, via Wikimedia Commons. https://commons.wikimedia.org/wiki/File:Chartist_Demons tration_Kennington_Common_Flyer_1848.jpg

CHAPTER TWENTY SIX - VACCINATION

Edward Jenner vaccinating patients in the Smallpox and Inoculation Hospital at St. Pancras: the patients develop features of cows. Watercolour after J. Gillray, 1802. Courtesy of Wellcome Collection. CC BY license.

Edward Jenner vaccinating a boy. Lithograph after E.E. Hillemacher, 1884.. Credit: Wellcome Collection. Attribution 4.0 International (CC BY 4.0).

CHAPTER TWENTY SEVEN – THE GREAT HUNGER

Manglewurzel, from Catalogue of flower and vegetable seeds, gladiolus, lilies, and summer flowering bulbs, with instructions for their cultivation, 1872. Public Domain via Wikimedia Commons.
https://commons.wikimedia.org/wiki/File:Catalogue_of_flow er_and_vegetable_seeds,_gladiolus,_lilies,_and_summer_flowe ring_bulbs,_with_instructions_for_their_cultivation_(1872)_(1 9959091863).jpg

Frontispiece from 'The Irish Small Farmer of 1847; Containing Ample Directions for the Cultivation of the Soil During the Present Crisis', by William Kelly, Cumming & Ferguson, 1847.

CHAPTER TWENTY EIGHT – THE THIRD REPUBLIC

Hôtel de Choiseul-Praslin au n°111 rue de Sèvres - Paris VI, by MBZT, public domain via Wikimedia Commons, licensed under the Creative Commons Attribution-Share Alike 3.0 Unported license. Retrieved 30-01-2020.
https://commons.wikimedia.org/wiki/File:P1240814_Paris_ VI_rue_de_S%C3%A8vres_n111_hotel_Choiseul-Praslin_rwk.jpg

Louis-Blanc assis en buste, de tr. q. à dr.: Carjat, Étienne (1828-1906). Photographe Publisher: Galerie contemporaine, 126, boulevard de Magenta. - phot. Goupil & C.e. - Cliché Carjat & C.e, rue Notre-Dame-de-Lorette, Subject: France -- 1848 (Gouvernement provisoire).
https://gallica.bnf.fr/ark:/12148/btv1b53014213d

"Vue intérieure de la salle de l'Assemblée nationale", Journées illustrées de la Révolution de 1848, Paris, 1849.
Ed. Renard. Public Domain.

L'Assemblée nationale est envahie. Arnout, Jules (1814-1868). Lithographe. New-York. Published by Goupil, Vibert & C° 289 Broad-wa'y - Paris. Goupil, Vibert & C.ie, Editeurs. - London. Published by E. Gambart & C°, 25 Berners Saint Oxford Saint. Bibliothèque nationale de France, département Estampes et photographie, RESERVE QB-370 (113)-FT4. 1848.

Beschreibung: Brauer, Franz: ¬Das¬ Opernhaus und der Zwinger zu Dresden: nach der Revolution im May 1849 / Gez. v. Franz Brauer. Lith. v. W. Bässler. - Dresden: Adolph Brauer; Dresden: Braunsdorf, [ab 1849]. - 1 Kunstbl. : Tonlithogr. ; 28 x 18 cm. Licensed under a Creative Commons Attribution-ShareAlike 4.0 International License.
http://www.deutschefotothek.de/documents/obj/90026307

Irish Famine Workhouse Scene, taken from Ridpath's history of the world, by John Clark Ridpath, 1907. Public domain via Wikimedia Commons.
https://commons.wikimedia.org/wiki/File:Ridpath%27s_his tory_of_the_world_-
_being_an_account_of_the_principal_events_in_the_career_of _the_human_race_from_the_beginnings_of_civilization_to_the _present_time,_comprising_the_development_of_social_(1474 9361956).jpg

CHAPTER TWENTY NINE - VICTORIA

Queen Victoria by Franz Xavier Winterhalter (1843). Public Domain via Wikimedia Commons.
https://commons.wikimedia.org/wiki/File:Winterhalter_-_Queen_Victoria_1843.jpg

Dublin Castle - Throne Room (1740) in State Apartments cc-by-sa/2.0 - © Joseph Mischyshyn – geograph.org.uk/p/3690310

The Queen's Drawing Room, Dublin Castle. Illustrated London News, August 11, 1849. Public Domain.

CHAPTER THIRTY – LAST DAYS AT PORTRANE

Caves at Portrane © Mark Devine. (CC BY-SA 2.0) via https://www.flickr.com/photos/majad3v/341333086/in/photostream/.

Evans Family Grave, Portrane © Gerard Ronan.

The Irish Zorro: The Extraordinary Adventures of William Lamport

GERARD RONAN

'Ronan's book is not only an excellent history book, it is a great read. Thoroughly recommended.'
Peter Berresford Ellis. *Irish Democrat*

'Sometimes, historical biography can be a dry read. Ronan's is anything but. He provides interesting insights into the lives of large Irish enclaves in France and Spain in the first half of the 17th century along with harrowing ones of those accused of heresy and subjected to the *auto da fe* of the Inquisition. Ronan's passion and sympathy for his subject shines through so it reads like a novel. A "must-read" for the new year.'

Ann Dunne. *Irish Independent*

'The life and adventures of this pirate, heretic and spy were stranger than any fiction.'
Bookworm. *History Ireland*

ISBN-13: 978-0863223297
ISBN-10: 086322329X

William Kelly of Portrane: Forgotten Hero of the Famine and Land War

GERARD RONAN

William Kelly was a modernizing influence on Irish farming, whose tillage practices and self-invented mangelwurzel bread helped save many lives in Donabate and Portrane during the famine. A leading light in the tenants' rights leagues of the 1870s, he was a council member of the Irish Home Rule League, one of the founding fathers of the Land League and a signatory to a pivotal document of Irish history. A champion of the poor, he faded from history following his death in 1881.

ISBN-10: 1999973828
ISBN-13: 978-1999973827

The Round Towers of Fingal:
Their Hidden History

GERARD RONAN

From tolerant Vikings to ambitious Huguenot's, feminist atheists to cultural pressure groups, the story of Fingal's round towers mirrors the development of the complex Irish identity. The men and women who built and restored these towers link them to multiple invasions as well as to Robinson Crusoe, the Book of Kells and Frankenstein. This book will change the way you look at these monuments forever.

ISBN-10: 1999973836
ISBN-13: 978-1999973834

Margaret Evans:
Poet of Portrane

GERARD RONAN

In 1798 Margaret Evans' husband, Hampden, was sentenced to hang for high treason. When his sentence was subsequently commuted to voluntary exile, she was forced to follow him to Hamburg and later to Paris, where she coped with her enforced exile and family tragedies by writing poetry for herself, her daughters and her female friends. Her writing permits us a very personal glimpse of her life as the wife of a leading United Irishman and provides a personal insight into the safe female space that 18th and 19th century women found in the writing and sharing of poetry. Margaret and Hampden Evans played a prominent role in the history of Portrane, and indeed of the United Irishmen, but little was known of their story until now, or indeed of Margaret's poetry.

ISBN-10: 1999973860
ISBN-13: 978-1999973865